HOW TC
W(

A compendium of essays by leading activists and writers
— essential reading for anyone trying to understand
today's global problems.

CW00458635

HOW TO SAVE THE WORLD

A Fourth World Guide to the Politics of Scale

Edited by

Nicholas Albery and Mark Kinzley

TURNSTONE PRESS LIMITED
Wellingborough, Northamptonshire

First published 1984

© FOURTH WORLD TRUST 1984

This book is sold subject to the condition that it shall not, by way of trade or otherwise, be lent, re-sold, hired out, or otherwise circulated without the publisher's prior consent in any form of binding or cover other than that in which it is published and without a similar condition including this condition being imposed on the subsequent purchaser.

Albery, Nicholas and Kinzley, Mark
    How to save the world.
    1. Associations, institutions, etc. — Social aspects
    2. Associations, institutions, etc. — Political aspects
I.   Title
306   HM131

ISBN 0-85500-209-3

Turnstone Press is part of the Thorsons Publishing Group

Printed and bound in Great Britain

'Human survival now depends on the swiftness with which our political, social and economic institutions can be made small enough for them to be manageable and more adequately responsive to human control.

Wars happen despite our intentions, not because of them; they are an inevitable product of the general giantist pattern of our collective lives and the explosive overspill of power it creates.

Hence any moves towards peace which do not involve a profound restructuring of the size and scale of our institutions are bogus and inconsequential, and by lulling people into a false sense that peace may be secured without such changes, are likely to be adding to the general pressures making for war. The purpose of this book is to begin the lengthy process of defining the nature of that restructuring and the means by which it may be accomplished.'

John Papworth
Editor of *Fourth World News*

WHAT IS THE FOURTH WORLD?

The Fourth World as a concept has caught the imagination of several groups worldwide and has been variously defined.

Since the early 1960s in Britain, *Resurgence, the Journal of the Fourth World,* has developed the very broad definition that we are using in which 'Fourth World' embraces small nations of under twelve million inhabitants, groups working for their autonomy and independence at all levels from the neighbourhood to the nation, minority groups, whether ethnic, linguistic, cultural or religious, and those in the fields of peace action, ecology, economics, energy resources, women's liberation and the whole spectrum of the alternative movement, who are struggling *against* the giantism of the institutions of today's mass societies and *for* a human scale and a non-centralized, multi-cellular, power-dispersed world order.

Contents

Introduction: The Politics of Scale

1 The Creative Disintegration of the State

2 Appropriate Technology

3 Education

4 Intentional Community

5 Personal Transformation

6 Right Livelihood

7 Agriculture

8 The Third World

9 Green Cities

10 War and Peace

11 The Fourth World Movement

Introduction: The Politics of Scale

I call the Fourth World into existence, but can you hear me?

JILL TWEEDIE

Extracted from Jill Tweedie's column in the London Guardian *newspaper.*

The phrase 'small is beautiful' has entered the language, yet you will find no reference to it or its originator, Fritz Schumacher, in any book of quotations or in any of even the most recent reference almanacs or dictionaries of modern thought. Nevertheless, Schumacher's *Small is Beautiful,* published in 1973 (and based on precursors from the early Fifties, especially Leopold Kohr's *The Breakdown of Nations*), was and is an international bestseller that has sparked off a worldwide movement among all those working for a decentralized autonomy and independence against the giantism of mass societies, whether ethnic, linguistic, cultural or religious; whether on a national or a neighbourhood level; whether in the fields of peace action, politics, ecology, economics, energy or women's liberation.

A human scale – that is the key. There is no doubt in my mind that many human ills and evils are intimately linked to numbers. Certain inner behavioural mechanisms enable us to regulate our conduct and our sense of worth but those mechanisms break down once the size of our communities grows too large and have to be replaced by mechanisms imposed from the outside, with varying degrees of force and varying results of individual apathy, alienation, violence and chaos. Overwhelmed by numbers, we lose the human scale and begin to commit the inhuman crimes that now threaten our planet.

Richard Leakey, in his television series *The Making*

of Mankind (*man*kind ?), produced compelling archeological evidence that early nomad hunter-gatherer tribes contained around thirty members, probably because that was the optimum number the surrounding environment could easily support and the minimum number necessary for human relationships. He also introduced us to the African tribe who, until thirty years ago, had remained nomad hunter-gatherers in groups of about thirty, with every member's voice heard in tribal decisions. Then, the tribe settled, increased in numbers, became herdsmen and property-owners, and now have a hierarchical system of elected representatives from among the powerful (i.e. the 'rich'). Thus have they changed from a democratic absolute to a society in which individual voices are drowned and disunion has begun. The original human scale has vanished.

Now, no one suggests that we can go back to wandering groups of thirty for the decisions necessary upon a crowded and complex planet. Nevertheless, some echo of that ancient human scale can and must be resurrected for our survival, because there is ample evidence that it is upon that scale that we still, today, operate in our own best interests.

John Papworth, editor of *Fourth World News*, is much concerned with redefining a workable human scale. He talks of the Ancient Greek view that the proper number for democratic decision-making was that in which 'one voice could reach to the edge of a crowd' and points out that in a community of, say, a thousand people, each person may claim one-thousandth part of the power to rule, but when nations become as large as, for instance, China, to say that each individual within it has one hundred millionth of the power to rule is a meaningless statement.

Therefore, at what stage in growth does the individual voice become meaningless? When is a group or a nation so large that the principle of democracy or autonomy remains just that – an ideological principle without basis in reality? Should it not be possible to apply the human scale to all existing structures without diluting political beliefs?

Today, many of us accept that we gain power only through numbers and, on one level, this is clearly true. No point one woman raising her voice for women's liberation, no point a few people demanding better wages, freedom for political prisoners or an end to nuclear deterrents. Power comes with movements, trades unions, organizations like Amnesty and the CND. Our rulers do not listen to a few voices but they are forced to take notice of thousands – that, in its way, is democracy.

The paradox is that overwhelming numbers also threaten democracy; a loss of the human scale undermines our sense of worth and purpose and participation and, worse, alienates us from each other, causing a disturbance in the human psyche that leads to mindless violence. In a faceless crowd, in anonymous cities, in vast multi-national companies, individuals lose the ancient checks upon behaviour. Instead of the human restraints engendered by shame, social ostracism or the simple you-scratch-my-back-I'll-scratch-yours impulse for personal survival that make unfettered greed and violence horrid aberrations, we lose ourselves in the crowd and shed, along with our identity, our very humanity. Buttons and mega-deaths are substituted for normal face-to-face conflict; pieces of paper make profits more important than the deaths of children. Somehow, in some way, we must struggle towards a two-tier system that incorporates both the power that numbers bring and the human controls that can only be achieved by breaking down vast blocks into manageable units.

As John Papworth says, the Luddites were not protesting against machines but against the power of those machines to disrupt, without argument, relationships, traditional skills, morality, culture and a sense of individual social responsibility. No one can predict exactly what the movements of the Fourth World can accomplish. No one imagines that a move towards a human scale can solve problems, only that it may make a start.

Giantism – public enemy number one of the human race

JOHN PAPWORTH

JOHN PAPWORTH is ex-Personal Assistant to the President of Zambia, founder of Resurgence *journal, Editor of* Fourth World News *and author of* New Politics.

We live in an age of protest mounted in a desert of ignorance. Today it is almost impossible to find any literate person who is not allied to one form of protest or another, whether it is with the various movements which append the word 'liberation' to their cause, to the struggle to assert a threatened or a fast-vanishing ethnic identity, to a whole complex of organizations protesting ecological despoilation or localized bureaucratic presumption, or to the numerous anti-war bodies (the current Peace News Diary lists the headquarters – never mind the branches of many of them – of no less than 130 'peace' organizations in Great Britain alone).

The effect of all this multifarious activity on the mainstream of events is negligible, the overall crisis of our civilisation continues to gather momentum with a seemingly inevitable progression towards collapse, and in their hearts many of the excellent people who involve themselves, and even devote their lives, seeking to arrest it, must surely feel at times that they are joined in battle against forces over which there is no prospect that they can prevail.

Very few, if indeed any, of the numerous protest movements which have surfaced over the past few decades appear ready to step back from their situation and to ask themselves leading questions about the dynamics that prompt the evils or abuses against which they protest, few seem ready to relate their protest or predicaments to the very existence of prevailing political forces or to make any realistic assessment of their prospects of successfully doing battle with them. Very often indeed they seek to identify with them! To protest in the dark seems enough, however futile it may seem to do so. The problems of war, ecological despoilation, the mindless rundown of finite resources, ethnic suppression and mass alienation are worse now than when all these organizations were first launched.

It is against this background of multiple ineffectuality that the concept of the Fourth World has emerged. If the major evils of our time can indeed be ascribed to a loss of citizen control over the governing mechanisms, if that loss of control stems from giantism, if indeed, giantism has become public enemy number one of the human race, then clearly we cannot begin to counter those evils unless we first address ourselves to this key problem of size.

Thanks to such writers as Kohr, Schumacher, Narayan, Goodman, Roszak and Illich, some common ground had been prepared and it was on the basis of their theoretical work that the Fourth World was launched. Our plans were ambitious, even if they were much less so than the nature of the human predicament warranted. We wanted to establish a large and continuing think-tank exercise in which people would relate their particular concerns to the *principle of the human scale* and then spell out how the people of our planet could assume control of the forces which are apparently bent on its destruction.

We of the Fourth World are challenging the assumptions of nearly every form of political and economic power that now dominates the globe, we are also challenging the basic assumptions that individuals nearly everywhere have about the way they view this power and how they act in response to it. But such challenges cannot be met except by the private response of countless individuals who determine in their hearts it is the right thing to do and then set about doing it. I have no doubt at all that they will emerge. I am confident that growing numbers will come to see that the Fourth World, the world of the human scale, is an answer to the paralysing inconsequence of the protest movement of the past generation, that they will come to understand that our global crisis is itself a product of a deep-rooted global malaise and can only be countered by an equally deep-rooted transformation of global outlook and action such as the Fourth World embodies.

Nor is this confidence solely a matter of faith; however much such faith may be needed, it is also a matter of taking due note of what is already happening. Even as these words are written there must be hundreds of thousands of modest, small-scale initiatives burgeoning all over the world concerned to combat the phenomena of giantism, to assert the supremacy of the human scale and in doing so manifesting, often quite unconsciously, an identity with the Fourth World. The reader who is curious is referred to Kirkpatrick Sale's encyclopaedic compendium, *The Human Scale* (pub. Secker and Warburg). Readers in a similar state of grace are also referred to the pages which follow, where attempts to define some of the parameters of the new thinking are made and some possible signposts of the new directions we need to take established.

It comes to this, a revolution in human consciousness is under way, perhaps one of the most important in human history, yet almost as though some instinctive and involuntary conspiracy were at work, its import is almost wholly unremarked by the main organs and channels of opinion.

Quite suddenly the idea has begun to invade popular consciousness that what is basically wrong with our political and economic institutions is not their political complexion or the failings of particular leaders who seek to run them, but their *size*.

Such an approach has the effect of side-stepping most of the points of contention in the current political and economic debate, points which have dominated Western thinking on such matters for nearly two centuries. If countries are too big, as for example China, Russia, India and the USA are too big, then nothing can be made to work properly, except fortuitously, since their bigness puts them beyond control. Beyond the control, be it noted, not only of their citizens, but of those who are supposed to be running them.

Yet if such countries are small enough to be sensibly managed by their citizens it does not much matter, within obvious limits, what political colouration they happen to acquire. As Professor Kohr has pointed out, San Marino has been a small independent communist state in the centre of Italy for decades, yet unlike the communist giants it is quite prosperous and poses no threat to anyone. In the same way tiny Liechtenstein, albeit capitalist, is also quite prosperous and no way a threat to its neighbours.

As yet this conceptual approach is still in its infancy; its protagonists lack cohesion (and perhaps they always will) and there is still not a single institution of learning or research anywhere in the world concerned to probe the problems of applying the human scale to our political and economic structures.

One reason for this resistance or indifference doubtless lies in the assumption that as a proposal for resolving many of our ills talk of the human scale is too visionary and impractical for serious consideration. This reaction does not stem from any lack of examples showing where the application of the human scale is both practical and successful, but from the current domination of the globe by giant nation states.

How, it is asked, are countries of the order of Britain, France and Italy, never mind the USA, the USSR, India and China, to be made subject to human-scale criteria? *How* can they be broken up? The question indicates a quite illusory belief in the permanence of these arrangements. Very few of the nation states of the world have a history of more than a hundred years, and most are of considerably more recent creation. They are the product of certain beliefs which prevailed when they arose, they will cease to exist in their present form when those beliefs cease to hold sway. Less than a generation ago the world was dominated by a number of giant empires. Where are most of those empires today?

Nor should we overlook that something like one third of the people of the world are already living in what we may call human-scale countries, that is, those with a population of twelve million or less. They include, it should also be noted, the richest, the most socially advanced, the most liberal, stable and peaceful nations of the world. The base already exists on which the Fourth World may be built.

Sometimes new thinking has such an explosive impact that after its initial reception there follows an interregnum in which the old thinking continues as if nothing has really happened. This seems to be the case with the appearance of the late Dr E.F. Schumacher's *Small is Beautiful*, first published in 1973. The title of the book itself has now passed into the language, but meanwhile a considerable readjustment of thought is still underway and the contributions published here are but a very modest indication of the scope and the extent of that change.

Those interested in how things begin will wish to take specific note of the date 1957, the year which saw the first appearance of Professor Leopold Kohr's epoch-making book, *The Breakdown of Nations. The Economist* described it as 'maddening', possibly because the reviewer could see no way of refuting its general thesis – that global wars are a product of state giantism and centralization – and yet wished to continue to hold on to the parameters of the old thinking.

Another date that may prove to be significant is 1966, the year in which *Resurgence*, the journal of the Fourth World, the world of small nations, small communities and the human spirit, was founded. Its earlier contributors included among others Leopold Kohr (of course), Fritz Schumacher, Sir Herbert Read, Paul Goodman, Theodore Roszak, Jayaprakash Narayan, Thomas Merton, Geoffrey Ashe and Ivan Ilich. Good names of people pleading a good cause, but in some ways the journal was ahead of its time and its modest circulation reflected its sharply minority stance. The success of *Small is Beautiful*, comprised in part of Schumacher's *Resurgence* contributions, was, in circulation terms, a shot in the arm. But by then, under a change of editors, it had ceased to be mainly concerned with the problems of the human scale.

Since then the number of books on the theme of the human scale has increased. Perhaps special note needs to be made of Roszak's widely acclaimed *The Making of a Counter Culture* which, in fact, preceded Schumacher's book by three years, and which was as important for the questions it posed as for the answers it sought to give in its discussion of the problems of the large-scale technocratic society under challenge from the rising generation.

No less important was the appearance of Sale's *Human Scale*, referred to above and of which Lewis Mumford wrote, 'If anything can arrest the total disintegration of world civilization today it will come through a miracle: the recovery of "the human scale" described in Kirkpatrick Sale's encyclopaedic book.' Its appearance, in 1980, coincided with the efforts of a small London-based group to establish what they called 'The First Assembly of the Fourth World'. This think-tank exercise on the problems of the human scale was envisaged as being an annual event which would engender papers on specific topics for serious discussion and spark off action as the conclusions might indicate.

Despite a plethora of papers, a number of them wildly unsuitable, a large (400) attendance and the setting up of twenty or more forums on specialist topics, the event can only be described as a glorious failure. Very few of those who attended seemed to be aware that the event was not just another get-together of the radically-minded cognoscenti, but an attempt to lift the entire debate on politics and the problems of war and social disorder onto a new level. Few seem to have read the general Declaration which all who attended received, and fewer still to have digested its implications; much time was spent on matters extraneous to the purposes of the gathering and far too little on matters which were germane to it.

Yet many of the papers, (some of which are included in this volume), were first-class discussion material and indicative not only of the extent to which the new thinking is spreading, but of the solid conceptual base on which it rests.

Subsequent Assemblies have focussed on single rather than multiple issues. In both Berlin (1982) and Larzac (1983) the theme was 'communes' and reflected in the main the concerns of their respective organizers. But it is possible, despite everything, that we built better than we knew at that First Assembly. In any event we may be sure that the attempt then started to establish some honest and clear-sighted parameters amid the intellectual ferment so characteristic of our time, will continue. What direction it will take may well depend in large part on the response this volume evokes from its readers.

Megasociety – a dictatorship of the executive

Dr KIT PEDLER

The late KIT PEDLER was the author of Quest for Gaia, Doomwatch *and* Mind Over Matter.

I will begin by asking what the greatest areas of social change in the next ten or fifteen years will be and to answer this I want first to distinguish two separate parts of the situation: social activity and the actual energy resource structure which underpins social activity. Social behaviour will, I believe, be forced into change without any choice by people simply because the basis of the industrial society no longer works.

There is neither the energetic nor the resource basis for it to continue in its present form, and a high proportion of the very large scale industries, which are still being planned, will never function. For example, British Steel will plan and build a new steel factory but it will not go into service for at least nine years, and by that time the energy and resource basis on which it was first costed will no longer be remotely valid; so the entire plan gradually becomes more irrational. For this general reason, there will be an enormous change in the way in which the industrial society functions, and many of the products which we now take for granted will no longer be there, because the materials and energy to make them will no longer be available. And this will inevitably force social change. I recently saw a juggernaut roaring down the motorway with the words 'Mother's Pride' written on it. Apart from the fact the product itself may be quite uneatable, why is it necessary to deliver this degraded product hundreds of miles across country when a local bakery can produce a more nutritious product without significant delivery charge? What will happen is that people will become more locally oriented and therefore large centralized industries will no longer be valid.

But will we be led or propelled into these changes? The

danger is that we shall be propelled, in which case there is likely to be quite a large scale social convulsion of one sort or another and many people are likely to get hurt. And whether it will be breakdown or revolution, it is the weak who suffer the most; the old and the young. But for years the political basis of our democracy, as we are encouraged to perceive it, has been apparently well established. And so if we are going to experience a social convulsion will our political system be forced to change fundamentally as well? I think that it will and the first idea to get rid of is that there is a Left and a Right and a Liberal. These are now antique ideologies and I now no longer believe that there will be any valid human centred ideology for a sustainable future. In a book I have written I call the necessary politics 'Gaianism', named after Gaia, the Greek goddess of the earth, because I hold that any valid political ideology for the future must, by virtue of the rapidly degrading planetary situation, be based on placing human need second to the need of the earth organism, the planet-wide life process. And this is not idealistic environmentalism. I am not an environmentalist, but I now believe that we will quite shortly be forced to recognize that we can no longer use the earth in the way that we have been, because it will simply fail to provide altogether. We will wake up one morning and find ourselves living on a dessicated cinder. In order to sustain the earth for the future, and to sustain ourselves, we shall be forced to orient ideology towards this aim. But another problem to face is that we do not have very much democracy left, either in the West or the East. Society is now dictated by the executive, people who were never elected; an autocracy of bureaucrats; and this situation is common to China, Russia and America, as well as in Europe. Political ideology has to change towards putting human need second. Victor Hugo called it 'La Grande Morale' – the idea that we should have a major extra-human ethic which guides everyday life in a very positive way.

But there will be danger in the way that we deal with the scientific and social future. Can we be optimistic that we are going to be able to make the change safely, bearing in mind the development of the more lethal technologies like nuclear energy?

The answer is yes and the reason is based on science. Top grade physicists are beginning to say things about nature and about the way in which the universe works, which are very different from the strictly materialistic views of the old scientists. They are beginning to consider the demise of the current science and the emergence of a new science which incorporates more ideas of human consciousness and mind. And this will come to have a much more benign influence. What some scientists are now saying is that beyond the pieces that they analyse there may be a whole. And in that whole there are some very optimistic changes for human beings should they become part of a more general social currency.

But timing is crucial to these changes. The longer it takes to make the adjustment, the harder the adjustment will be. On the other hand, to move too quickly could create an imbalance in society which itself could be difficult and dangerous to handle. And the danger would be because a polarity would emerge; reason against unreason. We have seen an appalling example of that recently in Iran, where a high-technological country ceased to exist overnight. It was replaced by an entirely irrational belief system, which has in no way improved the Iranian circumstance. And by analogy what I worry about is that during the breakdown, there might be groups of people who try to force irrational concepts and so do others great harm.

But getting back to earth, how can we deal with the environment, the awful urban sprawl that most of us live in? Are we going to wipe the slate clean and create an entirely new urban environment? Or will we continue to reshape and redevelop the old? If we look at the cities as they are built, it seems that man, after 5,000 years of evolution, has rediscovered the rectangle. Buildings are not really buildings any more, they are concrete realizations of a cost benefit analysis. But there is no reason why we should not take from the older architecture those principles which are viable for an energy-starved future.

For example, I lived until quite recently in a house that was started in the sixteenth century. It was built of old bits of wood which had been cut with an adze, it had plaster and lath in between, and there was not a single rectangle in the place. Over the centuries the house had simply adapted like the skeleton of an animal to the shape and movement of the earth. But in that great drought a few years ago, many houses in London cracked because the foundations dried out and they had no flexibility. So one can learn very simple lessons like that. The other day I read an extraordinary bureaucratic statement from the GLC saying that the average lifetime of a house is seventy years. Yet the house I lived in had been sitting around unchanged from the sixteenth century. So we do not need to wipe the slate clean; we just have to be more intelligent about how we choose technologies.

Many dreamers see us going into entirely new environments – building cities under the sea, or in space. But these do not have the slightest chance of appearing because of the energy resource base that would be needed to create them. It is rather similar to the economies of a North Sea oil rig; everybody enthuses as to how productive North Sea oil is, but they omit to bring into the equation the fabrication energy of a machine twice the height of Big Ben – all the steel and welding has to be paid for in energy first. The energy equation of an oil rig certainly does not work if you look at it as energy accountancy rather than cash accountancy.

Many of the theories about undersea cities are based on the assumption that the world's population will continue to show the same sort of doubling rate and exponential increase that people claim it is showing now. But there are big changes occurring, particularly in urban population.

Some diseases which I call the technogenic diseases – diseases which are generated by the technological society – are already showing signs of change. It may well be that the world's population will level out or even decline as a result of our own efforts. An American scientist said to me the other day that what we need to do now in order for man to survive is to take people as far away as possible from man-made molecules. In other words, what we are doing is very dangerous to our bodies.

But what about cultural development in the future, often a very depressing area to examine. Are there any hopeful signs?

At present we have a society which is, in my view, culturally sterile. If art, to use the old cliche, is a mirror of the age, then art is showing that sterility very clearly. We have people who really only have a talent for publicity coming to the fore as cult figures. I recently saw an exhibition of sculpture at the Hayward Gallery in which someone had put a block of stone from a quarry, complete with drill marks, on the stand as his own work. Now that seems to me to be a very significant exhibit because it was nihilistic. What the block of rock was saying was 'I'm desperate, what do I make of this piece?'. Like the pile of bricks in the Tate. And there is a similar trend in pop music. If we can begin to look at the world in a different way and put more of our own needs second, we might put some of the softness and attraction back into our art. People might even start painting pots of flowers again.

But are children at school being adequately prepared for a rapidly changing future? They are most certainly not. To me the reason for living is personal growth and the sort of education most children are receiving at school gives them no provision for that whatsoever. They are basically educated to get a job in the computerized society, a job that in all probability won't be there in the near future. They are not taught the personal freedoms or anything important for the full development of a human society. I would like to see pupils taught the basic subjects of food, warmth, shelter, health and politics, within which would come the three Rs as a natural consequence. But that, unfortunately, would create a free society, and that is the last thing that a dictatorship of the executive wants.

The work ethic is a very poor conditioning influence. We are on this planet to live and make the most of our lives. It just happens that the society we are living in fails to give any chance of this. Instead of throwing pupils on to the scrap heap at the age of sixteen or seventeen as they currently do, schools should be teaching children about life and what it offers, not just preparing them for a lifetime of work. Sooner or later the emphasis is going to change for all of us, because the idea of work will collapse. But the answer is not just more leisure or free time, it is the chance to lead a richer, fuller life.

The central theme to the changes that face us is that the mega-society takes away responsibility and choice. If you hand responsibility back to people they may redevelop choice. They may choose to live a much more humane and fulfilling life.

Fourth World principles

KIRKPATRICK SALE AND PROFESSOR LEOPOLD KOHR

These ten principles are the Fourth World equivalent of the ten commandments and represent the rudiments of political wisdom. They are derived principally from Kirkpatrick Sale's book Human Scale *and from Leopold Kohr's article in this book (see page 33). LEOPOLD KOHR is the author of* The Breakdown of Nations.

In summary:

The Beanstalk Principle (Sale):
For every animal, object, institution or system, there is an optimal limit beyond which it ought not to grow.

The Law of Peripheral Neglect (Kohr):
Governmental concern, like marital fidelity or gravitational pull, diminishes with the square of the distance.

The Law of Government Size (Sale):
Ethnic and social misery increase in direct proportion to the size and power of the central government of a nation or state.

Lucca's Law (Sale):
Other things being equal, territories will be richer when small and independent, than when large and dependent.

The Principle of Limits (Kohr):
Social problems tend to grow at a geometric rate, while the ability of humans to deal with them, if it can be extended at all, grows only at an arithmetic rate.

The Population Principle (Sale):
As the size of a population doubles, its complexity – the amount of information exchanged and decisions required – quadruples, with consequent increases in stress and dislocation and mechanisms of social control.

The Velocity Theory of Population ('Slow is Beautiful') (Kohr):
The mass of a population increases not only numerically, through birth, but through increases in the velocity with which it moves.

The Self-Reliance Principle (Schumacher):
Highly self-sufficient local communities are less likely to get involved in large-scale violence than those whose existence depend on worldwide systems of trade.

The Principles of Warfare (Sale):
(1) The severity of war always increases with an increase in state power. (2) War centralizes the state by providing an excuse for an increased state power and the means by which to achieve it.

The Law of Critical Power (Kohr):
Critical power is the volume of power that gives a country's leaders reason to believe that they cannot be checked by the power available to any antagonist or combination of antagonists. Its accumulation is the inevitable cause of war.

Most of the above principles are explained in more detail in the notes that follow.
Kirkpatrick Sale:

I am not saying that size – and its companion notion of scale, or sizes in relation to each other – is the *only* measurement to make in judging something. But it does make sense that it should be the first, and the central consideration, in as much as it is likely to affect, in one degree or another, all other considerations.

The Beanstalk Principle (Sale)
For every animal, object, institution or system, there is an optimal limit beyond which it ought not to grow.

It occured to me one day, looking at the drawings in a book of fairy tales, that the giant in *Jack and the Beanstalk* looked somehow more fragile than menacing. If the giant was, as he looked, about five times as big as Jack – five times taller, thicker and wider – then he would have to weigh not just five times as much, but five-to-the-third-power as much, five times in each direction. The giant would have been trying to support 125 times the weight on bones only 25 times as strong.

As the city planner knows, doubling a city's population means vastly increasing its area – since as its population increases arithmetically its space tends to increase geometrically – and it means services become increasingly complex, independent, rigid and vulnerable.

Size indeed, might well be regarded as *the* crucial variable in anything. More important than say, ideology – for a large disciplined party like the Communist Party in the Soviet Union is no better than a large undisciplined one like the Christian Democrats in Italy; both are unwieldy, unrepresentative, undemocratic, and inefficient, not because of their politics but because of their size.

Lucca's Law (Sale)
Other things being equal, territories will be richer when small and independent than when rich and dependent.

Communities are always much richer than they think they are. It is not smallness that deprives them of economic power and the ability to sustain themselves self-sufficiently, but on the contrary, their ties to largeness.

A study for an American supermarket chainstore shows that a firm with US $ 5.7 million in annual sales will export out of the local economy $ 332,160 more than a store owned locally. Multiply that for virtually every product and service, and you can see that the only difficulty with a community's wealth is that it doesn't stay there.

The little town of Lucca became one of the fiercely independent republics in the thirteenth century and for the next 400 years it was one of the most prosperous places on the entire Italian peninsula. It enjoyed a rich and self-sufficient agriculture; it was a major banking centre (still with no more than 15,000 people); was famous for its velvet and other textile manufacturing; was the home of recognised artists, musicians and writers. Today it is a forgotten backwater of 45,000 people, with a shaky industrial base (confined largely to jute and tobacco), the recipient of all that happens to the Italian economy of compounded chaos and inflation.

The Principle of Limits (Kohr)
Social problems tend to grow at a geometric rate, while the ability of humans to deal with them, if it can be extended at all, grows only at an arithmetic rate.

> Oversize appears to be the one and only problem permeating all creation. Whenever something is wrong, something is too big. If the stars in the sky or the atoms of uranium disintegrate in spontaneous explosion, it is because matter has attempted to expand beyond the barriers set to every accumulation. If the body of a people becomes diseased with the fever of aggression, brutality, collectivism or massive idiocy, it is because human beings have welded into mobs, unions, cartels, or great powers. If a society grows beyond its optimum size, its problems must eventually outrun the growth of those human faculties which are necessary for dealing with them.

The Population Principle (Sale)
As the size of a population doubles, its complexity – the amount of information exchanged and decisions required – quadruples, with consequent increases in stress and dislocation and mechanisms of social control.

> That seems perfectly plausible when we consider that in a group of 25 people there are theoretically 33 possible conflicts between two people at any given moment, and in a group of 10,000 no fewer than 50 million possible conflicts.
>
> Anthropology and history both suggest that humans have been able to work out most of their differences at the population levels clustering around the 'magic numbers' of 500–1,000 and 5,000–10,000. Anthropological literature indicates that it is when a population reaches about 1,000 that 'a village begins to need policing'.

The Self-Reliance Principle (Schumacher)
Highly self-sufficient local communities are less likely to get involved in large-scale violence than those whose existence depends on worldwide systems of trade.

> As physical resources are everywhere limited, people

satisfying their needs by means of modest use of resources are obviously less likely to be at each other's throats than people depending upon a high rate of use.

The Principles of Warfare (Sale)
(1) The severity of war always increases with an increase in state power. (2) War centralizes the state by providing an excuse for an increased state power and the means by which to achieve it.

> War is the health of the state... (Victory is incidental: many losing nations emerge from wars with more powerful governments). In fact what goes by the name of the defence of the citizens by the state may really be better thought of as the other way around.
>
> Moreover, in the course of attempting to provide its defence, the state exercises its own forms of coercion and violence. It conscripts young people and takes to itself the right to jail or kill those who resist conscription or desert after induction; it forces the wider population to pay for warfare and its preparation through increased taxation, which has never in history been paid voluntarily; it amasses an army that denies individual rights and freedoms through accepted methods of authoritarian control. And such a state, preoccupied with defence, begins to justify all acts in its name (as Presidents justify all crimes with 'national security').

The Laws of Scale

PROFESSOR LEOPOLD KOHR

LEOPOLD KOHR is the author of The Breakdown of Nations, The Overdeveloped Nations *and* Development Without Aid. *A further three of the Fourth World principles are among matters explained in the following article.*

The Law of Peripheral Neglect
According to the Law of Gravitation, the power of attraction diminishes with the square of the distance.

There are many variations of this law in the social universe as well. Marital fidelity declines with the square of the distance. So, as Konrad Lorentz has shown, does aggressiveness. Attentiveness, and the corresponding marks, diminish with the square of the distance a student sits from the instructor. So does familiarity with the environment which limits the reach of efficient government or the chance of pursuing war. What defeated Napoleon in Moscow was not lack of military power but sheer distance from the source of his power. The same was true of America's defeat in Vietnam.

It is this circumstance that has put barriers to the expansion of nations and empires, permitting other gravitational fields to form, with their own governmental centres, or forcing them to create sub-sovereign regional provinces on their own soil by giving them a degree of autonomy proportionate to their distance from the capital.

For beyond a given distance, even the most concerned and benevolent government is bound to treat its receding regions with ever increasing neglect. The law of peripheral neglect is the main argument for limiting the sway of central government, and for replacing the unitary state by a federal or confederal system of self-governing states, not by integrating but by duplicating the institutions of social life.

Central governments tend to counteract the inexorable workings of this law by increasing the central powers of government which simply increases authoritarianism and insensitive repression without diminishing the neglect of the periphery. As the law of gravitation is the law behind the multi-star system of the universe, so the law of peripheral neglect is the law behind a Fourth World system of a thousand flags instead of the single sun of a UN.

The Size Interpretation of History

Various theories attribute the cause of historic change to the intervention of great leaders, ideologies, accident or economic systems. Marx, who produced the best reasoned theory, attributes it to a change in the mode of production. This he considers the primary cause. What he fails to explain is why the primary cause, the mode of production, should itself periodically change. There must therefore be a still more fundamental cause. This is the periodically changing size of society.

It is this that accounts for the expulsion from paradise. Man became too numerous for the apple-picking mode of production. Each time a population reached a given critical size, it had to introduce a more effective mode of production – from hunting to agriculture, from handicraft to machinecraft, from muscle power to coal, to nuclear energy.

The answer to the world's economic and energy problem lies therefore not in the pooling of resources and increased vast-scale international co-operation and integration, but in reducing the size of society to a scale that can once again be handled with the available simpler food and energy resources: pedestrian power, intermediate technology, human senses instead of computers. Only in small societies can transport distances be reduced and traffic correspondingly slowed down to uncostly material-saving dimensions.

Nothing of this makes sense unless the Size Interpretation is assumed to be valid. As it explains changes in the mode of production, so it explains all other changes in what Marx calls the 'superstructure' – art forms, legal concepts, lifestyles, crime, juvenile delinquency, loss of identity, ideological, economic and political changes, inflation, unemployment, war. All have their own critical size when they erupt.

Critical Power

Critical power is the volume of power that gives a country's leaders reason to believe that they cannot be checked by the power available to any antagonist or combination of antagonists. Its accumulation is the cause of war, the inevitable cause of war, and the only cause of war. It makes no difference whether it is in the hands of good or bad leaders, aggressors or lovers of peace. As in the case of uranium when it reaches critical size, it explodes spontaneously, even if no one wants this to happen.

Hence, the only way to prevent war is to prevent the accumulation of critical masses of power. Since these can accumulate only in countries of critical size, it follows that what is needed is not disarmament, treaties, preaching, or re-education, but the division of the great powers into systems of sub-critical parts.

Critical Size
A nation reaches critical size when the cost of its upkeep becomes larger than the benefits derived by its citizens. There are four elements contributing to the increase of national size: a numerical increase in the population; an increase in its density; an increase in its integration; and an increase in the velocity with which a population must move as a result of its ever increasing integration in larger territorial units. So important is the last-named factor that what the present world really suffers from is not a numerical but a velocity over-population. Numerical over-population can be corrected by the sinister Malthusian Trinity of famine, war, disease; whereas velocity over-population requires the contraction of national communities so that a city's or a country's daily activities can once again be negotiated at a leisurely pace.

Slow is beautiful. It reduces the size of a population without a drop of blood being spilled. I have formulated this in what I have called *the velocity theory of population* which, in analogy to the quantity theory of money, reduces inflationary population pressure by reducing the speed of circulation. It is because of the mass and size increasing effect of speed that theatres must have emergency exits. If an audience panics and starts to run instead of trying to leave the theatre walking, it has the same effect as if the audience had doubled or tripled. In other words, exits must be adjusted not to the numerical but the *effective* size of an audience, that is, numerical size multiplied by speed.

The solution to the problem of critical size is therefore the same as that for critical power: cut down the overgrown national and territorial entities by their cantonization into systems of largely self-sufficient small communities which can afford to move slowly simply because they do not need to move fast.

Velocity Theory of Population
As outlined above, the mass of a population increases not only

numerically, through birth, but effectively, through an increase in the velocity with which it moves.

A nation is forced to increase its velocity when it increases its degree of centralization and integration by increasing the commercial and administrative contacts of outlying districts with the centre as well as with each other. Not only do more movements become necessary, but they must also be made at ever increasing speeds with the result that, aside from such areas as India, the world suffers today not so much from a numerical but from a velocity over-population, which can be solved through no degree of birth control.

What is needed is to slow down the pace of life, through autonomous regionalization, or a system of loosely-confederated small states whose citizens can once again resolve most of their daily problems in their own neighbourhood rather than by journeying to ever remoter distant government and supply centres.

This is also the only way of radically solving the energy crisis: not through the discovery and utilization of new sources of power such as nuclear fission, whether it comes from the sun or the earth, but through making the inexhaustible supply of muscle power economical again by contracting the theatre of our daily activities once again to the dimensions of farm and city life that existed in earlier periods.

Papworth's Laws of Political Dynamics

JOHN PAPWORTH

Elegant variations of the foregoing 'Laws' are to be found in this article by John Papworth, in which he argues that mass democracy is a contradiction in terms. John Papworth is the author of New Politics.

Whichever party group wins an election it is seldom the people, for their role in casting a vote in elections today is largely symbolic and akin to being asked to kick-off at a football match. In whatever direction they kick, or whichever side they may favour, it has no bearing on the subsequent progress of the game or its result. Quite other forces are at work.

Perhaps the matter may be put more simply in a series of propositions with a brief comment on each, and with the kind of modesty which prevails in academe perhaps I may be allowed to call them 'Papworth's Laws of Political Dynamics'.

LAW 1   As a political unit increases in numbers, the capacity of the individual citizen to control its workings declines.

Comment: Liechtenstein has a population of thirty thousand; ignoring age and franchise considerations, it may be said that each inhabitant of the principality has a one thirty-thousandth share in its affairs. China has a population of one thousand-million, so that each inhabitant of China enjoys, (if that is the correct verb to convey the pleasure of suzerainty over so stupendous a morsel), a one thousand-millionth share in its affairs. It will be clear that while the numbers in the principality bear some relation to democratic reality, in the case of China the statement is devoid of any meaning.

The question of deciding at what stage in the growth of numbers in a political unit the principle even of representative democracy based on a head count ceases to have any meaning is surely one of the most urgent confronting us. Some of the authorities who have considered the matter in detail, (and very few of them have), would opt for an upper limit of five million, few would put it at greater than twelve million.

LAW 2   A community may be defined as a political unit of such modest dimensions that the personal relationships of the members, and how those relationships become expressed in terms of morals and values, can take precedence over every other force.

Comment: The general guiding principle of community

life is enshrined in the command of Jesus of Nazareth, 'Love thy neighbour', and even, 'Love thine enemy'. This is not some idealistic and impracticable moral objective but the basis, perhaps the only basis, on which a community can long survive – for any community of which the members pursue their individual interests without regard to the general interest can scarcely be said to be an entity at all and is likely to be absorbed sooner or later by others where general social disciplines are more effectively affirmed and applied.

Gandhi's observation that 'you cannot have morality without community' is unarguable and when under the impetus of a growth in numbers other objectives (efficiency? higher productivity? faster transport? the mobility of labour?) are assumed to be of greater importance, the community, whether a rural village or an urban parish, is already dying, because such economic forces have already destroyed the economic basis of village life, and when we note that villages are the 'blood cells' of any civilization, the demise of the village can only be a prelude to the demise of the larger body.

LAW 3 A large political unit which lacks the organic, non-centralized structure of localized community life is called a mass society and as such cannot long endure. While it holds sway it will be chronically subject to wars, economic upheavals and other attributes of political decadence.

Comment: In the nature of things the members of a mass society cannot fail to be isolated, alienated and manipulated. The idea that in big cities governed centrally by the leaders of mass parties such people are 'free' is wholly illusory. Theirs is the freedom to be manipulated by forces they neither perceive nor control, forces which are using forms of power beyond the reach and, all too often, the understanding of those affected.

These forces are pursuing goals of self-interest and it is the power they are able to wield (citizen power the citizen is unable to exercise) which creates the clashes of interest which lead to wars (both 'hot' and 'cold'), to inflation, unemployment, ecological abuse and a general trend of events which is beyond control.

LAW 4   A mass democracy is a contradiction in terms.

Comment: A mass may be broken down into human-scale communities which are almost wholly self-governing. This can constitute democracy, but it is no longer a mass. Or, a large number of communities may be merged into a single mass no longer susceptible to self-government and governed instead by rival leadership cliques but such governance is no longer democratic.

LAW 5 The dimunition of the power of individual members of a mass society to control its workings is always accompanied by an increase in the power of the forces at the centre.

Comment: In Britain (for example), the general citizen body has long ceased to be the arbiter of public affairs; public opinion is now but one, and a minor one at that, of several forces playing upon the disposition of power. The upper echelons of the civil service, of the financial system, of the industrial giants, the leaders of parties and of trade unions and the top people in other spheres, whatever process of democratic selection some of them may credentially claim, are in no wise voices of democracy but of oligarchies of power. The preamble to parliamentary bills, 'Be it enacted by the Queen's most excellent Majesty, by and with the assent of the Lords Spiritual and Temporal, and Commons, in this present Parliament assembled', is paying court to a traditional view which ceased to be valid long before the Napoleonic wars. It is now the *values* which the oligarchic groupings at the centre need to promote (success, wealth, speed and 'efficiency') which dominate the lifestyle of a mass society, not the moral judgements of the citizens.

LAW 6   In a mass society power is almost always pursued as an end in itself.

Comment: The quest for power is as old as history, but in human-scale societies it is possible for it to be subordinate to considerations of morals, aesthetics and the general health of the political body. Today we live in mass societies inevitably dominated not by the human scale and by human-scale judgements, but by the machine scale and the assumed imperatives of machine-scale existence. This is why we are building townscapes which are horrible to look at and to live in; money, a form of power, takes precedence over any question of seemliness or beauty. This was not so in human-scale Renaissance Europe. In political life today a politician will only support measures which will give him office or help to maintain him in it. If the measures are good, the citizen may well assume the politician is using his power to buttress good morality. He assumes wrongly. The politician is simply using morality to buttress his power position.

LAW 7   If politically ambitious people in a mass society fail to pursue power as an end in itself they will almost invariably be replaced by others who do.

Comment: It will be noted that this law is a twin of one of the laws of the economic dynamics which states: 'If an entrepreneur fails to pursue profit as an end in itself he will be replaced by others who do.' This is why the Conservatives, the 'patriotic' party, abandoned patriotism and joined the 'United European' movement; the other power factors, mainly money, the media and militarism, put on so much pressure that Tory leaders who wanted office were forced to submit even if, as in the case of Mrs Thatcher, they were opposed to the whole idea. For the same reason, the Labour Party currently opposed to both the Government and 'Europe', will be unable to withdraw from the Common Market unless the other elements in the power equation decide after all that the whole game is unworkable (as it is) and that it is not worth the candle. At the time of the referendum, public opinion was against joining Europe. A ten million pounds propaganda campaign soon turned public opinion in favour. Public opinion is a factor to be manipulated; it is seldom itself decisive on any question.

LAW 8   In a mass society public policy is determined by private leadership groups, seldom by public opinion.

Comment: A failure to grasp the significance of this law has caused most of the horrors of the twentieth century. The Russian liberals thought they had only to get rid of the Tzar to usher in an era of progress and reform; instead they unwittingly helped to create one of the most horrendous tyrannies mankind has ever seen. They failed to see that if you do not control the base of society in the villages and urban parishes (as is quite impossible in a mass society), then you can have no influence on what happens at the top, for the top anyway is dominated by people questing for power *as an end in itself.* The same mistake is made by our World Federalists, Planetary Citizens, World Governmentalists, World Citizens, United Nations Associationists, to say nothing of the members of *any* mass political organisation. What happens at the top is either despite their intentions or because it happens fortuitously to correspond with what they want, because the power freaks are promoting it anyway in their own interests.

LAW 9 In a mass society mass movements of reform acquire the same characteristics of centralized control and personal alienation of members as the mass society itself.

Comment: This law is based on Michels' Iron Law of Oligarchy. The key factor here is size; with growth in the numbers of the unit the power of the individual to influence matters declines while the power-at-the-centre expands to a like degree. Party members are not served by party leaders in mass parties, they are manipulated, deceived or ignored. The party leaders want power and while the concern of the party member with morality and principle may be a factor to be reckoned with, it is seldom more, and never decisive. Mr Hugh Gaitskell could vow to the Labour Party (of which he was the leader) that he would 'fight, fight and fight again' to reverse a motion it had just passed in favour of unilateral disarmament. He vowed this to its face! He felt no need to resign because the conference had rejected a key plank in his leadership policy. The real basis of his power stemmed not from the individual members but from other sources.

LAW 10 Giantism, centralization and excessive speed now represent a doomsday triumvirate that has become public enemy number one of the human race.

Comment: None of the problems which constitute the current global crisis in human affairs is susceptible of resolution (1) unless the size of our monster states is reduced to a human scale of fragmentation around no more than twelve million, (2) unless even those units are conducted on the same principle of localized power such as is practised politically (but not, unfortunately, economically) in Switzerland, and (3) until the pace of events, especially in the sphere of production and commerce, is reduced to one which lends itself to genuine human control. Without such changes, would-be reformers, radicals, progressives, or whatever label may adhere to those who seek to improve matters, are merely whistling in the dark, while the forces which willy-nilly will drown the world in blood are gathering around them.

The Fourth World – local power for peace

JOHN PAPWORTH

JOHN PAPWORTH is Editor of Fourth World News.

Do YOU control your local bank?
If not, why not?
The power of money is one of the forms of power which governments use to pay for armaments and war. You may not even have a local bank; why not start one? A locally owned and controlled centre for all things to do with money; like insurance, pension funds, building society loans, mortgages. *They* can do it; why not you? Don't wait for the big banks to drop dead; besides, you may beat them to it. Keep the money and the profits in your village or parish.

Do YOU control your own local school?
If not, why not?
You may not even have a local school. Start your own! Let the power freaks know you have had enough. Insist on

controlling the schooling of local children yourself. Encourage your neighbours to join you. Campaign for full control of the local school board.

Do YOU control your own local hospital or clinic?
If not, why not?
Start your own centre of non-aggressive and non-poisonous medicine. Barefoot doctors do a great job in China; why not here?

Do YOU control your local police?
If not, why not?
The role of the police is to protect people, not to be an arm of the State to oppress us. That is why people have always seen a strong need for local control of police. Where is that local control today? With centralized computers, the police headquarters can now have an instant file on every single person (for all we know they may already have it) including your medical record, your bank account, your politics, your family history, details of your sex life and the names of your friends. The police role is becoming one of general surveillance of everybody. Don't laugh at the idea that we may become a police State; we are already half-way there. Insist on local control of local police – while you can.

Do YOU control your own local government?
If not, why not?
Central control of local government is part of the power used for war. You may not even have any kind of local government. Many villages and urban districts have no local government at all! They have been wiped out by giant schemes which ignore people. Which ignore us! The central government only allows local government to do what it permits. Turn it round. Insist central government only does what local people permit. The Swiss do this. Why not you? Don't wait for the others to do it; get on with it, before it's too late.

Do YOU control your local newspaper?
If not, why not?
The power of the press is used to buttress the power to make war. You may not even have a local newspaper; in

any case, why not start one? It need not be big or cost a lot, but it must be lively and full of fun as well as news. *They* can do it, why not you?

The only real answer to the abuse of national power to make war is local power for peace. Let us enjoy our celebrations for peace, and our protests against war. But peace is not just a celebration. Peace is a way of life. War comes from power we can't control. We need citizen power at local level. Non-centralized power for peace. That is the aim of the Fourth World. You can't join the Fourth World. There is nothing to join! You can only make it – by doing it! And by being it.

Laudatio for Leopold Kohr

JOHN SEYMOUR

JOHN SEYMOUR is the author of Self Sufficiency *and numerous other books. In 1981 the State Government of Salzburg in Austria honoured Leopold Kohr with the award of the Golden Ring and organized in his honour a symposium of international scholars on the theme of 'The Return To The Human Scale'. This is the speech which John Seymour gave to mark the occasion.*

Being uncompromisingly unacademic I find it very hard to consider my friend Doctor Leopold Kohr as an academic at all. I rather think of him as he was that hot summer's day on my farm in Wales when I was perched precariously on top of a load of hay on a wagon, having bales flung up to me by a gang of bearded desperadoes of the sort that used to frequent my farm in those days – when I suddenly became aware that the man flinging up hay bales to me did *not* have a beard – and was *not* a desperado (except perhaps in spirit) and was, in fact, none other than the celebrated scholar and author whom we have come here today to honour. And he went on throwing these heavy bales up to me for a long time – I got tired of it before he did in fact.

Or I like to think of him on the many convivial occasions, in many a convivial inn, or private house equally convivial, when we have talked and laughed half the night through.

My anti-academic attitude makes it difficult for me to take any pronouncement from the groves of academia seriously. I generally assume that the value of what a man says or writes varies in inverse ratio to the number of degrees he has got. And yet here is this person who has doctorates in Law and in Political Science, has obtained degrees in History and Economics, has studied at the universities of Innsbruck, Paris, Vienna and London, has held lectureships and professorships at Rutgers University, at the University of the Americas in Mexico City, the University of Puerto Rico, who has headed a research team for the Carnegie Institute, and who finished his official academic career at the University College of Aberystwyth – and in spite of all this he talks sense!

Mind you he has always worn his learning so lightly that it is difficult to believe that he is an academic at all. He speaks – and writes too – so amusingly that one's first reaction to him is always laughter. I look upon his writings as some of the most serious and important writings of our century, and yet I have never read one of his books without bursting out, many times, into laughter.

One does not expect to laugh at economics!

We call economics, in England, the *dismal science,* and I believe it is because of the advice of people who call themselves *economists* that the so-called Great Nations of the world are in such a dismal mess. And yet – here was a professor of economics who not only talked sense but actually made people laugh!

The Breakdown of Nations was published in 1957. It was decades before its time. My belief is that it was pretty well ignored by Professor Kohr's fellow practitioners of the Dismal Science. For one thing the ideas expressed in it were then quite *new* – what person who has spent a lifetime mastering *old* ideas is suddenly going to listen to new ones? For another thing the author made you laugh. What serious academic is going to take seriously the arguments of anybody who makes you laugh?

Sixteen years after the publication of *The Breakdown of*

Nations came that fine book *Small is Beautiful*, written by Professor Kohr's great friend (and mine, I am proud to say), Fritz Schumacher. Doctor Schumacher always generously acknowledged the debt he owed to Leopold Kohr. Leopold has got a hilarious simile which involves one man in a telephone box, and another man outside it, and they both share the same beard, and he uses this to illustrate his intellectual relationship with Fritz Schumacher, but you will have to get him to explain it himself because I'm sure I can't.

The point is – *Small is Beautiful* swept the world, and its influence will, one day, actually permeate the thick skulls of those who rule the Great Nations – that is if they don't blow themselves up first. No matter how thick their skulls are, presumably they are not thick enough to stop an atom bomb. These ideas are being accepted all over the world nowadays by people who are receptive to new ideas.

But when *The Breakdown of Nations* came out – just under a quarter of a century ago remember – the ideas in it were completely original.

There is a quotation in one of Professor Kohr's later books, *The Overdeveloped Nations*, from the American psychologist William James, which describes the classic stages in the reception of a new theory. First, the theory is attacked as absurd. Then it is admitted to be true, but obvious and insignificant. And finally it is seen to be so important that its former adversaries claim to have discovered it themselves.

I imagine that Leopold Kohr's central theory is at the second stage of development. I am longing for it to reach the third, for if it does not, and that pretty soon, I don't have any confidence in the future of our species at all.

I brought myself up partly on the writings of H.G. Wells. In those days he was considered way out in front by we lefties – but a raving socialist lunatic by such people as my step-father. Wells was to be content with nothing less than one world state. He was the apostle of the Enormous. His great wish was to see Mankind 'conquer nature' and 'turn it to his own uses'. This could only be done if the world had only one government – the government of the world.

Well obviously, nothing could be more dangerous than our present set-up of the world having effectively *two* governments – half of it being ruled by an old man in Washington and the other half by another old man in Moscow. The dangers of this are *quite* unacceptable – particularly when one considers the *quality* of the people thrown up by these two super-duper powers to rule themselves. Certainly there seems to be a Law (I wonder if Professor Kohr has missed it? I'm afraid he has not) that the *quality* of rulers varies in inverse ratio to the size of the mob over which they rule.

But a government of the world!

If one thing is obvious to me *now* it is that if there were such a government it would be despotism – it would be the biggest despotism that the world has ever seen – and it would be the most despotic. It would make Orwell's *1984* look like a kiddies' fairy tale. Give me Genghis Khan any day! Personally I wish to see no sovereign state bigger than the State of Salzburg. If the world ever achieves one government I want to get off it.

After all – what is it that we individual human beings want from our societies? Leopold hammers this in his writings again and again. We want food and shelter of course – but good food not factory-processed rubbish – and good shelter. We want security from being bashed over the head by our neighbours. And, beyond this, we want what Leopold is constantly talking about – we want *conviviality!* We want good fellowship, we want culture, we want fun! Leopold's books give us chapter and verse about this but really – do we have to name names of artists and names of countries – surely anyone of us here knows perfectly well that the poets, composers and musicians, artists, philosophers and writers whose work still gives us the most pleasure nearly *all* came from what were small countries...

I remember Leopold being attacked at a party by a friend of mine – a real old-fashioned Welsh internationalist socialist she was.

'Leopold' she said. 'Your piddling little small nations can't even provide the poor people with *bathrooms!*'

'Madam,' he replied, 'in Salzburg, which is a very small

nation, even the *horses* have been provided with a bathroom.'

And consider the architectural merits of Salzburg, and compare them with those of New York!

I come from a country which calls itself *Great* Britain. In what does its *Greatness* consist? It termed itself great because its armies and its navies went about the world knocking other people about. There's not much *conviviality* about that. Ah – but my true country – my *England* – that *was* great. In the days before its population reached eight figures, England produced Chaucer, Milton, Newton, Wren, and a thousand poets, prose writers, scientists in the true sense and people of other accomplishments of the very first and highest order. What has *Great Britain* produced? Elgar I suppose! As an exercise can anybody here think of one great poet whose work will survive a thousand years? Shakespeare's will, if the world does.

I don't want to live in a *great* country. I want to live in a civilized country, a convivial country, a free country and a *fun* country! A country in which the people have very limited and simple physical needs but high–high–spiritual aspirations. And artistic and intellectual aspirations too. I don't want my country to be *great* in the sense of largeness... And I don't want it to be *rich* either, or powerful, or – what all the *great* countries are in the world today – *dangerous*.

It was a disaster when the small states and principalities of Europe were knocked together into the so-called *great* nation-states. It has led to nothing but wars of the most brutal kind, to mutual fear and distrust, to stupid and megalomaniac 'rulers', to police states and graceless dictatorships. And it has wiped out so much variety – the diversity, the gaiety, the fun of life. I remember somebody saying to Leopold Kohr after he had been talking in praise of Salzburg – and of Oberndorf as he often does – 'You forget that all this glory was when Salzburg was part of an enormous empire! It was not a small state at all.'

'Ah!' said Leopold, 'but it was a *ramshackle* empire! It didn't do too much damage to the many small states that it was supposed to rule. It didn't try to suppress their languages, nor their cultures, nor interfere with their trade. They just went on as though it hadn't existed.'

Well I wouldn't mind being a subject of an empire provided that it was *ramshackle* enough. And it couldn't be too ramshackle for me. It wouldn't worry *me* if a lot of silly young men swaggered about its capital and danced the waltz with the young ladies to the tunes of the late Johann Strauss. But the empire I was a part of was anything but ramshackle. It was far too efficient. It penetrated to every corner of the lives of its subject peoples. It tried to teach them that their only hope of becoming 'civilized' was to forget their own religions, their languages, their cultures – and try to be as much like English gentlemen as they could contrive to be – even to the extent of playing *cricket*.

That empire has, thank God, collapsed into the dust and England is a far happier country without it. She has still hung on to one last little colony though – the colony of Wales. The country that is afraid to be a country. Leopold Kohr fought valiantly for that little country's integrity and independence all the time he lived there, and Mr Gwynfor Evans – the Leader of the Welsh Nationalist Party, who is sitting in this Hall with us now – told me how greatly he valued the work of Dr Leopold Kohr, as he stumped about his hills and valleys giving talks to people, writing pamphlets and articles and books – trying to give the Welsh people the courage to be themselves again. It may seem at the moment as if this fight is a forlorn hope, but history is full of forlorn hopes that have triumphed in the end. Witness King Alfred of England's fight against the Danish hordes. Victory goes to the side which *hangs on longest*.

I have been asked by Welsh Nationalists why I, an Englishman, call myself a Welsh Nationalist. My answer is that it is because I am an *English* Nationalist. Nay, I go so far as to say that it is because I am an *East Anglian* Nationalist! East Anglia is a big enough country for me. It is about as big as the State of Salzburg. I would like to see Wales get her independence so that England could get rid of her – and become a smaller country again!

Of course I want to see my country *great* – but I want to see it great in art, in true science, in conviviality and culture and fun! Not great size or numbers. *Quality* is what I value – and it varies in inverse ratio to size and number.

From a certain size that is. I'm not going to preach the Kohr doctrine here; I assume that every civilized person has read *The Breakdown of Nations*. If one has not let me advise him to hasten to do so. But I must point out that it is not smallness that Kohr writes about but *right size*. All good things know when to stop growing. Like noses or big toes, otherwise we would all look most peculiar and shoemakers would have a hell of a job. States, too, should know when they are big enough.

A state with but one citizen is not big enough. A state with twenty million is too big.

Leopold Kohr backs his arguments up with such a massive weight of evidence – historical, statistical and otherwise – that it must be hard for even the most Neanderthalic practitioner of the Dismal Science to refute him. His scholarship is daunting. But he does far more than just produce masses of evidence to support what he says. It is *what he says* that is so important and interesting.

I believe that this is so – that he has been so consistent in his message – because his aims have always been the right ones, and simple ones. He has never allowed his mind to stray from the purpose of it all, of all politics, of all philosophy. And that purpose is, in human terms, that all children, women and men should be allowed to lead a good life. It is not that men and women should be able to do things like flying to the Moon. True – to do that you have to live in an enormous nation-state. If that is your idea of the good life – to sit crammed into a metal capsule, sucking nourishment out of a tube like a baby, shitting into a plastic bag, then you want to live in a big nation. But if it's high quality of life that you want – then you want to live in a small one.

Oh yes – we're all decentralists now. At least in intelligent and progressive circles – we've all jumped on to the banana wagon. But whenever I hear my fellow trendies pleading for human institutions of a human size I think to myself: Kohr said that a quarter of a century ago and then nobody took any notice of him.

When the *great* nation-states slaughtered tens of millions of their own – and other peoples' – citizenry, smashed and devastated the heritage handed down by true civilizations, ruined the quality of life of the survivors throughout the entire world – people blamed every factor except the real one that caused it all. They blamed Hitler, they blamed Churchill, they blamed the Jews, the Communists, the Capitalists, they blamed the supposedly evil character of this or that people. Only Leopold Kohr, so far as I know, blamed the right culprit: he blamed the obscene *size* of the swollen nation-states.

The citizens of a tiny state would not *allow* their rulers, no matter how stupid these were, to drag them to destruction like that. Oh yes – wars there may be in a world of small states – wars there were when there was such a world. But they would be, and were, *small* wars, and short wars, and – hopefully and very often – comic opera wars. Wars are nasty, small or large. It would be fine if there could be no more of them. But nobody but a fool will claim to have ideas which are going to produce instant heaven-on-earth. But *huge* wars are obscene – and *they* are the ones waged by huge nations.

Before I started writing this talk I went round searching for some of Leopold's friends. I never *knew* a man with so many friends, and in such diverse places! We should found a Friends of Leopold Society, to take the place of the Freemasons or the Buffaloes. And I have come to the conclusion that in Wales, which is where I conducted my researches, to take the place I suppose, of the giant steel industry, the giant coal industry, and all other giant industries which appear to be going the way of the dinosaurs, there is growing up a new industry and that is the telling of Leopold Kohr stories. The man is becoming a legend in his time.

I can imagine that in the future Leopold will furnish the material for an Austro-Welsh equivalent of the Mullah Nasrudin. Apart from his unusual habits – this fairly mature philosopher used to *jog* to wherever he wanted to go around Aberystwyth – he could always be relied upon to say the most unusual things. Yes – very often they were pretty shocking things! At the height of the Watergate scandal, for example, and at a party of dons and their wives, when everybody was cluck-clucking about the awfulness of American corruption, and congratulating each other that such things could not happen in cosy little Great Britain, Leopold announced that ten per cent of the economy of any country *should* be corrupt – it oiled the works and everything worked much better! Whether he meant this literally or not I would not presume to say, but it certainly had the effect of putting an end to the cluck-clucking.

In spite of the honour I feel in being asked to come here to deliver a *laudatio* in this beautiful place – in this superb and truly-civilized city-state – I have to admit I feel a touch of resentment to you all! You have stolen away our Leopold! We like to think of him as living at Number Twelve Baker Street, Aberystwyth. Some of us may not have seen him very often but we liked to know that he was there – and he had the habit of popping up in the most unexpected places like a pantomime devil.

Well, if the Mountain won't come to Mohammed then Mohammed must go to the Mountain: and I must admit, if I have to emulate the prophet in this matter, I cannot think of having my mountain in a more splendid little country.

And when I say *little*, I mean no disparagement, but the very highest praise.

1 The Creative Disintegration of the State

Small is democratic

PROFESSOR LEOPOLD KOHR

This article is extracted from Leopold Kohr's book, The Breakdown of Nations.

Man's greatest happiness lies in his freedom as an individual. This is inseparably connected with political democracy. But democracy, in turn, is inseparably connected with the smallness of the collective organism of which the individual is part – the state. In a small state democracy will, as a rule, assert itself irrespective of whether it is organized as a monarchy or republic, or even as an autocracy. Paradoxical as this may sound, we do not need to go to great length to realize the truth of this proposition.

The small state is by nature *internally* democratic. In it the individual can never be outranked impressively by the power of government whose strength is limited by the smallness of the body from which it is derived. He must recognize the authority of the state, of course, but always as what it is. This is why in a small state he will never be floored by the glamour of government. He is physically too close to forget the purpose of its existence: that it is here to serve him, the individual, and has no other function whatever. The rulers of a small state, if they can be called that, are the citizen's neighbours. Since he knows them closely, they will never be able to hide themselves in mysterious shrouds under whose cover they might take on the dim and aloof appearance of supermen. Even where government rests in the hands of an absolute prince, the citizen will have no difficulty in asserting his will, if the state is small. Whatever his official designation, he will

never be a *subject*. The gap between him and government is
so narrow, and the political forces are in so fluctuating and
mobile a balance, that he is always able either to span the
gap with a determined leap, or to move through the
governmental orbit himself. This is, for instance, the case
in San Marino where they choose two consuls every six
months, with the result that practically every citizen
functions at some time during his life as his country's chief
of state. Since the citizen is always strong, governmental
power is always weak and can, therefore, easily be wrested
from those holding it. And this, too, is an essential
requirement of democracy.

While every kind of small state, whether republic or
monarchy, is thus by nature democratic, every kind of
large state is by nature undemocratic. This is true even if it
is a declared republic and democracy. It is therefore by no
means unnatural that some of the world's greatest tyrants
such as Caesar, Napoleon, Hitler, or Stalin arose on the
soil of great states at the very moment when republicanism
and democracy seemed to have reached a pinnacle of
development. French coins bore the inscription: *République
Française, Napoleon Empereur*, which was a contradiction
only on the surface. Any government in a great power
must be strong, and any great multitude must be ruled
centrally. But to the extent that government is strong, the
individual is weak, with the result that even if his title is
citizen, his position is that of *subject*. The mobile balance
maintained among the individuals of the small state
translates itself in a large power into the heavy stable
balance maintained by the colossal and dangerous mass of
people on the one side, and the equally colossal and
dangerous power of government on the other.

A citizen of the Principality of Liechtenstein, whose
population numbers less than fourteen thousand, desirous
to see His Serene Highness the Prince and Sovereign,
Bearer of many exalted orders and Defender of many
exalted things, can do so by ringing the bell at his castle
gate. However serene His Highness may be, he is never an
inaccessible stranger. A citizen of the massive American
republic, on the other hand, encounters untold obstacles in
a similar enterprise. Trying to see his fellow citizen

President, whose function is to be his servant, not his master, he may be sent to an insane asylum for observation or, if found sane, to a court on charges of disorderly conduct. Both happened in 1950. In 1951, a citizen spent $1,800 in eleven months in an effort 'to get the President's attention' – in vain. You will say that in a large power such as the United States informal relationships such as exist between government and citizen in small countries are technically unfeasible. This is quite true. But this is exactly it. Democracy in its full meaning is impossible in a large state which, as Aristotle already observed, is 'almost incapable of constitutional government'.

The chief danger to the spirit of democracy in a large power stems from this technical impossibility of asserting itself informally. In mass states, personal influences can make themselves felt only if channeled through forms, formulas, and organizations. It is these latter rather than the individual who become increasingly the true agents and asserters of political sovereignty, so that we should speak of a group or party democracy rather than of an individualistic democracy.

Three thousand ecoregions!

MAURICE GIRODIAS

MAURICE GIRODIAS is a publisher and author of Ecoregions.

A growing novelty in world politics today is the uprising of ethnic, cultural and religious minorities everywhere. This is usually described by the media as militant backwardness, violence without a cause, mindless destruction of life and property by a handful of young desperadoes.

But it is becoming increasingly difficult to minimize so universal a phenomenon. The Third World War with which we have been threatened for so long is indeed already upon us – as the War of the Third World, the War of the Minorities.

It has already been fought openly, with savage brutality in twenty spots or more: Northern Ireland, Palestine, Nicaragua, Basque country, Chad, Indochina, Ceylon, Sahara, the Philippines, Eritrea, Ogaden, Indonesia, Iran, Turkey, Cyprus, Lebanon, Pakistan, Afghanistan, Namibia, Kurdistan...

Elsewhere, it is still in the smouldering stage. The Western world has its own repressed or suppressed minorities – Bretons, Corsicans, Scots, Welsh, Gypsies, Eskimos, Blacks, Indians of North and South America – and millions of illegal immigrants in its festering ghettos. And on the other side, in the Soviet Union, we see the dominant Russian republic waging a gigantic campaign of racist infiltration and assimilation, with the help of the Party and of the Secret Police, against the Ukrainians, Tartars, Balts, Uzbeks, Turkmens, Armenians, Georgians, Bielorussians: in all more than one hundred smaller groups or nations.

It is becoming obvious that the nation-state is a relatively recent invention of Western society, even if it has been imposed on most of the world populations in recent years. The nation-state is founded on a number of social attitudes and ideas that are deeply abhorrent to most of the older cultures, which reject the materialistic goals of capitalism according to which land is just another commodity meant to be bought and sold at a profit. Land speculation is seen by Indians and Africans, and by most non-industrialized societies, as an absurdity but also as a crime against life. You cannot sell your land any more than your ancestors and your descendants, land being the one link which relates you physically and spiritually to them.

This divergence in perceptions supplies the key to the present division of the world. For instance, the colonial take-over of Africa at the end of the last century was accomplished for the most part as a vast land-buying operation, the competing powers sending their agents into the wilderness to sign treaties with local chieftains who gladly accepted a few worthless gifts in exchange for well-decorated, but to them meaningless, pieces of paper. They had no idea that they had just signed a contract and that their land now belonged to some distant power.

The same tactics were used by the Zionist pioneers in Palestine when they offered money for their land to unsuspecting Arab peasants. For the Fellahin, who were then driven away from their homes, that double operation of substituting paper for land, and then turning that land into a state – that could only have been the work of the devil. What was *money*? What was a *state*? What were those foreign laws which made such things possible?

For the White race, that form of legal structure appears as the only way that can procure a civilized way of life to all; the only lawful, acceptable form of social contract. However, for the rest of humankind – the vast majority – the nation-state is nothing more than the White Man's fantasy, an arbitrary institution totally foreign to human needs and to traditional practice.

The nation-state is not an advanced form of social structure. It does not serve the general interest but only the selfish concerns of the political class, of the military, the bureaucracy and the owners. Whether we consider the nation-state in its totalitarian version, or in the form of a presidential republic, it is obviously never at the service of 'the people', despite its claims, but only of the power hierarchy. By contrast, the ethnic group in harmony with its natural environment forms the basic unit of a potentially ideal society: and that unit I call here the ecoregion.

Model of an Ecoregional Society
Fortunately we have to help us a model which is a thousand times more helpful than the most ambitious theories: Switzerland.

From its creation in the thirteenth century as a defensive league, the German, French and Italian populations of Switzerland gave their common territory its political unity as a federation. Ever since the system has been preserved, and each group has kept its own culture intact, as witnessed by the number of dialects still spoken in isolated mountain villages. Each one of the twenty-five cantons or half-cantons has its own original constitution, and practices the most direct form of popular democracy; in three cantons the electorate meets every summer in a large field to legislate. By contrast, the central government in Berne acts rather as an administration, consulting the population by referendum to decide issues of even only moderate importance.

Switzerland has therefore given the proof that the classical forms of Greek democracy are still perfectly adaptable to a modern society. The country is one of the most advanced in terms of technology; and in spite of its small size, its five million inhabitants have enjoyed for centuries a unique level of prosperity. Whereas all the surrounding nation-states have gone through a continuous series of crises, wars and degradations of all sorts, the Swiss have managed to retain their balance and their neutrality. They have a modern, well-equipped army, and compulsory military training; but contrary to other nation-states, their citizen's army has a purely defensive role.

If one hesitates to consider the Swiss example, it is only because it puts to shame the history of all other nations. One will always reproach the Swiss for an excess of wisdom; their very success is crushing for their European neighbours, whose nationalism has cost them a terrible price in human lives lost in many destructive wars. But if the Swiss character seems guarded and somewhat withdrawn, the reason is, precisely, that with such neighbours they have remained for centuries on the defensive. Even their incredible wealth is a form of protection against the dangers of international life.

In terms of institutions Switzerland gives us a clear idea of the workings of an ecoregional society. The Swiss model could provide the solutions which Canada, Spain, Ireland, Israel etc. are unsuccessfully trying to find within their national structures.

These new formations are not seen as alternatives to the nation-state; the role of the state will not be eliminated, but transformed from centralist power to central organ of ecofederal planning and arbitration – which, incidentally, gives a chance to the political class itself to find a new definition, and fulfil many useful functions in the service of a rehabilitated, renovated national structure.

The human horizon, then, will no longer be limited to a few giant ghetto cities and some 175 nation-states; it will open onto three thousand ecoregions, each one a live, thriving centre of new culture. War and violence will be disarmed, since the misdirected energies which caused them will be put to a better use. The cult of growth which dominates our society will be redirected from acquisition to education; it will be replaced by a dedication to self-development which will give a new value to the successive ages of life. The very nature of the economy will change with its context; a life of genuine, convivial luxury will be accessible to all, for one tenth of the cost in work and time it takes today to live badly. The economy of waste and obsolescence, founded on such multipliers as credit, national and international marketing, advertising, storage and transportation of energy and goods, taxation, bureaucracy and useless war industries – all this will be replaced by small-scale, local industries, and high-level craftsmanship, thanks to which not only the environment can be restored, but our taste for life as well.

Localism v. Globalism?

As Michael Young of the Mutual Aid Centre wrote to the editors:

> *… Many people owing allegiance to the alternative movement … want as much 'self-sufficiency' as possible on the very smallest level. But they continue to use petrol from the Middle East, tea from Sri Lanka, sugar from Mauritius, ideas from Japan or Thailand laundered through California.*

We believe that the movement we are supporting for a new 'localism' in world affairs involving as it does the breakdown of giant nations, needs to be balanced by a sane internationalism.

We must evolve criteria and safeguards for the federalist and transnational structures that are necessary to give expression to the emerging 'one world' consciousness, and to confront the complexity of the planet's problems.

Any form of political or economic power which is not controlled by those affected by it is a threat to peace, or to freedom, or both. Genuine internationalism cannot therefore be seen as simply a matter of genuflecting before any international institution, even when it is ostensibly established to serve the cause of peace.

Questions that need to be asked centre on control: Who appoints whom? Who elects whom? Who hires and fires? Who decides policy? Who settles the budget? Who checks the books? And who controls those who make these decisions? Very few people have any real control over their own national (or even local) government, and such lack of control tends to surface in every kind of economic and political abuse, from exploitation and corruption to mass misery and war. Any body representing a multiplicity of governments is thus all too likely to be a compound of their defects rather than of their virtues. What new forms of internationalism can we create which will reflect our needs and be responsive to citizen control?

Pondering such questions has led many Fourth World writers, as the following articles demonstrate, to call for the decolonization of the American and Russian empires, the dismantling of Great Britain, and all nations with over ten to twelve million inhabitants; and an avoidance of all types of 'superpower' – whether expressed as a European Common Market, the United Nations, or a vision of world government.

Proposition 14, dismantling the federal government of the United States of America

RICHARD CUMMINGS

RICHARD CUMMINGS is a writer, poet and constitutional lawyer.

– Whereas the various communities of the United States of America have been obliged to surrender their ability to live and to function independently, and
– Whereas the individuals who live in these communities have been denied a meaningful say in the affairs of their common societies, and
– Whereas the two-party system, the electoral process and the entire present system of governance have ceased to be either effective or responsive...
– Therefore these communities, according to the will of the individuals who constitute them, hereby reassert their autonomy.

The current political system of the United States of America simply does not work. The remoteness of a giant and all pervasive bureaucracy alienates and angers the entire population, while elected representatives of the major political parties consistently betray their constituents.

Working in combination with this political paralysis is the power of the corporate bureaucracy, which is free enterprise in name only. It relies on the collusion of both the Democratic and Republican Parties as well as on government agencies to sustain artificial growth and, when necessary, unemployment.

The bankruptcy of existing ideologies, from left to right, makes it essential to seek solutions elsewhere. Decentralized community control through the use of direct democracy or the town-meeting form of government can effectively break down the monolithic structure into smaller, more manageable units which would be increasingly self-sufficient.

This process is actually underway. More and more communities, as well as the states, are demanding greater authority from the federal government and getting it. Direct democracy, through the process known as the Initiative and Referendum, whereby citizens can enact laws by themselves, bypassing existing legislative bodies, is in force in almost half of the states and in many cities and towns. The obsolete political parties are giving way to decentralized, direct democracy.

While this is happening, certain groups are actually seeking independence from the United States altogether, through secessionist movements or through movements for autonomy. The native Americans are most prominent in this movement, but throughout the country, various regions are asserting their independence.

The smaller, autonomous entities that are emerging are more likely to respond to alternative energy sources and appropriate technology simply because they are workable and ultimately less expensive. The end result could be a far more satisfactory way of life in the United States than the one the people have come to accept through a constant bombardment of television advertising. From consumers, they are being transformed back into human beings.

It must be noted that there is strong resistance to this movement. The entrenched parties and governmental structures will not yield easily. Also, certain groups remain fearful that this process could result in a loss of benefits and possible civil rights. The obvious answer to this is that it has been this very structure that has taken away the right to be human and that human rights can best be enhanced on a human scale.

Indian land claims and treaty areas of North America

WINOBA LA DUKE

WINOBA LA DUKE is an Anishinabe Indian who lives in Cambridge, Massachusetts.

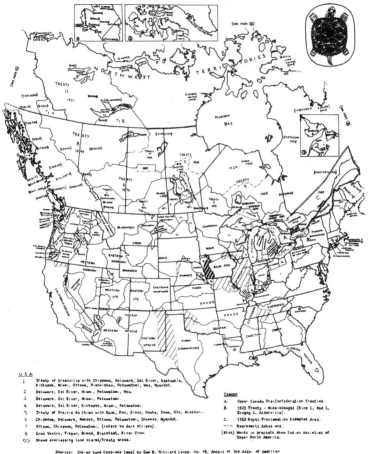

U.S.A.

1 Treaty of Greenville with Chippewa, Delaware, Eel River, Kaskaskia, Kickapoo, Miami, Ottawa, Piankishaw, Potawatomi, Wea, Wyandot.
2 Delaware, Eel River, Miami, Potawatomi, Wea.
3 Delaware, Eel River, Miami, Potawatomi.
4 Delaware, Eel River, Kickapoo, Miami, Potawatomi.
5 Treaty of Prairie du Chien with Sauk, Fox, Sioux, Omaha, Iowa, Oto, Missouri.
6 Chippewa, Delaware, Munsee, Ottawa, Potawatomi, Shawnee, Wyandot.
7 Ottawa, Chippewa, Potawatomi, (refers to dark stripes).
8 Gros Ventre, Piegan, Blood, Blackfeet, River Crow.
▨ Shows overlapping land claims/treaty areas.

CANADA

A. Upper Canada Pre-Confederation Treaties.
B. 1923 Treaty - Mississaugas (Rice L, Mud L, Scugog L, Alderville).
C. 1763 Royal Proclamation Exempted Area.
--- Represents Adhesions.
(BYAR) Words in brackets show Indian societies of Upper North America.

Sources: Indian Land Cessions (map) by Sam B. Hilliard (supp. no. 16, Annals of the Asso. of American Geographers, Vol 62, No. 2, June 1972); Current Affairs Atlas 1979-80, Pub. Macmillan Press; and maps from "Left Out? The Indians and the Canadian Constitution" (National Indian Brotherhood of Canada/Survival International) and "First Nations, States of Canada & United Kingdom: Patriation of the Canadian Constitution" (Constitutional Committee of the Chiefs of Alberta). 1981 © CIMRA

A reproduction of this map is available from Northern Sun Alliance, 1519 East Franklin Street, Minneapolis, MN 55404; or from CIMRA, 218 Liverpool Road, London N1, United Kingdom. Current prices on application to the appropriate address.

This map could be called the indigenous North American view of bioregional succession. The treaty and land claims areas you see here are not exactly how it was BC (Before Columbus), but the basic outline of land areas and native nations. This may clarify some of our miseducation. First, the map shows how and why native people lived in distinct territories, areas which are essentially bioregions. Second, it shows that North America's reigning governments – Canada and the United States – are, according to the 'host nations', on shaky grounds. In other words, very little land in North America is *not* under the question of who has legal jurisdiction. This could be a powerful tool for all of us.

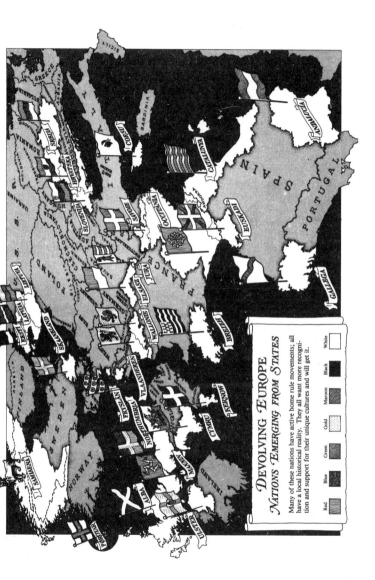

DEVOLVING EUROPE
NATIONS EMERGING FROM STATES

Many of these nations have active home rule movements; all have a local historical reality. They all want more recognition and support for their unique cultures and will get it.

Red   Blue   Green   Gold   Maroon   Black   White

This map is available from *Co-Evolution Quarterly Journal.* For current subscription information write to *Co-Evolution Quarterly,* Box 428, Sausalito, California 94966, USA.

The common market – another superpower?

JOHN COLEMAN

JOHN COLEMAN is the author of Coleman's Drive *and an activist in Alternative movements.*

The Common Market represents the greatest piece of political centralization since the formation of the United States of America. It has come into being with distinct American encouragement and money. This was pointed out by Professor Swann in his *Economics of the Common Market*, a book on the EEC Commission's reading list. At the same time a great deal of anti-American feeling was exploited to get the Common Market going. When opposing giantism it is difficult not to fall into the trap of becoming like it!

Monopoly capitalism learnt the advantages of eliminating state boundaries through the American experiment. Monopoly chains were able to spread through the length and breadth of North America. Their ambition is to cover the globe. They are in the process of creating a world of free trading blocs within which national boundaries are rendered meaningless.

A great deal of the accepted wisdom in the State Department of the USA has its origin in the German geopolitical thinking of the earlier part of this century. Professor Karl Haushofer published an article in 1933 in the *Journal of Geopolitics* (Munich University) entitled 'Small States have no Right to Exist'. In it he actually said 'The survival of small states is a clear sign of world-political stagnation.' His work not only influenced Hitler, it also influenced Hitler's enemies and fostered the kind of political thinking which created the Common Market. George Orwell became acquainted with this kind of thinking at the World Federalist conferences he attended and *1984* was prompted by it.

Significantly the work of Fritz Schumacher arrived on the scene at the very time when this kind of giantism was rolling ahead almost unopposed.

While many of us believe that we need freedom of enterprise at the local community level, we also know that this may best be protected by more, not fewer, trade barriers. Ecologically and conservationally there are distinct disadvantages to industrialized countries taking in each other's washing machines and other mass-produced goods. We don't wish anyone to be short of the real necessities of reasonable civilized life, but we cannot agree with masses of throw-away manufactured goods being carted around the world in oil-burning lorries and ships.

For those of us who are against the Common Market on the grounds of size there is the question of whether the United States and the Soviet Union would not also be better dismantled. I believe it will be much harder to dismantle the United States than the Soviet Union. The USA, like the EEC, rests on an economic, commercial foundation. The Soviet Union exists on a much more brittle governmental structure which would probably not hold together without a strong military threat from the United States. Both governments, however, extract tremendous advantages in the actual governing of their peoples from the military threat coming from the other side.

The EEC, despite all its protestations about peace, is coming into being as a gigantic military-industrial complex, using a real or imagined Soviet threat to frighten its populations into accepting the loss of self-determination that the formation of such a power bloc necessarily involves. Mary Kaldor wrote after the 1975 Referendum:

> Britain's decision to stay in the Common Market has opened the way to an increasingly close integration of our defence policy and arms industry with those of the other member states. Over the next decade in fact we may see the rapid development of an EEC based 'military-industrial complex', which national governments will find almost impossible to control.

The essential reason for Britain joining the Common Market was summed up in the Heath Government's White Paper just prior to entry in 1972: 'Together we would be able to tackle the technological problems which would be too big for any one of us.' The EEC deliberately aims at giantism and high technology and is a virtual haven for those massive multinational corporations which straddle the world and aim to break down all natural communities, whether through capitalism or socialism. The summarizing chapter of the White Paper went on to say that through the development of the high technologies we would be in the best position to help the Third World. What it meant was, to help the Third World to become another power bloc like the EEC and the superpowers.

In fighting giantism we need a strategy. Regionalism can easily turn out to be the decentralist's Trojan horse. Supergovernments, by breaking up national governments into small pieces, can pick off the pieces one by one, leaving all the real decision-making at the continental bloc level. (We have been hearing a lot lately about the EEC speaking with a single voice on foreign policy).

Our strategy must be to use the nation state to hold out against an even greater centralization, and *within* the setting of the nation-state start to work towards decentralization to regions and local communities. We want to hear as little as possible about 'speaking with one voice'. At its best the nation-state did represent the strivings of the communities which comprised it. Its downfall came when it began to represent the strivings of power-hungry leaders with imperial visions.

We are told that the smaller countries of the Third World want all the 'advantages' of the so-called advanced industrial world, but the leaders of our industrial nations, with their own commercial benefit in view, have been instrumental in seeing that those countries get leaders who voice the desires they themselves have. They talk of aid to the Third World and by it, in the main, they mean giving their own people's (taxpayers') money to Third World countries so that those countries can buy equipment from the giant industrial corporations of the West. This is simply a process by which the Third World is forced to become a mirror image of the Industrial World. What we need to do is to hear the voice of the Fourth World in the Third and indeed in all the world.

The dumping of the surpluses produced by the Common Agricultural Policy has the effect of destroying the simpler agriculture of the Third World and is thus forcing it along the path towards centralization and high technology. Above all it aims at a system of competition that will in the end, if it is allowed to follow its present course, impose uniformity and centralization on the whole world. This was pointed out by Hugh Stephenson (Business Editor of *The Times*) in his book *The Coming Clash*:

> For large-scale modern industry, most especially at the high technology end of the spectrum, must increasingly be part of an interlinked and international network of production and sales. Otherwise it will not be commercially viable. The choice, within the present structure of nation-states, is therefore limited. Either the political and social framework is adjusted to suit the requirements of large-scale industry, or a social experiment is conducted outside the mainstream of industrial advance.

This is the real choice for those who oppose the Common Market. It is also the real choice for those who champion the alternative course. Not to follow the alternative course, 'the experiment outside the mainstream of industrial advance', is to throw whole nations, their people, their traditional industries and their patterns of employment at the mercy of competition from the multinational giants who have the latest and fastest at their disposal and who hardly need people. Opposition to the Common Market cannot merely be based on the cost of food — though it is interesting that the Greeks were required to eliminate a high percentage of their small farmers as a condition of entry, while rich little farmers within the industrial framework of Germany and France are supported to the point of doing extreme damage to natural agriculture in the Third World – nor can it be based on excessive budgetary arrangements. These can be changed. The real question is whether people exist to serve large-scale industry and the governmental structure it entails (and everything about the EEC shows that this is what it is) or whether industry exists for people. John Silkin put the same point another way when he said that the Labour Movement came into being to ensure that Capital served Labour, and the grassroots of the Labour Party showed that they understood this instinctively at past Labour Conferences by voting against the Common Market and for human survival (i.e. against nuclear arms) and thereby made themselves, whether they knew it or not, part of the Fourth World. Their leaders will probably evade their decisions – as the leaders of almost all organizations seem to be doing at the moment – unless the power of 'Fourth World' thinking becomes an irresistible force.

Thus, in conclusion, we see the EEC as part of a global competitive power bloc system in which decision-making is deliberately and systematically being moved further and further away from the people who live under it, which is destroying natural agriculture in the world, and whose reckless momentum towards high-technology carries with it a military development which is sweeping the world and will be the final means of putting down opposition to it, whether in capitalist or socialist countries, the final means used by the big to put down the small.

Dismantling the United Kingdom?

GWYNFOR EVANS

GWYNFOR EVANS was President of Plaid Cymru, the Welsh nationalist party, from 1945 to 1981, and is an ex-Member of Parliament.

Dismantling the UK is very different from decentralising, regionalising or federalizing the UK. On the face of things it appears no more than a pipe-dream. No powerful unitary state has ever been federalized, let alone dismantled.

Nevertheless, given certain conditions the dismantling of the UK could prove to be possible.

The UK is a unitary state. It has the biggest population in

Europe under one government. It is the most highly centralized state in Europe, not excluding France. These facts both indicate the extreme difficulty of dismantling it and also indicate why it should be dismantled.

The UK has one legislature for nearly sixty million people. Switzerland has twenty-six legislatures for nearly six million people. The millions of those governed by the UK belong to different nationalities which preceded England. For centuries in the past violence was used to bring them into union with England, whose population composes 82 per cent of the whole.

A feature of the huge, centralized unitary British state is the enormous power of its civil service. It works hand in glove with a few of the top politicians and the press, leaving Parliament, except on odd occasions, with very little power. The hugeness of Britain results in a bureaucratic democracy in which the bureaucracy has far more power than the people.

Their power is centralized in London, where every decision is made which affects the whole of Britain, or, to take the case of Wales, every decision which affects the whole of Wales. This is brought out in Anthony Sampson's *Anatomy of Britain*, which is described as an examination of 'The British Power Structure'. One gets the impression that nothing of importance happens outside London, that everyone of importance has a London home; that, in fact, London is Britain and Britain is England, and that the sedulously fostered Britishism is the old English chauvinism. Anyone concerned with the dismantling of Britain must face the fact that British is English, that Britain is in practice England. From the standpoint of this article it is not an unhopeful fact.

Since the last war in particular there has been a tendency among politicians, journalists and historians to call Britain a nation. The first thing to establish is that Britain is a state. If Britain were a historic national community, dismantling it would be permanently beyond our powers. It would be indestructable. But Britain is a state, not a nation, so that we are British nationals only in the sense of being British citizens as we see on our passports. Britain is so huge a state that even a sense of community is absent in its day-today life, though much is made of the Royal Family, their deaths and entrances.

The British Empire used to be called a nation. Imperialism is the extension of the power of the state over the land, resources and people of another country. This extension of the power of the state, as in the case of Ireland, Scotland and Wales, was pursued at the outset mainly for military reasons. Then prestige came to play a big part, as it obviously still does. Economic reason then gained prominence. The colonies, internal and external, were exploited as rich sources of a monopoly. Welsh natural resources have been brutally exploited, as were her people in war and in the economic depression between the wars, when 500,000 were transferred to feed English industries which were calling out for them. They were state labour fodder. A.J.P. Taylor says 'the history of the English (*sic*) state and of the English people merged for the first time' with the Great War.

From the standpoint of dismantlement there could be no better news than that Britain is a state not a nation. The English nation cannot be dismantled although its government can and should be federalized, but the British state is a political construction which can, given the will, be dismantled.

Military defence no longer depends on size, though defence spokesmen constantly give that impression. Their emphasis is on Britain retaining her role as a Great military power, possessed of what they call an independent nuclear deterrent. But am I wrong in thinking that what is in the back of their minds is not so much defence as prestige?

How soon can the people be awakened to the fact that Polaris, Trident, Cruise and the rest are not about defence, but prestige; and that Great Britain is an anachronism; that there is no place for it even in the Common Market; and that there is no excuse in today's world for keeping nearly sixty million people, all capable of governing themselves in small entities, under one government? They will discover, I hope, that their life is being trivialized. Human life is not about power and glory and prestige, and when they make this discovery, which nuclear weapons may help to force upon them, they may begin to think of replacing the huge, centralist bureaucratic state by small organisms of human size, each with its own beating heart. Perhaps it is the very depth and extreme dangers of the human crisis which will compel new widespread thinking in which the most fundamental questions about men and women will be asked.

We must begin with the fact that the human person is each one of supreme value, that his infinite value should govern all our actions; that the idea that Great Britain can stock-pile and at some point in time fire a nuclear missile which will kill hundreds of thousands of children and other innocent people is one we cannot tolerate. If that is how the UK keeps itself intact, then the sooner it is dismantled the better.

Community must be fostered wherever it is found, and created where it does not exist. It is here, at the roots, that the dismantling of the UK begins. Community consciousness must be fostered in the neighbourhood, whether urban or rural, the region and the nation.

The value of fostering national community consciousness in small nations, and ensuring for them self-government, is seen by comparing the unhappy experience of Wales with ten or a dozen small nations in Northern Europe, from Austria through the Scandinavian countries to Switzerland, which have thriven economically and culturally.

In none of these nations was it possible to separate the national culture from the economy, industrialization, urbanization, politics, transport, new techniques, formal education, the press and especially now television. The dismantling of the UK involves dealing with all these and more. It involves building up powerful opinion from below, and especially the strengthening of communities with shared values. It is a political task, and nothing great is achieved in politics without organising like-minded people in a way which has political clout.

Most fundamental is a sense of community and a strong loyalty to it; and this must be expressed politically. This is essential whatever one is trying to achieve, whether it be a vibrant local community, a viable region, full-blooded federalism, or national self-government. I admire the work done by a company of Cornish people to maintain what they consider to be a national community and to revive its language.

Although centuries of psychological and structural violence have alienated most Scottish and Welsh people, one fears, from a warm loyalty to their nations, yet it is their political nationalism that still offers the best chance for initiating the kind of radical reconstruction we wish to see in these islands.

There is a fluidity in the political, economic, military and international situation which could lead to major changes. Should the people opt for a non-nuclear future, that would be a revolutionary change of consciousness, giving Welsh and Scottish nationalism their great opportunity.

What do they aim at? A partnership in these islands of free and equal nations, in no way subordinate one to the other in any aspect of their domestic or external affairs, but freely associating in a Brittanic Confederation which would supervise common services and discuss matters of common concern, much as the Nordic Union does. There would be no economic separation in the sense of having frontiers and tariffs and passports. People, goods and capital would be able to pass back and forth as they do today; and one assumes that we would be in the EEC if England is there. A solution for the intractable problems of the counties of Britain might be found in this.

It is the Scots and the Welsh national parties which are in the vanguard in furthering this civilized policy. The practicality of the Fourth World vision of the England of the future depends almost wholly on the measure of success they achieve. The dismantling of the British state occurs when the Scottish and Welsh states don the mantle of statehood. When it does occur it could prove to be the death knell of the lingering imperial–militarist tradition which has prevented creative moves towards small democracies of human size in England.

DISMANTLING THE UNITED KINGDOM?

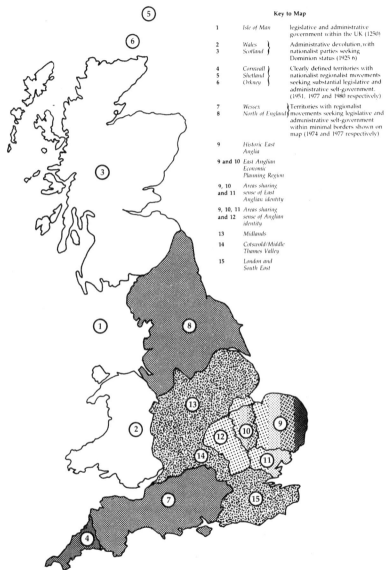

Key to Map

1	*Isle of Man*	legislative and administrative government within the UK (1250)
2	*Wales* }	Administrative devolution, with nationalist parties seeking Dominion status (1925 6)
3	*Scotland* }	
4	*Cornwall* }	Clearly defined territories with nationalist regionalist movements seeking substantial legislative and administrative self-government. (1951, 1977 and 1980 respectively)
5	*Shetland* }	
6	*Orkney* }	
7	*Wessex* }	Territories with regionalist movements seeking legislative and administrative self-government within minimal borders shown on map (1974 and 1977 respectively)
8	*North of England* }	
9	*Historic East Anglia*	
9 and 10	*East Anglian Economic Planning Region*	
9, 10 and 11	*Areas sharing sense of East Anglian identity*	
9, 10, 11 and 12	*Areas sharing sense of Anglian identity*	
13	*Midlands*	
14	*Cotswold/Middle Thames Valley*	
15	*London and South East*	

Dates refer to achievement of self-government (Isle of Man), or to foundation of nationalist/regionalist movements.

This map is reprinted from *The Regionalist* magazine. For current subscription information write to Davyd Robyns, 55 Eaton Crescent, Swansea SA1 4QN, Wales.

Bioregionalism – the politics of place

MARK KINZLEY

Mark Kinzley, co-editor of this book, is a community activist in Redbridge, North-east London.

Until now thinking about the methods of transforming society has been dominated by two strategies: winning power through electoral politics and influencing those already in power by means of pressure groups.

As to the first, some of us have come to feel that it is both impossible to win power in this way, and that even if it were possible it would not be desirable. We fear that any environmentalist government would be an authoritarian government, that decentralization cannot be imposed from the centre downwards except by creating a plethora of local centralized governments, that achieving a New Age society is a slower and more profound process, a learning process. How can you go through a learning process merely by gathering in a mass movement? Fighting elections might even be said to be 'playing their game', embracing the mechanism that has been laid out to entice and absorb us. The real power does not lie in the institutions of central government, but in the structure of society. It has been said, for example, that 'Peace is not just an absence of war', as those who call for government action seem to think, but rather 'Peace is a way of life'. Further, in going through the political process we accept the principle of postponed reward – so that ends and means immediately become divorced. What good can come of this? And the reward, of course, is postponed indefinitely.

As for pressure groups, it has become a commonplace to say that single-issue groups cannot challenge the prevailing paradigm as a whole. John Papworth has written very effectively in his article 'Giantism – Public Enemy Number One', (p.18) 'Very few, if indeed any, of the numerous protest movements which have surfaced over the past few decades appear ready to step back from their situation and to ask themselves leading questions about the dynamics that prompt the evils or abuses against which they protest.' He goes on: 'The(se) problems are worse now than when all these organizations were first launched.'

So it is time now to look for a small way, and it is from America that our new inspiration is largely coming. In a past issue of *Resurgence* Gary Snyder said in an article called 'Thoughts from America': 'How much do you need to be in touch with networks of people of like interests?... Too much talking back and forth between people who agree with each other, without actually doing something, is not healthy; and to do something you have to be specific to a place.'

This is exactly it, 'Bioregionalism' – the politics of place. All over America far-sighted people are declaring the boundaries of their bioregions ('a geographical terrain and a terrain in consciousness.') People are setting out to cultivate deliberately the dying or not-yet-born culture and identity of their bioregions – this is called 'Reinhabitation' or 'Intentional Community'. A deliberate and self-aware element is entering in, which is new in history. Perhaps it is only those 'nations' which lie awkwardly across bioregional cultures and ecologies which are aggressive, seeking to contain their internal instability by forever expanding, both militarily and in terms of their economies.

And what is to be the method of bringing the bioregions to the fore? It is by founding alternative institutions locally – Skills Exchanges, Learning Exchanges, wholistic health centres, alternative local currency, alternative businesses dedicated to Right Livelihood, Community Land Trusts, alternative energy projects etc. Look after the economics of independence, and the politics will take care of itself. To re-apply a quote from the organizers of the coming North American Bioregional Congress:

'To begin this fundamental reformation it is not necessary to declare oppositional or adversarial stances toward existing human-centred systems. Neither is it necessary to seek official recognition of a formally established alternative organization. Rather we just begin by calling the Congress, and setting its natural and self-organizing coordinative function in conscious motion.'

Learning to live-in-place

PETER BERG and RAYMOND DASMANN

PETER BERG and RAYMOND DASMANN are involved with the Planet Drum Foundation, a Californian-based organization which stresses the importance of 'bioregional' awareness.

To live-in-place is to follow the necessities and pleasures of life as they are uniquely presented by a particular site. It is the opposite of making a living through short-term destructive exploitation of land and life. In many bioregions of the developed world natural systems have been severely weakened. The original wealth of diversity has been largely spent and altered toward a narrow range of mostly non-native crops and stock. Chronic misuse has ruined huge areas of once-rich farm, forest, and range land. Wastes from absurdly dense industrial concentrations have left some places almost unlivable. But we now know that human life depends ultimately on the continuation of other life. Living-in-place provides for such continuation. It has become a necessity if people intend to stay in any region without further changing it in ever more dangerous directions.

If the life-destructive path of technological society is to be diverted into life-sustaining directions, the land must be reinhabited. Reinhabitation means learning to live-in-place in an area that has been disrupted and injured through past exploitation. It involves becoming native to a place through becoming aware of the particular ecological relationships that operate within and around it. It means understanding activities and evolving social behaviour that will enrich the life of that place, restore its life-sustaining systems, and establish an ecologically and socially sustainable pattern of existence within it. Simply stated, it involves becoming fully alive in and with a place.

Reinhabitation involves developing a bioregional identity, something which most of us have never possessed. A bioregion is both a geographical terrain and a terrain of consciousness – a place and the ideas that have developed about that place.

A bioregion can be determined initially by use of climatology, physiography, animal and plant geography, natural history and other descriptive natural sciences. The final boundaries of a bioregion are best described by the people who have lived within it, through human recognition of the realities of living-in-place. All life on the planet is interconnected, and there is a distinct resonance among living things and the factors which influence them that occurs specifically within each separate place on the planet. Discovering and describing that resonance is a way to describe a bioregion.

Useful information for reinhabitants can come from a wide range of sources. Studies of local native inhabitants, in particular the experiences of those who have lived there before, both those who tried to make a living, and those who lived-in-place can contribute. Reinhabitants can apply this information toward shaping their own life patterns and establishing relationships with the land and life around them. This will help determine the nature of the bioregion within which they are learning to live-in-place.

Our real period of discovery has just begun. Bioregions are barely recognized and it is still an anxious mystery whether we will be able to continue living within them. How many people can a bioregion carry without destroying it further? What kinds of activities should be encouraged? Which ones are too ruinous to continue? How can people find out about bioregional criteria in such a way that they will feel that these exist for their mutual benefit rather than as an imposed set of regulations?

People have been part of the life of their bioregions for a long time. The greatest part of that time has been a positive rather than negative experience for other life sharing these places. In describing how as many as 500 separate tribal republics lived side by side in California for at least 15,000 years without serious hostility toward each other or disruption of life-systems around them, Forbes (1971) points out a critical difference between invaders and inhabitants.

> Native Californians ... felt themselves to be something other than independent, autonomous individuals. They perceived themselves as being deeply bound together with other people (and with the surrounding non-human forms of life) in a complex interconnected web of life. That is to say, a true community. All creatures were brothers and sisters. From this idea came the basic principle of non-exploitation, of respect and reverence for all creatures, a principle hostile to the kind of economic development typical of modern society and destructive of human morals.

Reinhabitants want to fit into a place, which requires preserving the place to fit into. Their most basic goals are to restore and maintain watersheds, topsoil, and native species, elements of obvious necessity for in-place existence because they determine the essential conditions of water, food, and stable diversity. Their aims might include developing bioregional cultures that celebrate the continuity of life where they live.

There needs to be a massive redistribution of land to create smaller farms. They would concentrate on growing a wider range of food species, increasing the nutritional value of crops, maintaining the soil, employing alternatives to fossil fuels, and developing small-scale marketing systems. More people would be involved, thereby creating jobs and lightening the load on the cities.

Forests have to be allowed to rebuild themselves. Watershed-based reforestation and stream-restoration projects are necessary everywhere that logging has been done. Cut trees are currently being processed wastefully. Crafts that use every part of the tree should be encouraged – they would employ a greater number of regional people. Fisheries have to be carefully protected. They provide long-term rich protein, if used correctly, or a quickly emptied biological niche if mishandled.

Reinhabitory consciousness can multiply the opportunities for employment within the bioregion. New reinhabitory livelihoods based on exchanging information, cooperative planning, administering exchanges of labour and tools, intra- and inter-bioregional networking, and watershed media emphasising bioregional rather than city-consumer information could replace a few centralized positions with many decentralized ones.

The bioregion cannot be treated with regard for its own life-continuities while it is part of and administered by a larger state government. It should be a separate state. As a separate state, the bioregion could redistrict its counties to create watershed governments appropriate to maintaining local life-places. City-country divisions could be resolved on bioregional grounds. Perhaps the greatest advantage of separate statehood would be the opportunity to declare a space for addressing each other as members of a species sharing the planet together and with all the other species.

The above article is extracted from *Reinhabiting a Separate Country: A Bioregional Anthology of Northern California*, edited by Peter Berg, published by Planet Drum Foundation, PO Box 31251, San Francisco CA 94131, USA.

Direct democracy

PETER CADOGAN

PETER CADOGAN is a 'social inventor', ex-National Secretary of the Committee of 100 and founder of the East-West Peace People.

The Monster at the Centre
After marking time constitutionally for about a hundred years we are now going backwards. The Welfare State of the Fabians and the pump-priming of the Keynesians have both been tried and found wanting. We have exchanged economic poverty for many for social, political and

spiritual poverty for most. We have solved countless material problems by means of science and technology but socially we are the victims of conventions that no longer work. The solution is direct democracy. As Patrick Geddes put it in his 1912 credo *What to Do*: 'For fulfilment there must be a resorption of government into the body of the community. How? By cultivating the habit of direct action instead of waiting upon representative agencies.'

The theory and practice of direct democracy is both personal and political. Direct democracy is new in its contemporary form and as old as the assemblies of ancient Athens and folk-moots of Anglo-Saxon England. It has nothing to do with votes. It signifies a clear break with the desperately tired values and procedures of parliamentary party politics, representative government generally and bureaucratic officialdom.

All previous forms of government in civilized societies have either been variants of the master-slave relationship or have relapsed into that condition as the result of conquest. Direct democracy is different in kind. It is the constitutional form of incipient classlessness. It exists all round us, many of us practice it quite regularly but we are conditioned not to recognise its meaning and therefore not to give it a name. Its very simplicity is one reason why it eludes people. They are led to believe that important new truths have to be difficult and complex, when the opposite is the case.

The traditional way of approaching a problem under the conditions of representative or *indirect* democracy is to locate an MP, a local Councillor, a Civil Servant or a Local Government Officer, tell him about it, pressurize him if need be (letters, leaflets, deputations, demonstrations etc.) and wait for him to produce the answer and solve the problem. Indirect democracy accepts a we–they situation. It means elections, representatives, officials, petitions and power-groups that tend to have an interest in a problem or a project to the extent that there are votes, or kudos, or jobs or money in it. Human needs, long-term thinking and a little thing like 'the truth' are liable to have a poor time of it unless there is a powerful lobby organized in their defence. Every 'advance' tends to mean more taxes, more reliance on the centre and more helplessness at the periphery. Faced with the horrors of nineteenth-century self-seeking society (given its vast achievements in other directions) the new fabian democracy seemed to work, but eventually the Centre became the monster that devoured its supplicants. It is that situation we are in now.

The Redundancy of the State

The State as such has certain irreducible functions. First law, including legislation for such social services as public opinion is effectively able to demand; second order, the coercion of an enemy or the civil population if need be; third, the raising of such money as may be necessary to make the first two possible. If it can be shown that these functions are either destined to become redundant or that they can be better served by non-State agencies, then the case for the redundancy of the State will have been made.

Most political and social services can be organized and paid for regionally. There is thus no good reason why the present position should be allowed to continue wherein most taxes are raised centrally and local authorities are 65 per cent dependent on handouts from on high. This kind of bureaucratic centralism makes nonsense of democracy. Local authorities today have two choices ahead of them, the first is to accept a future as mere branch offices of Whitehall, the second that of self-financing regional autonomy.

The present order of things can be reversed. All taxes can be raised regionally and the regions then provide such funds as they think fit for whatever national functions they, the regions, deem necessary.

The present chaotic, unmanageable and dispiriting system of direct and indirect taxation has nothing to commend it. We should scrap it in favour of a single tax on production at source. The advantages would be endless: most of the present tax-collecting machine would be redundant; tax-fiddling and the tax-fiddling industry would die a natural death; the perks and expense account racket would be pointless; countless problems would not so much be 'solved' as abolished. There would be immense gains in terms of incentives for employers and

employed alike, paper work reduced to a tenth of its
present scale, burdens on development removed, normal
time and overtime paid in full, vast improvements in
industrial relations and production – and all taxes paid not
from what is earned but in what is spent. Clearly the bare
essentials of living would carry the least tax (some perhaps
none at all) but after that the rate would be steeply graded.

Politics in peacetime turns on taxation decided by the
Cabinet in consultation with principal civil servants and
other advisers. The Treasury is the key and the Prime
Minister is its First Lord. Constitutional fiction has it that
the Prime Minister's mandate is a majority in Parliament,
the story being that Parliament, and thus the electorate,
has the final say. In fact, of course, neither Parliament nor
the electorate have anything of the sort. The required
majority gets to Parliament by means of an elaborate
exercise in public and party manipulation, the methods of
which have been perfected over the years since 1830.

At required intervals the party machines see to it that in
every constituency the voters are presented with two or
three carefully vetted candidates, men and women who
have made politics their career, and who will do what they
are told by the Party Whips. The occasional rebel who gets
through the net does not affect the issue and he can be
dispatched at leisure. In professional politics success is
measured by getting and retaining seats and office.

In matters of substance everything depends, or used to
depend, upon the Leader. We enjoy (or suffer, as you
please) uncrowned, elective, monarchical government and
voting is an act of personal-political abdication in face of
concealed absolutism. The monarch of today, however, is
only a caricature of his former self by virtue of the growth
of a government machine that he cannot hope to control.

Every five years, in commutation of our legitimate
decision-making powers, we are given a ballot paper to be
dutifully inscribed with the mark of illiteracy. And we
allow ourselves to be deceived, we who wonder that our
forebears could ever subscribe to trans-substantiation!

No elective monarch of No. 10, no matter how
enlightened, can cope with the needs of the last quarter of
the twentieth century. It is not a question of personal

merit. No one, and no Cabinet, can ever again hope to govern Britain. The task is too big, too complicated. For years now we have had an Administration but no Government. The helm is stuck and no one will ever move it again.

The central task of politics is to bring about the redundancy of No. 10.

The Death of Party Politics

The foundation of local politics is to be found in the Ward. At present it will have three councillors, but it is frequently hard to find even those. For what, after all, is the prospect before any man or woman who might offer his or her services – the party rigmarole that has to be observed to secure nomination, the considerable risks of backbiting and petty jealousies, the mock battle with an opponent, the insane monosyllabic parade round the doorsteps, endless time, trouble and expense to get on the Council, and then what? The party whip (albeit of less consequence than at Westminster), too many committees to serve on, too little time to digest masses of information, a feeling of powerlessness *vis-à-vis* the Town Hall and an extremely limited opportunity to do what one is good at. The result is that good people don't bother — life is too short — the system generates political animals as such, cut off from ordinary mortals. If we get insensitive local government is it to be wondered at? That it works at all is due to a great deal of lateral thinking, the power of the voluntary lobby and the professional integrity of good local government officers. Formal democracy has become a degenerate myth.

Is it to be wondered at that so many Councillors are pensioners, builders, trade union officials and a diminishing number of men and women with private means? The mainstream of the community flows elsewhere and inevitably power concentrates increasingly in the hands of full-time officials and the men of Whitehall to whom they are answerable. If, nationally, the prospect is that of *Big Brother* v *The People*, locally the same situation tends to recur as *The Town Hall* v *The Folk*. Both contests have to be resolved.

Direct democracy can transform this situation. There needs to be an answer, different in kind, at Ward level. The whole ramshackle nonsense about political parties and elections is expendable. The volunteers have to replace the representatives. The number of Councillors per ward should be increased to seven or more and constitute a Ward Council. (The boundaries of wards and parishes should be rethought round the natural perimeters of actual communities; the ward and the parish should be the same.) Elections are not called for.

Men and women are invited to stand for the Ward Council i.e. to volunteer. The conditions of volunteering need to be stricter than with the present nomination procedure and to require the signatures of a dozen or so local residents who are asked to recognise the public importance of what they are doing since their 'candidate' is almost certain to become a Councillor. The names of all signatories should be published.

If the number of volunteers is equal to or less than the number of Councillors required they are all automatically declared accepted. If the number is greater then names are put in a hat and the first seven, or whatever it may be, are chosen.

The result will have important new consequences. There will be a vast number of people who can then volunteer to man the Committees of the various agencies of local government. They will be able to take the proper measure of their own time and talent and the community will have the advantage of the services of its best people. Party politics will die out and instead we shall have schools of thought and divisions of opinion on creative and flexible lines. The local government professionals will meet their equals on every committee and local government will have arrived, belatedly, in the twentieth century.

(The above article is extracted from Peter Cadogan's pamphlet 'Direct Democracy', available from him at 1 Hampstead Hill Gardens, London NW3. Current price available on application to Peter Cadogan.)

All power to the community

STUART DAVISON

STUART DAVISON is a professional archaeologist, and ex-chairman of the Ecology Party's Bedfordshire branch.

Principles

1. The principal units of government should serve areas with which people can identify; and be sufficiently small for individuals to exercise reasonable influence over their elected representatives.
2. Governments or councils at levels other than that of the principal units would exist only to provide forums for cooperation between principal units.
3. There would be a Constitution to provide safeguards for the ecological balance in society.
4. There would be a Bill of Rights to safeguard the basic human rights of individuals and prevent the oppression of minorities.
5. The method(s) of election of representatives should be such that any council or parliament is truly representative of the people it serves.
6. Councillors and MPs would have to satisfy strict residential qualifications, and would be paid a salary and/or expenses.

Long-term Aims
1. The precise areas served by principal units of government would be determined by plebiscites, but would be likely to be comparable to present-day Parish/Community/Town Councils, (hereafter referred to as a 'Community Council').
2. Community Councils would have responsibility and powers in all fields of government, and would exercise or delegate these responsibilities and powers in accordance with the wishes of the people they serve.
3. Such taxes as would exist in a fully decentralized ecological society would be collected and administered

by the Community Councils.

4. Services or facilities which it is felt cannot be provided by a single community may be provided by a group of communities through the agency of a Joint Council.

5. Joint Councils would only embrace those responsibilities and powers delegated to them by the member communities, by whom they would be financed and to whom they would be accountable. There would be no nationally-imposed restrictions on the size or shape of areas served by Joint Councils, these being determined by the nature of their functions, and subject to the approval of a plebiscite.

6. The Community Councils could employ a permanent executive ('civil service') to administer services in which 'professional specialization' is advantageous (e.g. hospitals); otherwise services could be provided by the entire population on a rota system.

7. Joint Councils would not be empowered to employ a permanent executive.

8. The Federal Parliament would function in a similar way to a Joint Council, with clearly defined areas of responsibility (e.g. diplomatic representation, pollution control, natural resource management). It would be a single-chamber parliament, but policy would have to be ratified by a consensus of Community Councils. The Federal Parliament would employ the necessary personnel to undertake its approved responsibilities.

9. The Judiciary would exist separately from any level of government, with courts at levels intermediate between the Community and the Federation to act as arbitrators in the event of disputes between communities, or between Joint Councils. There would be a Supreme Federal Court to judge cases of dispute between communities and the Federal Parliament, and to act as the ultimate Court of Appeal. Civil and criminal cases would ordinarily be heard by the Community Courts.

10. Community Councillors would be required to reside within the area they represent, and would be

compelled to resign upon leaving the area for which they were elected. After five consecutive years of service, Councillors would not be eligible for re-election until a further two years had elapsed. Councillors would be paid a salary and/or expenses such as would be necessary to ensure an income equivalent to the Community Average Income.

The above proposals were drafted by Stuart Davison for possible inclusion in the Ecology Party's manifesto. The manifesto itself can be obtained from ECO, 36/38 Clapham Road, London SW9. Current price on application to the Ecology Party.

2 Appropriate Technology

Technology as if people matter

GEORGE McROBIE

GEORGE McROBIE is the author of Small is Possible, *the sequel to E.F.Schumacher's* Small is Beautiful.

Schumacher and a group of his friends set up the Intermediate Technology Development Group in 1965.

To give more concreteness to the work programme indicated by the words 'intermediate technology', we emphasize four criteria : smallness; simplicity; capital cheapness and non-violence.

Non-violence in this context refers to modes of production which respect ecological principles and strive to work with Nature instead of attempting to force a way through natural systems in the conviction that unintended damage and unforeseen side-effects can always be undone by the further application of violence. All too often, one problem is 'solved' by creating several new ones.

The established trend of technological development is towards ever larger scale, towards giantism. This is considered to be justified by the 'economies of scale'. But large scale production units can be economical only when certain conditions are satisfied: a high market 'density', for instance, or a highly efficient low-cost transport system. When these conditions (and others, such as skill in large-scale organization, management, buying, and selling) are not satisfied, the so-called economies of scale become illusory. In fact, large-scale then tends to act as a principle of exclusion: only people already rich and powerful can embark on new productive enterprises; the small man is excluded, reduced to the position of a job seeker – and when there are not enough jobs provided by the rich and powerful, he has no possibility of becoming productive.

It does not take great scientific or technological creativity to take a further step in the direction of complexity and capital-intensity. This means nothing more than following the established trend. But when the demand is made to search for smallness, simplicity and capital-saving, the normal first answer is that 'it cannot be done'. Experience shows that – not everywhere, but over wide ranges of application – this answer is simply wrong. It *can* be done, but it requires a more original Research and Development effort than is normally forthcoming. The road to the cheap and simple solution often demands the deployment of the most sophisticated thought processes and calculations, and can be successfully travelled only with the help of the latest and best research equipment.

In industry and agriculture we have developed highly capital and energy-intensive technologies – which has led to an increasing centralization of economic power in our societies, an ominous trend if one accepts that economic and political power tend to be closely associated.

Over the past 150 years, but especially during the past quarter of a century, we have progressively de-skilled society. In both industry and agriculture, energy and capital have been substituted for human skill and creativity. We must now start to *re-skill* society, and we already know that one of the most effective ways of giving a free rein to human creativity and ingenuity is through the small enterprise. Experience shows that there are many opportunities within the existing level of demand to start small firms at quite modest levels of capital investment.

Seven years ago, we started a unit to promote appropriate technology in Britain, and as part of its activities we have been helping to form a network of Local Enterprise Trusts throughout the country, with the most rewarding results in terms of the variety of firms started, the variety of their products, and their creation of productive and satisfying jobs for local people.

The choice which now inescapably confronts the industrialized countries is either to continue on what Schumacher called 'the onward stampede' with technologies that are ever more capital intensive, centralized, people-excluding; or to take stock, and turn towards technologies that are smaller, decentralized, more frugal in their use of resources, people-involving – and therefore sustainable. In this respect, at least, the rich and poor countries of the world have more in common than is generally supposed.

Wean the boffins from their addiction to nuclear energy

SIR KELVIN SPENCER CBE, MC

SIR KELVIN writes: 'I was a backroom boffin myself. Later I had the job of striving to control other backroom boffins, and found how difficult it was to wean them from over-specialization.'

For the past forty years or so I've lived in a Devon village whose roots are deep in history. The ancestors of many here are commemorated on churchyard tombstones going back for centuries. Right up to the mid-twentieth century the village was a self-contained community, self-reliant for whatever was felt to be necessary. All able bodied people contributed in some practical way to the general well-being, and got satisfaction out of doing so though the money was small. Till the 1950s we had no electricity, no mains water, and no drains other than earth closets and a few cesspools. Transport was without benefit of the motor. Such coal as was used, mostly for the limekilns, came by boat from Wales. It was dumped on the beach at high tide and carted away on the ebb. The village had all the necessary trades such as blacksmith, baker, carpenter, plumber, builder, cobbler, fisherman, and of course the local postman.

Over the years I've had many a chat with the old folk. Some, now of course dead, whom I knew, were born as long ago as the 1850s. In these chats I often brought the conversation round to the old days and how much things had improved since. Most admitted, of course, that in many ways life was now easier. But they all told me that life was better in important ways then than now. There was more neighbourliness, and children had a happy life finding their own amusements in the countryside. The gist of their musings was that in the old days life had meaning and purpose which, in some way, had faded since. Not just for them, not indeed for them at all, but for the younger people around them.

This sensible and healthy self-sufficiency has now nearly gone. Nearly, but not quite. Every now and again snow or a flood cuts us off from the outside world for a few days, and it's cheering then to see how readily folk get back to traditional ways, but this is becoming more difficult with every year that passes. We're moving fast towards dependence on mass-produced supplies and services from other regions and from abroad.

Technology at present nearly always leads to more centralization, with vital decisions which affect us all being taken behind closed doors by fewer and fewer people, and most of them knowledgeable only over a narrow field. We are fast drifting towards a totalitarian state. The technique this time is not Hitler's antisemitism, but the need to trust to a small minority of experts the running of more and more complicated machinery and processes. Centralization of mass-produced necessities means that a very small number of people can hold the country up to ransom, whether they be the workers themselves taking industrial action or terrorists. To safeguard some of the more vital centralized activities, a measure of personal security vetting is becoming common, quite alien to our traditions. For the first time in our history we now have a permanently armed police force. It is only very indirectly responsible to a Minister and Parliament, its master being that powerful Quango the Atomic Energy Authority. In theory of course that Authority is democratically controlled. But no Minister could force his views on an uncooperative AEA without action involving legislation, with all the delays that involves.

We've had practical warnings of things to come at Windscale a few years ago : the plant where fuel for nuclear power stations is manufactured. Had the strike there continued for a little longer with access for essential supplies and servicing being denied, the cooling ponds might have evaporated dry and clouds of radioactive gas and smoke would then cause havoc to health and life over an indeterminate area. Nuclear energy is unique in the extent and duration of the damage it could cause accidentally.

The way forward is not to renounce the benefits of technology but to harness technology wisely, to make it an aid to wise living. At present it is too often indulged in as psychotherapy for its addicts. To use technology wisely one of the needs is to promote decentralization instead of tamely accepting more and more centralization. Whenever some activity can be done on a small scale locally, with proper concern for the deeper values of life, it should be done on that scale. Technology will have to lend a hand to achieve this in most cases. No doubt the economists will point out that in terms of what they call 'real resources' it is better for many activities to be done on a large scale. Don't be misled by their dismal science. It's been said that if all influential economists were laid out in a straight line, head to tail, they would reach...no conclusion. True, perhaps. But alas many tentative conclusions of theirs have promoted wrong action. Our faltering national affairs testify to this. Their mistaken idea of 'real resources' leaves out the higher values of life, those values which mankind has lived by for centuries but seems now to be forgetting.

It is up to us to wean the boffins from their high technology to something more in keeping with our genuine needs. The goal is plain : to evolve a way of life that embraces the good features of village life but eases its drudgery and its hard physical work. In doing this we will not only benefit ourselves but also the under-developed countries. Their problems all involve technology on a small scale: use of natural sources of energy in penny packets for such purposes as pumps and some electrical aids to daily life; better sanitation; simple and healthy housing made from local materials with local skills.

It is cheering to note how many groups have sprung up to pioneer this new kind of technology. It holds promise of being just as intellectually exciting and challenging as any of the high technologies that now monopolize too much of the country's brainpower. But appropriate technology will continue to be derided, alas, by the old-in-mind. Leave them to muddle along for the time being with their *in*appropriate technology while we youngsters fashion the post-industrial civilization. That, as I see it, is the challenge which the young-in-mind are facing. The struggle will be hard and success may be slow to come. The establishment will oppose – that clique of clever influential folk who lack vision. If enough of us work with knowledge and dedication we will make the transition from our decaying industrial culture to something better, and will achieve this with less disorder and with a happier outcome than if we leave it to the establishment. It can be done. A good start has already been made. Lend a shoulder to the wheel.

(The above is extracted from an article which first appeared in 'Natural Energy and Living', No 9.)

Currencies based on trees not gold

ROBERT SWANN

ROBERT SWANN is a key figure in the Institute for Community Engineers and the E.F.Schumacher Society.

It is up to us who are the advocates of appropriate technology and small scale to become the inventors of an appropriate technology for money. It is vital to us because all the other appropriate technologies with which we are involved depend eventually upon a proper and decent exchange system. When the national currencies fail through runaway inflation or for whatever reason, we may survive in some fashion through barter or labour exchange systems. But if we are to expand and grow and become not merely a counter culture or New Age portion of the larger culture, then we must replace the present money system with a new one in which all of the attributes which we value (cooperation, self-reliance, community, etc.) can become the growing and dominant part of the entire culture. Such would be the direction of the work on which we must concentrate in order not only to survive the coming currency collapse, but to develop an 'economy of permanence' in Schumacher's words.

A local currency (appropriate scaled currency) should:

- be consistent with customary practices (cash, checking, accounting systems);
- be redeemable in real goods of every day value;
- though based on local production, be a universal measure of value;
- be controlled by the community, perhaps through a non-profit bank.

I would suggest that we consider using some form of energy as the unit of measurement and as the reserve currency for redemption purposes. The so-called energy crisis has made it clear to almost everyone that energy is the key factor in all forms of production and in meeting the needs of society as a whole. In this respect, gold, as the traditional form of reserve currency, is being replaced by commodities which provide essential energy. Thus oil is referred to as 'black gold'.

But if we're looking for a universal form of energy to use, where do we look? Obviously, the most sought after forms of fossil fuel energy such as oil are as poorly distributed and limited in supply about the earth as gold. What is needed is a form of energy which is both renewable and as universally available throughout the world as possible.

My proposal is that we consider using some convenient measure of wood energy which can become the standard unit of measure and which can be used for redemption purposes in order to establish a local currency which also has universal value. We might begin, for example, with something as simple as cord wood. I realize that the energy component of cord wood is variable and might not be ideal, but if you compare a cord of wood with the US dollar in terms of its constant value, the cord comes out way ahead. I only suggest this is a way to begin, we will have to perfect it as we go along – perhaps an index of different kinds of wood or use one ton of dry wood. Consider also that besides being used on a worldwide basis as a primary source of energy, wood is also used for other basic needs – fruit and nuts for food, lumber for building, and wood can be transformed chemically into plastics which substitute for metals.

Briefly, let's project a scenario of how we might start such a local but universal money and banking system. A group of organisations such as cooperatives, community development coporations, community land trusts, local merchants, small businesses, etc. could form a structure which could establish a joint account in a local bank with each of the member depositers. Deposits in the bank would be in terms of US dollars initially. Once sufficient capital were established, the surplus could be used to invest directly in a commodity of intrinsic value. This could be gold or silver, but I am suggesting investing in energy, and the best source of energy available almost anywhere is trees. Therefore the surplus would be invested in forests or directly in cords of wood, and set up for a community land trust to manage and control. As a sufficient potential supply of cord wood from the forests becomes available, each depositor would then be issued a certificate (or note) measuring the value of his/her deposit in energy – or cordwood. This would mean that the deposit would be redeemable in cordwood. With a ready and continuing supply of cordwood to 'back' their currency, the group would then be in a position to 'issue', or provide credit for projects of real productive value within the local community.

The most pressing need I can imagine for a local and regional self-reliant economy is the invention and establishment of an appropriate exchange system such as I have described. Yet such a system, because it is based on a universal measure of value like a unit of wood energy, could, at the same time, become the key to establishing eventually a world-wide system. For it is obvious that while on the one hand we are at an historical point where local and democratic participation in the economy is essential to our economic survival and to our humanity, it is also clear that we live in a world which is rapidly moving towards a one world economy. This new, appropriate system would consist of thousands of small, primarily self-reliant regions exchanging or trading directly with each other using a common unit of exchange. Thus the foundation for a true world economy would emerge.

Convivial Computing?

ANDREW PAGE

ANDREW PAGE is a 'consultant in information technology' at the Dartington Institute, Devon.

Fourth World thinkers such as Leopold Kohr argue that any system big enough to require a computer is too big, that computers are the tools of a mass society overloaded with information. Andrew Page, however, here argues that computers could be used in the service of decentralized communities, for work sharing and instant voting. Whether or not Andrew Page is naive to trust in a computerized Utopia, it remains true that many of his excellent ideas would work equally well without computers, given a neighbourhood of sufficiently 'human scale', under about a thousand inhabitants.

A Community Communications System

A projection into post-industrial ways of life and means of livelihood

The Community Communications System is conceived of as being owned and operated by the community which it serves. Each subscriber would have at home, workshop or office a console consisting of two visual display units, channel selectors and a keyboard for video and cable TV reception (including a local channel), and such other facilities as wordprocessing, electronic mail, tele-banking, teletext and viewdata.

Instant referenda
A further advantage of the Community Communications System (CCS) is that feedback on people attitude's towards various issues affecting community life could be gained by means of opinion polls and referenda conducted electronically via the CCS. Prioritization and courses of action could also be thereby determined. Working parties on specific issues could be rapidly recruited by use of this two-way communications facility which would be closely integrated with local discussion programmes on the local cable TV channel.

Each person, many jobs
Among its functions, the CCS, coordinated from a local Cottage Office, is designed to assist a close match in the community of available work with willing hands, and, in particular, to allow for flexible working hours and job sharing. Within a post-industrial society with a high degree of local feedback and local control and coordination of materials, resources, jobs and services, it should be possible for each person not only to find work, but also to find different kinds of work. The expectation in this proposal is that given the information and incentive most people would select a *predominant* (rather than *exclusive*) occupation. A normal 'job' might fill two or three days per week. In additional working time, one could select various part-time, short-shift jobs as would be listed (and frequently updated) on a CCS videotext channel.

This would promote a way of life and means of livelihood in which, at least to some degree, everyone is a teacher, a health service worker, a street-sweeper, farm labourer, construction worker, worker in waste recycling, road maintenance, alternative energy production, a policeman, a fireman, legislator, government bureaucrat, etc. Such multiplicity of occupations is possible by virtue of the tasks being simplified, the responsibilities immediate, local and small scale. And most importantly each person works both as a boss (in a few jobs) and as a worker (in many).

Neighbourhood service

The CCS not only allows people to set their own working hours in diversified occupations; in addition the CCS is used to recruit sufficient staff per work shift if too few people volunteer. This latter use is described here as the 'On-call Programme'. All residents agree to be on-call for shared amounts of time, just as is the case now with select professions: doctors, nurses, airline personnel, etc.

The CCS allows extension of on-call procedures to any and all occupations. All enterprises coordinated by it generally recruit the majority of staff positions, even for supervisory persons, on a part-time short-shift basis. Some people reserve shifts in advance, but many wait until they specifically want to work and then switch on the 'Immediate Vacancies Programme' on CCS and select an occupation in which there is an immediate need. Obviously this system of self-selection of work shifts and occupations requires an additional policy to ensure that work crews in essential service occupations are adequately staffed. Therefore, all residents elect time periods in which they will be on-call in addition to their self-selected occupations and work shifts. This on-call responsibility pertains to any occupation at any level which an on-call resident is capable of doing. Highly skilled specialists are on-call not only for occupations within their speciality, but for 'unskilled' work as well. The CCS allows that the on-call procedure be entirely fair. The computer supplies to the persons working as CCS Coordinators a list of names of residents such that the first persons – the persons whose names will be at the top of the list – to be called for a particular work shift will be those who were least recently contacted for on-call work. Having completed an on-call shift, your name then goes back to the bottom of the list.

Post-Industrial Leisure

Increasingly today, as people are encouraged to specialize in highly skilled professions, who, then, will be left to do the menial physical work which in fact, will be the last to be automated? The answer allowed by the CCS is: just those same highly skilled persons – on a part-time short-shift basis in addition to their predominant occupation. The policy of providing part-time short shift work in many different occupations allows that such work be accepted even as a form of leisure. Street-sweeping eight hours a day, day in and day out, constitutes drudgery, but street-sweeping for a few hours every few weeks could be enjoyable, as physical exercise, an occupational diversion from predominant responsibilities, a productive form of socializing with other work crew members. The CCS encourages close community integration, providing a basis from which people may more genuinely understand each other and each other's work, and appreciate all that it takes to maintain their community.

The idea of work takes on an entirely different character in which the social aspects predominate. The effect of the CCS is to return direct control of life to the *local* community and to each individual. Work, education and leisure are reintegrated. People practise various skills at the same time as they are learning new ones. Waste of time and labour are minimized. Challenge and new experience are every day occurences. Expansion of individual potential is a normal universal expectation. One's local community rather than someone else's factory is the centre of existence.

3 Education

Education for what?

MICHAEL DUANE

MICHAEL DUANE was formerly headmaster of Risinghill Comprehensive School, North London.

Durkheim's formulation of the function of education – to transmit to the younger generation the forms of knowledge, the skills and the social values prevalent in the parent society – embodies the truth that is easily observed in history, *viz*, that every society seeks to perpetuate itself. Since the social systems of the Western industrial societies incorporate occupational and social class divisions differentiated by wealth, privilege, power and access to education, the inculcation of social values stresses the right of the upper classes to rule, respect for private property, respect for a religion which emphasizes humility and obedience to 'the will of God' and disregard for material possessions. Religion for the lower classes becomes a form of internalized control; for the upper classes it is used as a ritualized adjunct to legitimize the exercise of state power.

In accordance with the principle of the sub-division of labour, the system of education is grouped according to the functions that the pupils will exercise in adult life. For the ruling classes there are the public schools with a highly selective entry based on social class and achievement in the preparatory school, highly qualified teachers, themselves from upper-class backgrounds and Oxbridge. They are taught in small classes with intensive coaching and individual attention to develop high linguistic skill in all its forms – language, mathematics, science, music, art – in preparation for their social function of controlling a highly complex society in which many and varied forms of knowledge have to be coordinated.

The professional and semi-professional classes are educated in state grammar schools or, more recently, in the higher streams of 'comprehensive' schools. Their teachers come from similar backgrounds and usually have university degrees in the subjects they teach. Again there is much stress on linguistic ability in many forms, stress on uniforms, punctuality and conformity – in preparation for the disciplined and respectable life of the professional. Religious activities in school emphasize spirituality and morality in service for others, as a preparation for their future life. The curriculum is geared to examination success for entry to the university and professional training.

The manual working classes attend secondary modern schools or the lower streams of comprehensives. The average size of teaching group is more than double that in the public school. Their teachers rarely have university degrees and commonly have no more academic qualifications than five 'O' levels taken at secondary school. They spend an average of eleven years (5 – 16+) in education as against more than twenty years (3 – 23+) for the professionals who go on to higher education and professional training.

A particularly disturbing feature of the education system is that it fails to develop among the lower social classes the wide range of linguistic skills that are necessary not only to the control of a modern society but to full participation in such a society. It is not, therefore, surprising, indeed it is inevitable, that crime continues to rise. The mass media, especially television, reveal facts about our society hitherto only available to the sociologist, facts such as the blatant discrepancies between the styles of life of rich and poor.

Something other than educational reform is necessary. The change to a 'comprehensive' system of schools (a system that excluded grammar, public and other private schools!) has dramatically fallen short of its declared objectives and has continued to maintain, in disguised forms, the divisive methods and effects of the old tripartite system. Research reveals that every national system of education, without exception, reproduces in its structure, its objectives and in the disposition of its resources, the essential features of the parent society. Schools that seek more human objectives have to do so outside the state system, like Summerhill. State schools that try to do this are closed or forced to conform to the 'normal', like Risinghill or Tyndale. Individual teachers can create small democratic enclaves within their own classrooms, but they must be careful that the children are not heard addressing them by their christian names! They can refuse to beat their pupils or to send them for the cane, but the most determined opponents of the abolition of corporal punishment in schools have been until recently the teachers' unions!

When Christ said 'Love thy neighbour *as thyself!*' he spoke from the context of a small closely-knit community under Roman dominion but still bound together by tradition and personal esteem. When John Dewey said 'What the best and wisest parent wants for his own child, that must the community want for all its children. Anything less is ignoble; acted upon it will destroy our democracy,' he spoke from the experience of the small, recently-pioneer community founding a new, democratic nation. Plato's educational treatise was written as his solution to the problem of how to create a just and stable Republic.

We cannot formulate aims for education without postulating a society in which those aims will be realized. If we formulate aims such as 'joy', 'sensitivity', 'democracy' or whatever, we must create a society that will give expression to those aims. Hitherto we have been chained by cumbersome nineteenth-century systems of production and control. Modern forms of energy and communication make vast agglomerations of people, machines or materials unnecessary. We have the techniques to recreate small communities where we no longer know people only as 'workmates', as 'doctor' or 'policeman' or 'milkman', but where we know them as people rather than as functionaries, with all their strengths, weaknesses and individualities, and to create such communities even within our existing cities.

We should have to reassess our objectives and methods

in all our activities, but such reassessment would come, not from bureaucrats working on élitist assumptions, but from the communities themselves having regard to their most urgent needs. I do not doubt that love and freedom – whether we call them 'mutual aid' 'cooperation' or 'community action' – will figure high on our list of priorities. Under such conditions it would be possible that we might be tempted to share what we have with the most needy; that we might resist the urge to rob others; that we might fail to see the point of making nuclear weapons and maintaining vastly expensive and unproductive navies, armies and air forces that if unleashed could only produce Mutual Assured Destruction; that we might be the richer for not burning up our resources of timber, oil and minerals at a prodigal rate and for valueless ends such as military prestige. We might then discover that the enemies against whom we had been preparing to defend ourselves existed largely in our own heads.

Many, many small communities have so lived for centuries before the arrival of industrial man. Perhaps we ought to look again at those communities that, without benefit of our scientific knowledge to keep disease and hunger at bay, yet so often lived lives characterized by joyous gaiety and concern for one another. Hitherto we have tended to think that Small is Savage or Small is Bleak. Perhaps with more intelligent use of modern knowledge we could begin to realise that Schumacher had more sense than he was given credit for when he said 'Small is Beautiful!'.

Why aren't free schools spreading?

CLIVE DAVIDSON

CLIVE DAVIDSON used to teach at Kirkdale School, in South East London. This is a staff and parent cooperative for children from three-and-a-half to eleven years old.

Some people argue that since most free schools have to charge tuition, this leaves poor kids in the lurch. True, but only partly. Free schools are important agents of change, both as a training device and as a model. When they work well, other people in the community understand what they are doing and want them for their own children. This can put pressure on (state) schools to start some such schools of their own .... or it may bring closer a time when independent schools with no tuition (fees) and non-selective policies, no weeding out of children – at the door or later – will be considered 'public' and supported from tax funds on the basis of the number of students attending.

John Holt *What Do I Do Monday?*

The early alternative schools, Summerhill, Monkton Wyld and Kilqhuanity, are, and have always been, fee-paying. The schools of the sixties and seventies, wanting to open their doors to all children, made serious attempts to obtain state funding. Local education authorities responded by offering funds to deal with their failures, i.e. school refusals. Not wishing to become readjustment centres, alternatives have refused such offers in order to maintain their status as viable schools for all.

The schools since the sixties have looked to the private sector for funding, and trusts and charities have at least partly supported most of the alternatives that have appeared, and in many cases, disappeared again, in the last twenty years. But although schools such as White Lion have been able not to charge fees, and others, by subsidizing their fees with grants from various sources, have been able to keep them low, the problem of funding alternatives has been the most effective check on their growth.

Obtaining funds from the private sector is a time-consuming and skilled task. Only those groups with sophisticated programmes or at least one individual familiar with the intricacies and protocol of the grant-making organizations have been successful. White Lion have had singular success. They were set up with clearly defined aims by people equipped to deal with bureaucracies and they work in what is clearly a 'deprived' area worthy of philanthropic concern. Less professional efforts such as those by Leeds, also working in a deprived area, and Kirkdale, which can make no claim to the social needs of its children, have failed.

The effort and skill required for fund-raising programmes have been a drain on the resources of alternative schools. Their workers are required to devote vast amounts of energy to ensuring the survival of their projects, making their jobs unbearably demanding and few can stand the strain on the poor wages they receive for more than a few years.

Very few parents are prepared to commit their children to a school that is likely to disappear overnight. Since alternative schools have not grown in the last ten years, the demand for them is neither seen nor felt by the authorities. Successful alternatives have either been fee-paying or in deprived areas so that they are seen as either select institutions for an élite or rehabilitation centres for social casualties.

The situation at present is unsatisfactory. While there is a growing interest in alternative schools and a tacit recognition of the success of their methods by the authorities in the fact that many truancy units are run on alternative lines, no new alternative schools are appearing and those that exist remain either 'private' or 'charitable'. It is important that existing alternative schools continue as training devices and models but there needs to be some breakthrough in their funding if they are to grow and become more efficient agents of change.

There has been some useful exploitation of the government's youth employment programme, most notably by Leeds, obtaining a £25,000 Manpower Services Commission grant to set up an adventure playground. White Lion's school has a substantial grant from Islington/Hackney Urban Aid Programme. Kirkdale has always been a self-help group, a cooperative of parents setting up and maintaining the kind of school they want for their children. But while they can offer some support to members less able to contribute, the resources of this school are strictly limited. Each of these schools sees itself locked in a debilitating struggle for survival. They and the others will undoubtedly continue, carried by their momentum and because of the commitment of the individuals involved, but there is little prospect at the present time of alternative schooling being offered to more than those wealthy enough, or lucky enough to live in Leeds or London.

The hundreds of copies of *How To Set Up a Free School* and the Campaign for State Supported Alternative Schools have failed to produce a single offspring. This suggests that in spite of the wilful avoidance of figureheads by the latter-day alternatives, even these were set up by particular individuals of some expertise in response to particular circumstances. The problem of funding alternatives ensures that most projects are stillborn, and of those that make the first stage, most die an early death. Fees are in breach of the egalitarian principles of the schools, while the success of White Lion and failure of Leeds and Kirkdale to obtain charitable grants suggests that alternatives are at the mercy of Big Business and those able to gain access to their faceless philanthropists. Alternative schools continue to keep alive an idea of democracy based on equality, justice and love – it is vital that they do so – but their influence on society is in proportion to their numbers. The spread of alternative schools is likely only to follow the introduction of some kind of state provision, such as in Denmark, whereby small groups are able to set up 'Little Schools' on state funds.

The question must be asked as to why the state has refused to fund alternatives? The answer is not hard to find. The history of alternative schools is a history of attempts to bring about social change. By offering individuals freedom in their formative years and encouraging them to become questioning, independent and self-reliant, as adults they are likely to demand freedom that the state is unwilling to give. Funding of alternative schools is a commitment to widespread social change, a commitment no local authority has been prepared to countenance. As Michael Duane wrote after the refusal of the Doncaster Education Authorities to continue funding the Connisbrough experiment in introducing progressive education into a state school, they 'dare not even begin to move from the established forms of education and forms of authority. Those who placed them in power would disapprove'.

What is then to be done? Alternatives need to be supported in every possible way because of their value, as John Holt has said, as models, training devices and influence on the community. What is needed more than the advice contained in *How to Set Up A Free School*, is hard cash. The A.S. Neill Trust, set up to raise funds for alternative schools from private sources, failed to produce more than a handout. The Campaign for State Supported Alternative Schools conference in May this year decided to concentrate its efforts on influencing political opinion. White Lion are the most likely to breach the blockade by gaining ILEA funding. Their effort needs strong support in whatever way they may ask.

Finally, it may be the kids themselves who decide the issue, voting with their feet. As John Aitkenhead of Kilqhuanity says:

> There's a new element today that is forcing people to consider alternative schools and that is the extent to which kids have taken the law into their own hands and refused to go to school. In the poorest parts of big cities the teenagers are refusing in huge numbers to attend. Now the schools they are willing to attend you could call *progressive* or *alternative*, and the education authorities are beginning to recognize that.

(The Campaign for State Supported Alternative Schools can be contacted at White Lion Free School, 57 White Lion Street, London N1. They supply an action pack on setting up free schools.)

Start your own education system

MARK KINZLEY

MARK KINZLEY, co-editor of this book, is a community activist in Redbridge, North-east London.

It isn't hard to found a Learning Exchange. I started one without any previous experience or expertise. I began by founding a committee. I soon learnt that this was an entirely inappropriate tool for the job! It was like trying to crack a walnut with a pneumatic drill. Sensing that it was getting nowhere fast the committee drifted apart, and I got on with it on my own. The first thing was to find a group of people willing to participate, because I needed a core of subjects to start with, which I could offer other people in order to get them to join. I found a self-help group at my local drop-in centre for the unemployed, but you could find a social club for old age pensioners, a local branch of Education Otherwise, or a group for young mothers etc...

I passed round a sheet on which the group filled in their name, address and subjects they would like to learn and teach. Already at this point I had a Learning Exchange! From a group of about twenty people, some interested, some not, I had about thirty entries, ranging from teachers of cabinet making and motorbike mechanics to learners for computers and soft-toy making. I simply filed, typed up and photocopied the entries under the headings 'Teachers Wanted' and 'Teachers Offered'. Above I typed in explanation:

REDBRIDGE LEARNING EXCHANGE

Is there a subject you would like to learn? You can get tuition *absolutely free* by writing to the Exchange. I will send you the addresses of people who want to teach the subjects you want. It's then up to you to arrange to meet, perhaps in the teacher's home.

Is there a subject you could teach? Do you have a hobby you could share? Could you teach any of the subjects mentioned in the 'Teachers Offered' column (several teachers are needed for each subject)?

Please say if you prefer to learn/teach with one person or with a group. If you are old or handicapped, for example, you are recommended to be in a group.

Because the teaching is given for fun and friendship and not for money, neither the Exchange or any organization distributing it can accept responsibility beyond arranging initial contact, so I recommend you start a trial 3 lessons before coming to a longer arrangement. Shop for what you want.

Send all entries for the Exchange, with four SAEs to: Mark Kinzley etc. If you don't get a response from a contact let me know so I can remove him/her from my files. If the Exchange fails to get you a local contact make copies and distribute this sheet locally.

Having created this leaflet I started distributing it. I tried giving it to shoppers in the High Street, I experimented with putting it through letter boxes, I tested the response from stories in the local press. I have to say that all these approaches brought me little response. I learned that the most effective method is to ask the Borough Librarians of this and surrounding boroughs to distribute my leaflets through their internal postal systems to all their libraries. That way only interested people pick up the leaflets, which is a far more efficient use of them. Note also that a poster in a library, as opposed to leaflets, gets zero response – in my experience anyway.

But you can only do so much through libraries. It beefs up the entries on the Exchange so that you have a real product to offer, but from libraries alone you won't find the Exchange reaches 'take off'. The next stage is to phone up the ministers and vicars of local churches and ask if you can give a talk on the Exchange to social groups centred on their church. If you write instead, you won't get a response, not because they're not interested, but because they are too busy. Talking to social groups can gain new entries for the Exchange, but more important, you may persuade the group to assume responsibility for printing and promoting the leaflets in their community, and perhaps at a later date they might take over the filing of entries for their area.

Starting a Learning Exchange you do meet a lot of

apathy, and in the early stages you must expect to work hard for every new member, often explaining to them personally. Francis Sealey, who started the amazingly successful 'Community Network' which is described elsewhere in this section, had to persist with just forty members for a year before his exchange really took off. I visualize the hurdle as being that you have to reach a critical size of membership before the amount of gossiping by members about the Exchange becomes self-perpetuating. During the long haul up to that, the problem isn't the work involved, since when you actually look at it there really isn't very much – only sending off some SAEs of a morning and occasionally supplying a batch of leaflets. But the problem is learning to 'persist gently', to make sustained effort. To do this you must learn to resist fantasizing about the future – if you don't go up you can't come down.

Remember also that if the Exchange is a success it won't all have to fall on your shoulders. If you gain enough members you can advertise to form a fund-raising committee – jumble sales, coffee mornings for Exchange members etc... Should you ever have to drop out entirely they can take over. Once the Exchange covers a large enough area you can decentralize the whole thing by getting someone to take over the production of the Exchange for his or her half of the total area. You are then entitled to print on the back of the two exchanges:

> This Exchange is part of a network of exchanges. The first exchange in this network was founded in (e.g.) the London borough of Redbridge in 1983. When it covered a large enough area someone from the far half came forward and offered to take over the production of the exchange for his half of the total area. By regularly swapping its own entries with the immediately neighbouring exchanges in a network of exchanges, each exchange covers the surrounding areas but not the entire network beyond the immediately neighbouring exchanges. Because all entries are thus duplicated in neighbouring exchanges, should any exchange collapse any one of a number of exchanges can expand to fill the gap, and later split again. The network is thus very stable. It grows like splitting cells. In time, the network will extend

to all the coasts of Britain. Do you want to help this Exchange to split? If so, please get in touch.

Community network – a licence for neighbourliness

PETER MARTIN

The following is from an article in Time Out *magazine about a mutual aid group in London N13.*

Of all the longings people have, perhaps the commonest is a longing for community: to engage, to use and to be of larger use, to make better sense of how you live, where you live. But to travel out from the privacy of home into the daily world of work is to pass through a no man's land. Home and work represent two different cultures with different and apparently irreconcilable moralities, and between them this vastness where community should be.

Whatever the reasons, there's a sense of longing in the big city, a lack of feeling of belonging that isn't just explained by British reserve and a coldish climate. Move into a city or a suburb, and you may only get half a dozen chances to cement your future relationship with your neighbourhood. If you're cautious or marginally different your're likely to be marked down as snotty or some kind of pariah – and if you're too fulsome, just watch them run the other way.

However, people living in and around Palmer's Green, N13, have begun to crack all this with a piece of social genius called Community Network. 'Network gives people that initial *excuse* they need to get started with one another', says Fred Melvin, 74, resident of the area since 1938. 'They might want the badminton or to join one of the food co-ops. Or they might want the children's workshop or the under-fives information service or the babysitting circle. Or someone else might want to do a Network skill-swap – you know, I'll teach you bricklaying if you teach me accounting or the piano.

'With my father being in the army, we moved around a lot when I was young, but I've never seen a community like this one. It's all classes, races and ages, and it *works*.'

Built up in the 1930s, Palmer's Green's swish new pebble-dash and front-room parquet was immediately desirable to bank officials, accountants and solicitors who, while tending their regulation roses, would address each other as 'Smith' or 'Parker' – very public schoolboy democratic. Wives with delicately powdered bums held semi-formal coffee-mornings, and popping in for a chat, although frowned upon, had not yet been elevated to the level of incest.

Over time, Palmer's Green inevitably attracted a more anxious aspirant class – thrusting insurance chappies with motor cars on the never-never and toffee-shop Tories who knew exactly what was 'naice' and what wasn't. Gradually, the original residents began to head for less trampled pastures, and 'Mon Repos' boards in oak and pokerwork, glassed-in front porches and house numbers artfully spelled out – as in 'One-O-Five' – became the norm. Widows in reduced circumstances huffed past their lower middle class neighbours and whispered bitterly about how the place had 'gone down'.

By the early 1960s, Palmer's Green had come to comprise what social planners loved to call 'a good cultural mix' – a preponderance of working and lower middles, a 'leavening' of barely aspirant liberal middles, plus pockets of Greeks, Turks and Pakistanis. Fascinating though it may have looked on paper, it was in fact a limbo land of public smiling and private unease.

Network's founder Francis Sealey is an ex-school teacher and Open University programme producer who, having become increasingly browned off with traditional Labour Party socialism and having immersed himself in the writings of Illich, Schumacher and Kropotkin, began to look at the problems of society and change from a different standpoint.

'What was common to all these people was the idea that change could take place within society if it began with regeneration within the individual. Doing is setting up your own alternatives and creating from new forms of organization in which individuals are important enough to make a contribution to their own lives. Hierarchies prevent this happening either because they tell people what to do or somehow oblige them to ask for what they want. What's missing is authority exercised not vertically but horizontally – person to person – and achieving what we want by cooperation. After 1974 I was thinking a lot about these things and, by '78, how to get all that going here.

'We started,' Sealey explains,

'from the broadest conceptual framework – a belief and a desire to create a mutual aid society. To find people with common interests – yoga or a children's book group or a sports or wine club – and put them in touch with one another. To find people interested in co-ops – food, or crafts and so on. To find people willing to offer each other different services – English conversation for people whose first language isn't English; a phone-in advice service; an information bank of where to go and how to get things done locally. Overall, of course, we were attempting to initiate a concept and a spirit of community that would, after a time, become self-generating.

Central to the whole idea was this one of the learning exchange. At the moment, skills and knowledge are exclusive, protected, hoarded, and only held to exist when institutionally recognized. But if the incredible wealth of skills and knowledge already possessed by the community could be shared in some way – person to person – this would be the real, non-institutional cement of a Network.

In our original Network application form we included a questionnaire asking people what skills or subjects they would like to learn – plus what skills and subjects they might pass on to someone else; and from that we could put in touch people with skills to swap. When we'd got our first 40 people, we wrote out the whole list of skills wanted and on offer, plus the types of groups and clubs and co-ops people wanted, and included all this on our next run of application forms.

By June 1979, when membership was nearing 200,

Network turned itself into a democratic organisation, with a constitution and an elected management committee. By June 1980, membership was up to 500.

When the Sealeys' own sitting room could no longer bear the strain, Network moved into premises tucked just off the corner of Palmer's Green High Street. The tiny back room became the Network office – its files open to all members and its bi-monthly magazine hand-cranked on an inky duplicator. The equally tiny front room is now the community shop, run on a co-op basis, selling mainly baby clothes and local crafts.

Dave Beetlestone does Network's posters and magazine artwork, organizes bazaars, runs the craft shop, and is generally known to put himself usefully about.

> I *hate* joining things. But what really excited me and drew me in was community action. Network is such a range of things pooled together, when you participate you become a member of something which is the very opposite of exclusive in its interests and breadth. You actually feel the links through the community becoming deeper and stronger. In the magazine we advertise and give space over to other groups – Friends of the Earth, the National Federation of OAPs, the local racial harmony people, the Enfield women's group – so that they can explain what they do.
>
> I'm impressed how self-generating Network is now. There's a woman sent in some feminist-type poetry to the magazine and, out of that, she's getting her own group together. One thing just leads to another.

Membership is now well above 1,000 and still rising...

Jane Ballard, a conference secretary, moved into Palmer's Green just last December.

> I got to know about the Network because people in this flat before me hadn't cancelled their subscription and the news letter was delivered to me. Before, in Mill Hill, I knew no one. People see you rushing out to work, you're instantly classified, and that's usually the end of it. But, now, it's as if I've lived in Palmer's Green for years. Once I went along to the Network office where all the files are and was told, 'Look up what you like'. It was like being given the keys to the whole community.

Because Community Network is so many different things to so many different people, it is an impossible phenomenon to assess. Although political in the most fundamental sense, there's no drawing any straight ideological lines through it. For every whiff of resurgent Christianity it gives off, there's another to make Robert Owen smile in his grave. While its theorising often sounds hopelessly middle-class, you've only to step into a Network social to discover an altogether more complex reality.

Network's lateral exercise of community authority, on a person-to-person, neighbourhood-to-neighbourhood basis, certainly feels evolutionary. It may even be revolutionary in that, unlike a classically structured organisation, its content determines its form.

The development of its learning exchange is a case in point. Until a year ago, between thirty and forty new people each month were putting in for a skill exchange of some kind but only about half of these were managing to do it. Shyness was part of it. A free give-and-get contract requires initiative. The introduction of a token system has eased the situation somewhat. Some objected, of course, on the grounds that tokens contravened the spirit of Network, smacked of dreadful consumerism, etc. With and without tokens, swaps nonetheless continued.

But still not enough. So someone suggested trying a few short courses – putting small groups of people wanting a particular skill in touch with an individual willing to provide it. Twelve courses were the result in Autumn 1981. Such has been the subsequent demand for similar courses – seven or eight every month, it works out – that Network has just inaugurated its own educational council. It now seems likely that Network's other mushrooming activities – entertainments, co-ops and enterprises, communications and media perhaps, and certainly its social services – will beget their own councils.

Except for a one-off grant of £1,500 from the GLC and another £450 from a charity to get its English language service going, Network is self-financing through annual subscriptions, monthly dances, plus less regular big events like the recent International Week, jumble sales, and the community shop – in all, generating between £1,500 and £2,000 a year. 'This year,' says treasurer Fraser Michaelson,' it'll probably be up to £3,000. For one thing, we're now offering a duplicating service through the community shop.

'Beyond that Network could go any which way. There's already a group of people talking about a Network credit union. And there's no reason why Network couldn't do its own conveyancing. Still early days yet.'

Never having sought out the local authority for help, Network now finds *itself* being sought out. Local librarians, impressed by Network's access to up-to-date community information – its under fives information service is a case in point – are looking for a more closely cooperative relationship. Equally anxious for community access, some social workers have also plugged into Network, if only unofficially. All of which raises the question of whether or not Network is shoring up – and thereby perpetuating – the inadequacies of the local authority. 'Certainly there's a division of opinion about this among some of our members.' Sealey says 'Some argue we ought to press on with our education and our social services but also attack the local authority. Set up a Network Education Area, say, and a Network Services Area which are *better* – as a result of which it would be nice to say to the local authority: "Why don't you disband?"

'But Network isn't about abandoning authority at all. It's about abandoning the unresponsive institutional variety and putting personal authority in its place. And it's about cooperation. The National Childbirth Trust, for example, put on a course with us, and there's no reason why they shouldn't do so again. Because without us, they wouldn't be able to put on so many courses; and without them, we wouldn't be able to answer the local need.'

As for Network's future, Sealey reckons there's no way of telling which way it will go. 'We're becoming a little top-heavy now, and when membership reaches 1,500 or 1,600, it'll probably be time to decentralize. It might even work out, eventually, that 500 people in a smallish area is the optimum membership for a Network. I can certainly see a time when we have three or four Community Networks, each autonomous but having access to each other. If you needed something, it would be nice to punch up Haringey Network on a computer and see if they could provide it.'

(Community Network can be contacted at the Network Office, 13 Aldermans Hill, London N13.)

The Academic Inn

PROFESSOR LEOPOLD KOHR

LEOPOLD KOHR is an Honorary Fellow of the Academic Inn, London. The inspiration for this new London 'university', founded in 1983, came from the following article.

When the fascist regimes rose in Europe, scholars could continue their work by taking refuge in countries whose universities remained unaffected by government pressure. They could go to France, Canada, the United States.

But since then, a new and infinitely vaster danger has arisen to unfettered academic activities. This is the irresistible pressure emanating from the explosive dimensions of modern mass societies which can educationally be accommodated only by universities of vast scale. (* see page 134).

Though these are no less destructive to scholarship than tyrannical governments, one can no longer escape their strangulating effect, as was possible under fascism, merely by taking refuge in other countries. There are none left which do not share the mounting pressure of their increasing multitudes. Geographically, only flight to another planet could solve the problem.

Yet, there is one last way out. This is for scholarship to change its location not geographically but institutionally; to flee not from the earth to another planet but from the university to another establishment, an institution which by nature is immune to persecution (a) from mass pressure

because of the intrinsic smallness of its material frame; and
(b) from ideological pressure because it exerts a dissolvent
effect on all solidified ideas as a result of the fragmentizing
radiation to which it exposes everything. This institution –
the last refuge of the humanities – is the inn.

Freedom may disappear from the town hall, the church,
the theatre, the campus, under the intimidating weight of
Orwellian mass-enforced conformism. But once you enter
the inn – the last *public house* in the original sense of the
term, as it was also the first – and begin to sip your drink,
you also begin to feel liberated from the fear-inspiring
pressures of life *extra-muros*, venturing once again to utter
what is really on your mind, and continuing to do so as
long as you remain in the protection of its disinhibiting as
well as tranquillizing walls.

And so will others who join you in the fellowship of
'drinking associates'. In this way, their spirit rendered
tolerant as well as tolerable, the conditions are created for
the revival of unfettered conversation which, in proper
academic fashion, have as their purpose less the defence of
positions held than the search for new approaches to truth,
and the exploration of unknown continents beyond the
horizon.

Even if one of the 'drinking associates' is a secret agent
joining for the sake of spying, it will make no difference.
For to be a good spy, he too must have a drink; and if he
drinks, he too will become disinhibited and tolerant and
truthful, as was the case with the Austrian policeman
during the Schuschnigg regime. Arresting a citizen in a
tavern for having referred to his government as 'lousy', he
answers the evasive trespasser who claimed he was talking
not about the Austrian but the Chinese government.:
'Don't tell any tall stories, friend. There is only one lousy
government – ours. You go to jail.'

It is because of the effect which the companionship of the
tavern table has, first on the truthfulness of the 'fellows',
and then on the heightened chance of coming a step nearer
to truth, that the inn may not only turn out to be the last
refuge of the humanities. It was, in fact, the very place in
which the humanities were born.

The first universities of the Western World, the

academies of ancient Athens, started out as fellowships of the drinking table. To this day, the most hallowed institution symbolising the academic mode of production is the symposium, which is Greek for 'drinking together', (*syn* standing for together, and *pinein* for drinking). And to this day the great English law schools are called inns – Lincoln's Inn, Gray's Inn – in which, as is appropriate for an academic tavern, the chief degree requirement is that the student must not have passed that many examinations but attended that many dinners and as one of them woefully remarked, have eaten them too. It is therefore not surprising that Samuel Johnson, the greatest inn-scholar of them all, should have said: 'There is nothing which has yet been contrived by man by which so much happiness is produced as by a good tavern,' and as one may add, so much wisdom as well.

However, as Ortega y Gasset's revolting age of the masses has destroyed the essence of the university, it has also destroyed the essence of the good tavern. It has turned it from an extra-parliamentary meeting place into a dispensary of liquid tranquillizers and a high-speed refuelling station offering television along with the mustard on the hot dogs. And instead of lifting its guests from the limbo of their faceless anonymity, it returns them to the street with even less identity than they had when they entered.

So the first task in recreating what may be called the *Academic Inn* as a breeding ground of scholarly thought is to restore to it the essence of the good tavern which, to qualify, must offer not only good food, good drink, good service, and good accommodation, but also good conversation.

To ensure the latter, three requirements must be fulfilled in an age in which unorganized spontaneity and initiative are no longer such self-generating products of conviviality as they were at the time of Samuel Johnson.

1. In the first place, the guests must have the certainty that there will always be two or three individuals present who are likely to provide the spark for thought, dialogue, and discussion. As a university catalogue announces that Professor Johnson will lecture this semester on linguistics

Monday and Wednesday at 10.am. in classroom 17, the menu of the Academic Inn will inform that Samuel Johnson has his beer or cocktail every day at 5 p.m. at table 2.

This will be his only duty. There will be no programme, no other routine, with any guest wishing to join, joining his or the table of any other Johnsonian staff member, who happens to be in residence for a few days, weeks, or a month or two. If the 'star' is in no mood for talking, his table companions may be encouraged to converse by his mere presence. And if they too fail to come into the appropriate mood, they will enjoy an hour's silent musing and contemplation while watching the reflection of fireplace and setting sun in their glasses filled with brew or Churchill's 'amber liquid'. From there on, the chain reaction of conversation, sparked by musing silence or animated talk, will continue into dinner and after-dinner hours.

2 The second requirement concerns the nature of the guests, who need not necessarily have an academic preparation, just as the pilgrims to a religious shrine do not necessarily have to be graduates of a theological seminary. But as it is with pilgrims, they must be attracted to the Academic Inn not only by the sizzling steaks and the excellent service they are sure to find in its halls, but by the conversational spirit of the place, the *genius loci*, which is likely to take possession of them irrespective of whether they participate actively or passively. This should be strong enough to bring them from as far away as a good bouillabaisse is able to haul a Frenchman from half across France not so much for the stimulating effect it has on his stomach as on the sparkle of conversation which good food unfailingly releases in an animated mind. What identifies the guest of the Academic Inn is thus that he is *animated* – a spirit that is academically 'charged', not one that is necessarily academically 'educated'.

3 Finally, the Academic Inn must have the architectural frame that makes it conducive to fulfilling its special mission to offer an ideal enclosure for producing the numerous unplanned encounters which are statistically necessary for minds to be cross-fertilized and a given

number of new thoughts to be born. This is why the foremost physical amenity of the great colleges of Oxford and Cambridge has always been the convivium of a sumptuously conceived Common Room and the companionship of a great Dining Hall where the scholars drink, and eat, and speculate together under the stimulus of a splendid piece of architecture symbolising at the same time the university and the inn.

The only question is: would the idea of an Academic Inn appeal to a wide enough public to make it practical? Having held forth on the subject for two decades, I have rarely encountered a person whose enthusiasm could not be aroused *upon the instant* by the thought of such an institution.

It not only appeals to scholars who, after all, have long experienced on their own skins the subtle effect which the increasing dimensions of their working environment – too many students, too large a faculty, too big a physical plant – exert on the tenuous body of academic freedom which, commanding over no armed forces, are not equipped to withstand such pressure; it also appeals to the average person who sees in its convivial informality a compelling inducement to continued post-graduate education such as he would not seek under the more formal circumstances in which it is conventionally offered.

Indeed, so positive and instantaneous is the response to the idea that a Scottish lady reacted quite typically when, hearing of the as yet unborn Academic Inn, she immediately asked to enrol her two sons, aged 3 and 5, to secure a place for them in proper time, as is customary with Harrow and Eton, where parents enrol their children when they are conceived. And the late Howard Gossage, the genius of American advertising, actually proceeded with putting the idea into practice with a series of seminars in the magnificent frame of 'Timber Cove Inn' in January 1969. Had it not been for his premature death a few months later, I have no doubt that, once the prototype was established, the idea of the Academic Inn would as rapidly have spread across the world as the idea of music festivals once it was successfully tested in Salzburg and in Bayreuth.

Finally, there is the question of finance. Well, one of the main advantages of the Academic Inn, protecting it from interference on the part of those furnishing the funds, is that it is an *inn*. This means that, once established, it will live not from donations but from the income gained by competent innkeeping, that is by offering, aside from conversation, the best in food, drink, service, and accommodation. If this can support the engagement of singing stars by attracting those who love music, it should be able to support also the hiring of talking stars by attracting enough of the enormous crowd which would enjoy conversation if it discovered where it can be found.

The main financial problem concerns therefore, not the running but the *setting up* of the first academic inns. And this should encounter no great difficulty either, considering that the second main feature of the institution – besides being a good tavern – is that it is also an eminently academic enterprise. As a result, it should be possible to persuade some of the foundations dedicated to the advance of learning and knowledge to make the funds available for the establishment of the first prototype of an institution in which, in this age for, of, and by the masses, the humanities are as said, most likely to find their last refuge.

Besides interesting educational foundations, it should also be possible to engage the financial support of those most closely connected with supplying the inns with their most essential raw-material – the brewers, wine growers, and liquor distillers.

Suffering, as they are, from a congenital guilt complex because of their association with dealings in intoxicants, they have – instead of demanding homage from the public for relieving their daily miseries with Johnsonian joys of living – long tried to appease their bad conscience by supporting cultural activities such as the St. Louis symphony orchestra or the splendid Carlsberg museum in Copenhagen, hoping that their name will evoke Beethoven and Praxiteles rather than a wicked glass of beer.

Now if the producers of intoxicants are so ready to support orchestras and exhibitions of art which do not dispense liquor, they should be all the more willing to support a cultural establishment such as an Academic Inn where, in the hallowed fashion of the Symposium, 'drinking together' forms part of the proceedings, being the scholar's most ancient mode of production. (This is why in the renowned Princeton Institute of Advanced Studies, the only duty of the fellows is to sip together their daily cups in the common room.)

Moreover, once a first Academic Inn is set up with the help of a great brewer (possibly even carrying his name as Copenhagen museum carries the name of Carlsberg), other brewers, distillers, and wine growers will be forced by the psychological laws of competition to follow suit for the same reason that, once a bar installed television, all the others, alas, had to follow suit in quick succession.

In short, the financial problem of the Academic Inn is not one of running but of establishing it, and of establishing not all inns but merely their first few prototypes.

*The reason why large-scale universities are by nature contrary to the scholar's mode of production is not difficult to understand. In the place of universality, they are bound to foster a degree of specialization which soon loses track of the other segments that make up the circle. In the place of the spontaneity of conversation, which brings forth great thought as a result of a given statistical frequency of intellectual chance interaction, they foster the ritual regularity of planning and organization which is necessary for carrying out ideas but often prevents them from being born. And instead of individual diversity which produces creative energy through the random movement of unassociated free particles constantly colliding with each other, they foster the formation of stifling organized gluts out of the too many members which, at a given collective size, become available to the different ideological species.

Thus if 5 per cent of the members of an academic community belong by statistical law to the species of frustrates that believes in the use of power in a scholastic environment – in which power is about as productive as it is in church when a congregation tries to wrestle a concession out of the Lord – they would number 25 in a small university of 500 students, 50 in one of 1,000, and 100 in one of 2,000, a mere sprinkling which, like salt in a soup, would actually enhance the dialectic flavour of an establishment of learning.

But in a university of 20,000, the same 5 per cent would

number 1,000 – a chunk which, if it becomes organized as a band, is large enough not for flavouring but for ruining the soup, even if all the rest were lined up against it. And the laws of social gravitation will cause a number of that kind to become organized as a band of storm troopers against whom there is not *legal* resistance of the sort that is available against the threat of government intervention in non-dictatorial countries since, in contrast to governments, organised gangs cannot be restrained by court order.

Characteristically, during the most recent riots in March 1970 at the University of Puerto Rico, or any other place for that matter, it was not the government, not the police, not the administration, not capitalism, not imperialism which tampered with the freedom of teaching, learning, and research. It was the organized bands of students which, like imperialist invasion forces, occupied classrooms and barred the gates of the temple in which *truth* is supposed to reign, not power.

Ecologically, human glut-formation and the rise of ideological cartels which large universities foster in the place of individual scholarship under which even the most tenuous plant has a chance of survival, is therefore the primary cause leading to the ultimate destruction of academic freedom and, with it, of the very idea of the university itself which, as the name indicates, must be a haven for all intellectual pursuits, not only those backed by power and appealing to the palate of the multitude in season.

(Details of future Academic Inn meetings in London can be obtained from 24 Abercorn Place, London NW8; and readers are encouraged to apply this idea in their home areas.)

4   Intentional Community

The conservation of identity

IOAN BOWEN REES

IOAN BOWEN REES is author of Government *by* Community *and Chief Executive of a Welsh county council.*

The essence of the kind of community upon which one can base a unit of government is the feeling of belonging, a feeling which must be more than sentimental and carry with it a sense of responsibility and an opportunity to participate. The feeling of belonging is itself in the last resort subjective and communities should thus be expected to identify themselves. Not that they can always be identified by a snap referendum or poll. A deep sense of belonging carries with it a sense of history (acquired or inherited) as well as a striving for a common future. One cannot 'disenfranchise the dead'. Simone Weil calls the destruction of the past the greatest crime of all, 'le plus grande crime', and maintains that its conservation should be an 'idée fixe', while a recent Council of Europe paper maintains that public participation is likely to be futile without 'local centres of cultural history and imagination'. The ever growing mobility of society is a problem here. In law one not only disenfranchises the dead but enfranchises in their place recent newcomers who have had no opportunity to develop a sense of local identity. This is not an argument against the importance of the local political community, however. If anything, it is an argument against mobility. Even where we have to accept mobility, it is an argument for placing more emphasis upon developing the sense of community where a man actually lives. It is good to see that, in Western Germany, firms have to pay taxes in the far flung places where their

workers live as well as in the places where their factories
are located.

Variety is beautiful

If the idea of community is subjective it follows that
communities will come in a variety of sizes. Variety is at
least as beautiful as small, but the sense of belonging is
inevitably more intense in a small unit in which everybody
counts. The ideal size of local authority is a will o'the wisp
and the arguments for large authorities have been grossly
exaggerated in recent official reports. One must
nevertheless concede that there are some advantages in
size. Almost everyone accepts that hospitals should serve
greater areas than general practitioners, secondary schools
than primary schools, if only because specialist doctors
and specialist teachers cannot find enough customers in a
small area. Ivan Illich is now challenging the need for
schools and for hospitals – there is much in what he says
about education – but most of us will have to plan for the
existence of these institutions for some years! In any case,
rather than dwell on the arguments about size, it is more
important to say something about the nature of the
argument itself. Big units and small units are not
alternatives. The earth itself will always be some kind of
unit, as will the smallest parish, whatever political clothing
it wears. What is crucial is not the size of unit but the
nature of the relationship between the small, the medium
and the big. Those of us who value small nations and small
communities do not see them as self-contained Tibets. On
the contrary, we tend to see the world as a federation of
federations and a nation as a community of communities.
The essential difference between us and our predecessors
is that we strive to build wide units from the bottom up
rather than from the top down. Like Proudhon, we prefer
the contractual relationship to the authoritatian. We
recognise our responsibility to our neighbours and to the
World. What we cannot tolerate, even in the smallest
parish, is to be treated, in Proudhon's phrase 'comme
population conquise'.

Big units are more parochial
Another point that needs making is that parochialism no longer has anything to do with parishes. During the last few decades the problem of narrow perspectives has been turned upside down. People in the most sparsely populated parishes in the Balkans can catch television programmes on genetic engineering. There is now nowhere in Gwynedd or Dyfed where Welsh-speaking children should have any difficulty in attaining as acceptable a standard of English as if they lived in England. On the other hand, so pervasive are the mass media, there is no part of Gwynedd or Dyfed (the strongholds of the Welsh language) where it is easy for Welsh-speaking children to acquire an adequate standard in their own language. The situation is now so topsy turvy that a child is more likely to acquire the trivial from his wider horizons and the substantial from his own narrow community. Over large areas of rural Wales, practically every child in a certain age group can sing, in Welsh translation, a poem by Goethe set to music by Schubert. This is because Heidenroslein was recently a set piece at the Urdd National Eisteddfod, a kind of knock-out competition in which the first round is usually in the child's own classroom. How many of these children have acquired anything better from world television than a passion for Starsky and Hutch? Paradoxically only the small unit is broad enough to bring together into one community people of different professions, tastes and levels of brow. To find the new parochialism we must look at centralized professional organizations, trade unions, voluntary organizations and pressure groups. Again, the sheer size and complexity of large political units compel them to grant wide autonomy to the various services and professions. A small unit has a much greater chance of being a microcosm. Is not self-government for Wales more likely to enrich our lives than self-government for water or for British Rail?

What is progressive?
In the last resort, those of us who believe in enhancing the power of small communities do so because we believe

breeding free men to be more important than anything else, more important even than conserving the natural scenery which is the most fitting background for such men. If the free men do not always see eye to eye with us on priorities we must accept the rough with the smooth. There is always a risk in people having more freedom. Yet even in the short run, the transfer of power to small communities is far from likely to be a total disaster. For one thing, a community council with the primary responsibility for its own district will have a new and different role and a change of role often brings a change of attitude. Again, a shift towards democracy would create much more pressure for making civic education part of the basic curriculum of every school. And of course, if the people of power and influence who wish, for example, to be able to holiday in unspoilt countryside cannot get their way by stringent planning legislation centrally imposed, they will find another method. If they cannot order a farmer not to start a caravan site, they will pay him not to start one. In other words, there will be a change of emphasis from the authoritarian to the contractual method of regulating society. One interesting case in a Swiss Canton, the Grisons, contains the germ of a more equitable method of controlling development in under-developed country areas. About thirty years ago, a hydro electricity company wished to include in one of its schemes the Silsersee, a lake set in incomparable scenery. The local commune of Sils Maria who owned the lake, had virtually absolute power to decide the matter and was much tempted by the royalties which the project could provide. So the conservation societies raised a fund, outbid the electricity company and entered into an agreement with the commune whereby the lake could not be developed for ninety-nine years. Not only was the scenery preserved but an impoverished rural community was given substantial financial help. Country dwellers should always be on their guard against the urban or professional appeal to standards: much of this talk is sheer hypocrisy. What the conurbation really wants is something for nothing and in a world which only produces enough food to feed (by American standards) one-third of the population, the fair and sensible way to conserve mountain scenery is to make labour intensive farming pay better than either ranching, keeping caravans or mining.

Again, though most truly democratic communities tend to be conservative, who is to say in the long run what is progressive? In 1911 the Grisons (a referendum democracy) passed a law stating 'the driving of automobiles of any kind or type, passenger cars, trucks or motor cycles is forbidden on all highways in the canton'. In 1925 the law was relaxed in favour of public service vehicles such as ambulances. By 1932, after being accused of being the most backward part of Europe, the people of the Grisons eventually gave way. Hardly forty years went by before Swiss towns began to ban the motor car. There are now over fifty traffic-free towns in the Swiss Federation. In Britain, schemes for dealing with urban traffic are now costing literally hundreds of millions of pounds per city. In Western Europe as a whole we shall at the present rate, according to the Royal Institute of International Affairs, need by the end of the century 72 per cent of all the oil in the world – and this allows for increasing use of nuclear energy. Who can say today that the people of the Grisons were benighted when they banned the automobile in 1911?

The financial crisis which compels cuts in local government services in the United Kingdom today is an indirect result of a world crisis in natural resources. It is likely to get worse. At the same time a crisis in moral values leads people to expect more and more for less and less. If only because no government can possibly do everything that people now expect of it, it is now essential to maintain the local community as an active political unit. In such a unit, there is at least some hope that the spirit of self-help and of local identity and pride can be maintained. The conservation of the Welsh language and its dialects, the conservation of the special identity of all the varied communities of English-speaking Wales, are much more than flag waving and self-interest. We cannot hope to create a European or a world community in which human beings count without fostering a practical sense of community in every small locality. The world now influences every small community. It is time that small communities influenced the world.

Communes – the outward form of a movement in consciousness.

DENNIS HARDY

DENNIS HARDY is the author of Alternative Communities in Nineteenth Century England.

The alternative society (or 'counter culture') has been defined as a search for a free society, emerging in a 'struggle against violence and exploitation where this struggle is waged for essentially new ways and forms of life'. It embraces a notion of 'freedom' which rests not simply on the ability to do what one wants, nor even on the ability of others to do the same – but also on a shared consciousness of the limits of individual action. If there is one thing that can distinguish the communes of the 1970s it is, perhaps, their role as 'the outward form of a movement in consciousness'. How much can one do and have without transgressing the freedom of others, and without destroying natural conditions in the process? In raising consciousness, communes provide both a base from which to understand mainstream society, and an environment within which to work something different.

The need for new initiatives is, arguably, more urgent than at any time in the past. In a world threatened with nuclear war, famine and disaster, 'cooperative communities are not merely something it would be nice to have – if we don't build such communities there may well soon be no living persons left to cooperate with'.

So what lessons can be learnt from past experiments, particularly as they relate to achievements in the use of land? The first is an encouraging point – namely, that experimental communities are most likely to occur when mainstream society is failing in one way or another. The seventeenth-century Diggers, for instance, gathered support against a background of suffering on the land, coupled with a wider political instability; the Utopian Socialists and Chartists offered a response to alienation encountered by a new urban working class; while pacifists in the 1930s turned to the land while nation-states prepared for war. Few would dispute that we are currently living through a crisis period – military, economic and political – yet the hopeful side is that in a dialectic of social change, this is precisely the type of situation that will spawn radical alternatives.

More specifically, what will they do? For a start it can be expected that the principle to underpin them will be that of 'decentralism'; it is this which has been evident since the late-1960s, and which remains a prime force in alternative thinking. It is a principle which is applicable to all aspects of living – to forms of government, to the arrangement of services, to technology and to farming. Communitarians will continue to express a preference for small farming units, developing intensive organic techniques of production. Lessons will be learnt from the Third World, just as experience in new agricultural methods can form more fruitful exports to developing countries than armaments.

There is an urgent need for cheap small-scale technology in all parts of the world, and new communities can provide important seed-beds for its development. For all their limitations in achieving total utopia, past communities have undoubtedly proved to be sources of innovation – especially in farming. Time and again they showed that yields could be greatly increased through systematic methods and heavy manuring, compared with the systems they superceded. Otherwise cynical visitors to the Owenite community of Harmony Hall, or to the Chartist estates, paid tribute to the successful farming of the communitarians. Likewise, one historian, in trying to account for the relative longevity of American religious communities, pointed to the excellence of their farming as a critical factor. In terms of innovation, though, pride of place belongs to the socialist and anarchist communities of the 1890s, where the perfection of new methods of intensive cultivation were very much the order of the day; a dispersed landscape of 'fields, factories and workshops' depended on a radical rearrangement of farming and land tenure.

Sure, it was also part and parcel of the story of experimental communities, that they often ran out of money, they suffered from poor leadership, there were factions within them, and outside pressures were strong – and these are all problems that are likely to recur. They have been relatively few in number and, in direct terms, have made only a marginal impact on the rest of society. Yet, at the same time, they have always represented a considered and holistic challenge to orthodoxy. Usually within a wider matrix of political dissent, experimental communities have highlighted weaknesses in mainstream society as well as charting new routes. They have represented 'par excellence' a model of direct involvement, which for their participants has time and again proved to be a unique and valued experience.

The imperfections of present society open the way for further experimental communities. It is not that they have the capacity to change the world themselves, but when times are right they can at least act as a catalyst. In this respect, the words of one of the early cooperators retain an important meaning for modern ears: 'A new community would be like a pebble thrown into the centre of a pool; village would succeed village till the circle would at last embrace the whole country'.

A ten-year-old commune

PATRICK UPTON

PATRICK UPTON lives in a commune at Laurieston Hall, Kirkudbrightshire, Scotland.

This is about a commune ten years on. I've lived in it for most of its life. I'm one of those who came in as honorary ex-teenager and now look down from my aloof thirty-one years of age on the 'teenage' lives of the commune's newest members.

We grew out of the optimistic sixties as one of the many attempts to translate the freedom to make our own lives into practice. Communes were the place where daily life could be non-authoritarian, cooperative, sharing, loving, utopian, for ourselves, where the personal was political. No more separate families, separate houses, separate consciousnesses, we'll do it *together!*

So we did, taking our past lives with us, and our present belongings and utopian visions, and plonking them all into the word 'commune'. There was a kind of relief in knowing that we were not totally new. There was some knowledge of the Diggers, of nineteenth-century American communes. But we were going to be the ones who did it right. Whatever it was. That was hard to discover, hard in that our visions were only fuzzy, hard in that it became painful discovering and dealing with the many different visions we developed.

We helped the initial clean sweep by moving to the country, giving up homes, careers, friends, familiar places and habits. To the local people we were the hippies from London; our attempt at rebirth meant nothing to them. We were very introverted, developing our lives round the 'commune'. We began to learn to share meals, to use rotas, to share skills, children, money and love. We were social change specialists, looking to the solutions to our problems in new ways of doing things, new living areas in the house, more meetings, sorting out directions. The initial enthusiasm of our new lives gave us the sense that we ought to be able to do anything we could imagine.

For several families and individuals it took a lot of courage to leap into a new life with no parameters beyond those which we decided, no social conventions or contracts other than our own. Sharing all income and expenditure and having a common source from which to draw money for personal use, as much as each person saw fit to, trusting each other. This system of finance has worked well for ten years. Trust is a keynote. Without it we would disintegrate into rules and petty restrictions, malicious gossip and outright enmity. But with it comes honesty, honestly to say when you are feeling pissed off by somebody's actions, to praise each other, to trust that each individual is working for the good of the commune, to see the health of the group in the health of the individual.

Sometimes it's all very hard work. It just gets impossible to see the goodness, to see what is here rather than what could be. As a group we did hit a period when there seemed no way forward, no breakthroughs. Learning therapy techniques has helped us by teaching us to release our feelings, whatever they are, and feel OK about them, to feel supported, to risk and see others do the same. To challenge and be challenged without the seeds of bitterness lingering inside. Sometimes still we can't do any of this. As a group we seem to get into a blue funk or a brown study or something. Well, we're better at seeing this, at being patient and taking hold of opportunities to shift out of them.

More than anything for me, therapy has helped me to appreciate each individual. A negative charge often laid against communes is that everybody has to be the same. I think we have had times when we did seek a false form of equality from each other, whereby we are sure that nobody is getting a better deal than anybody else because we all do the same share of the same things. Some of that expectation carries through, particularly with respect to food preparation, wood collecting for warmth, and cleaning. But elsewhere we've got a lot better at seeing and respecting the different nature of each individual's contribution to communal life. It's not easy. Old world values of forty hour weeks, 'real' work etc. don't disappear overnight.

So we're still learning what's good for us. We're still finding out what we're capable of, what works for now, and what doesn't... I expect we always will be. The important point seems to be, to be clear about what we are doing, not to shroud our activities in a theoretical haze. The way we cared for our children is a demonstration of our changes. When we all came here the children had to come: they were thrown in whether they liked it or not. We probably didn't take enough notice of this, trying to make them communal children – to eat together and be with each other just like we were trying to. But they had their own pace and ideas. Our theories soon flew out the window, partly also because as established parents we can find it pretty difficult to give up that special connection with our own offspring to some untried communal theories. And that's how it stayed for a long time, with different children being primarily worried about by their parents and the occasional close lover. One time they chose to all sleep in the same room – something we never got round to – but now they nearly all have separate rooms. (A sign of their getting older). A lot of good things and some easy relationships, but never quite getting to grips with the utopian vision. Except that now we do have our first truly collectivized child. Before birth he was planned to be cared for by six adults who have chosen to develop relationships with the child, to have weekly meetings to share experiences etc., and this is what we do, and it works beautifully, with another baby soon to be born into a similar set-up. So why not before? Because we didn't know ourselves and the realities of living together well enough to do it. Because there has been no parent who felt confident and safe enough to ask to share that much, because we had too many younger children to make that sort of space. Lots of reasons. It feels great now. It feels like we've reached a point where the practice is easy as we're ready for it.

We're a tribe who've uprooted ourselves and are settling again. In settling, we're establishing new ways of doing and being – our own traditions, myths and rituals. At the same time we try hard to be flexible, to avoid rigidity and dependence on specific patterns.

The way we meet together is a good example of our development towards excellence. From the start it was important that we operated by consensus. It was part of our vision of 'commune'. It meant a commitment to reaching an agreement acceptable to all and not just the majority. But starting with this commitment didn't automatically mean that we had great meetings. We still suffered from dominance by the articulate, unclear decisions, too long, too late and large meetings, boredom, and so on. It was easy to blame meetings per se, and not realize that they are totally dependent on how we conduct them and tend to be as good as the energy we put into them. We learnt to try splitting business meetings from people meetings, but found it hard to separate all the issues. Gradually we've developed more awareness, and learnt techniques from elsewhere. We know that size is important, so we sometimes use small groupings. That an agenda planned well in advance helps, that giving time limits to certain issues helps. We hear each other more clearly by 'going round' more often, giving each a turn to speak on the issue and many more things. Which all make meetings less scary, less tedious and alienating. Despite knowledge of all these things we sometimes fail to use any of our awareness and have awful meetings. But we know we've only got ourselves to criticize if we do.

Similarly we've changed from being a commune of about twenty people who lived and ate together and tried to work together, to a commune *and* a wider cooperative with several small living groups and kitchens, some under the same economic umbrella, some separate. We've recognised the strength of diversity, in letting people find just that way of collective life which suits them best. We've found through practice that a living group of five or six seems to be the most comfortable size for most people. These are the 'new' families: each living group has its own identity and methods of support for the people who live in it. It's fluid and belongs intrinsically to the 'extended family' which is the cooperative as a whole.

The work we do has similarly diversified. From our beginnings when we sought to make our income largely from people coming for conferences, we have moved to getting cash from woodstoves, knitting, building and selling plants. At the same time we have got better at producing more from our own land. We do work that we want to do to support a standard of living that we choose, and 'standard' for us includes a lot about having control of our own lives.

This commune seems as far away from national government as could be. The government will happily speak of 'we' meaning fifty-five million people, whereas almost no-one in the commune would dare to speak for anyone else at all. But what do communes have to offer to nations seeking to decentralize? Sometimes it seems as if the very extreme nature of communes such as this one means so little to the majority of people. And yet the skills and sensitivity we've developed are applicable to all forms of human interaction. We've chosen to challenge just about every aspect of our own lives: and by so doing recognize clearly that the greatest statement of our politics is the way we live our daily lives. We give ourselves a great deal of attention. Sometimes we seem overly introverted. Sometimes it seems futile dealing daily with vegetables, wood, cows, children, emotions, finances etc., when the only sensible thing is to be out there stopping the Bomb. But there has to be something marvellous for the Bomb to miss.

The commune I have been describing is alive and well and very much an accepted part of the locality – one local described us as 'clever, but all right'. We interact with the other farmers by swapping our labour for their machinery, hay or whatever. Money doesn't change hands much. Our children go to the local schools. We drink at the pub. We are different, and want to be, but we're not *apart*. We share the same problems of being alive in the 80s, but have chosen our way of going about living. My desire would be to connect more closely with people so that the word and idea of commune is not threatening. Just as cooperatives are beginning to be seen as an answer to unemployment and traditional capitalist shortcomings in business, so communes can achieve that status as regards daily life and the traps of the modern family. Not for all, but for some, communes can be a much more likely way of life.

Neighbourhood autonomy zones

NICHOLAS ALBERY

NICHOLAS ALBERY is a member of the Green Town group which is planning an experimental new village in Milton Keynes, UK.

Peter Kropotkin wrote in *Mutual Aid:*

> Self-jurisdiction was the essential point (of the commune) and self-jurisdiction meant self-administration... It had the right of war and peace, a federation and alliance with its neighbours. It was sovereign in its own affairs, and mixed with no others.
>
> In all its affairs the village commune was sovereign. Local custom was the law, and the plenary assembly of all the heads of family, men and women (!), was the judge, the only judge, in civil and criminal matters...
>
> (In medieval towns) each street or parish had its popular assembly, its forum, its popular tribunal, its priest, its militia, its banner, and often its seal, the symbol of its sovereignty. Though federated with other streets it nevertheless maintained its independence.

A new community could well act as a model for the rest of society of what such drastic non-centralization nowadays could be like.

Each community or neighbourhood (up to a maximum of 1,000 inhabitants) could have the sort of powers now reserved to local councils, and more besides. For many purposes, such as running schools, it might well decide it needed to confederate with other neighbourhoods. But it would always retain the right to secede from such arrangements, and even to secede from the nation itself.

Within the neighbourhood many powers could be dispersed still further, to the clusters of eight or so households – these clusters could make their own decisions about design guidelines, allocating vacant houses and workshops, and care of communal facilities. They would be small enough to reach decisions informally, and there would be less distinction at such an intimate level between the 'joiners' and the 'non-joiners', the politicos and the apathetic. If cluster decisions couldn't be made by consensus, a two-thirds majority would be required.

Decisions made in clusters would be subject to veto by a simple majority at a neighbourhood open meeting.

Other desirable aspects of a new community would be:

- It could provide access to land and property for those with virtually no capital, like a Western Shanty Town for voluntary peasants.

     You could start off living in a tent if you wished, and gradually add walls and services as you could afford them.

- A New Community (or new council estate for that matter) should provide opportunities – a festival? work camp? summer school? – for would-be residents to get to know each other, to ground their visions, and to form preferred clusters of eight households or so *before* installing themselves on site.

     Likewise to join an established New Community, you would first have to find a cluster where a two-thirds majority was prepared to accept you.

     Neighbourhoods will be much less bleak places to live and far more distinctive in nature, once they consist of a network of friends and friends of friends.

- Almost every house needs to be big enough for at least two nuclear families. Then if they choose to continue living separately, so be it, but at least they have the opportunity to maximize use of space and to minimize isolation by sharing common rooms if they wish.

- The main principle of taxation within the neighbourhood would be 'No Taxation Without A Say In The Allocation'.

     Individuals would be consulted by ballot or by meeting as to how their share should be spent.

- There could be a two-tier dole system. A basic rate as at present for those who are unemployed. And a luxury rate (perhaps tied to a labour credit system) for unemployed people prepared to work within their neighbourhood, either on set tasks or doing work of the individual's own devising (approved by the local neighbourhood committee).

- Most of the communal land, as Andrew Page has suggested, could be parcelled up for individual stewardship. So at the age of thirteen and a half, for instance, you might undergo a little ritual and ceremony, whereby you thereafter undertook responsibility for looking after a particular tree or corner of the public square.

This way there is tender loving care of public property, as with the woman who carpeted her public telephone kiosk and put curtains in the windows.

There is a need for *Free Autonomy Zones* – a small-scale New Community equivalent of the Conservative's 'Free Enterprise Zones' and with the same advantages; but also acting as zones for social experiment, in which planning and building regulations would be advisory rather than compulsory, with mixed use – residences and workplaces – and open to any business accepted by the zone and employing less than twenty workers.

5 Personal Transformation

Where to start?

THEODORE ROSZAK

(The following extract is taken from Theodore Roszak's book, Person/Planet, The Creative Disintegration of Industrial Society.*)*

Smallness cannot guarantee the quality of life and of human relations in any institution. We must start somewhere else, and that can only be in the motivations and sensibilities of people. The problem of scale is finally not in our institutions, but in ourselves. Or rather, it is in our institutions because it is first of all in us – in the amount of alienation, in the degree of impersonal interaction we are able to tolerate. If we ignore this basic experiential dimension of the problem, there is no hope of solving it at some higher institutional level or in the realm of pure theory.

At the level of human relations, then, what we are concerned with is not, in the first instance, the experience of size, but the experience of *mystification*. That is the heart of the matter. The greater the amount or intensity of mystification, the greater the violation of our personhood. For mystification is, essentially, an imposition of false identity. It is the act of manoeuvring people into somebody else's conception of who they are, what they are, the roles they are expected to play, the feelings they must feel, the limits of ability, allegiance, personal worth they must respect. Mystification is aggression upon the spiritual autonomy of others; it is inevitably a depersonalizing assertion of hierarchical status based on the assumption that there is an authority somewhere in the world that has the right to assign and to enforce identities. This violation of personhood can take place on a vast social scale – as in the case of a governing elite imposing its privileged political position upon the subservient populace of an entire empire; or it may happen on a scale as intimate as the relations between husband and wife, parent and child. Wherever people are intimidated or manipulated into an assigned identity, they are being mystified. They are being tricked into forgetting that they are persons born to the right of self-discovery.

Only a culture of the person will teach us that we are not mere fractions of an anonymous mass whose every need and response can be collectively anticipated. From that sense of uniqueness we draw the sensitivity to detect, and the strength to resist the insistent pressures of mystification.

But to know that we *have* a voice of our own – that is something we must learn outside the institutional framework, from sources that can only exist unofficially, moving elusively about and between the formal structures of society as a fluid medium of Socratic inquiry and therapeutic work. For this we turn to teachers and healers, counsellors and situational companions. Here is where we acquire the surest defence of our personal rights, which is the knowledge that our identity is born from within, not imposed from outside.

All of us who have been touched by the adventure of self-discovery must face our convivial responsibilities directly and steadily, perhaps even before our personal quest is complete. We must come to see that what we experience in ourselves as the emerging need of the person is the Earth's urgent cry for rescue. Our proper response to that cry is to scale down the structures and institutions which endanger the living variety of the planet: to name their evil, to resist it, to expunge it. Specifically, we must openly declare that there is no place in a world of persons for monopolistic and multinational corporations, for the maniacal middle-class religion of merchandise, for genocidal military establishments, for continued urban expansion, for state socialism, for overbearing public or private bureaucracies, for technocratic politics. The declaration must be true to our style; it must be our original way of being political – perhaps working along the lines of cooperating networks, by way of spontaneous and leaderless consensus, openly, non-violently, by friendly persuasion and gentle strength, with every intention of winning over rather than trampling down, of recycling our institutional materials rather than simply destroying them. But the declaration must be made. For no-one can go on indefinitely hiding from the crushing pressures of the urban-industrial dominance in ashrams or growth centres, lamaseries or rural communes, therapeutic workshops or monastic retreats. Sooner or later, the empire of cities will impinge upon our solitude, break through our defences, and swallow us alive. There is no wilderness so remote, no corner of the world so private, that the Earth will not be able to remind us of her sufferings by the stink in the air we breathe, the poisons in the water we drink, the haze that veils the sun and stars from our eyes – and remind us, too, of all the human miseries such ugliness implies.

Gently persist

SUNNY SALIBIAN

SUNNY SALIBIAN lives in Cambridge, Massachusetts.

I hope I will not elicit too much scorn, especially from feminists, if I venture to scrutinize the phenomena of 'the pick-up' and 'the line'. It is true that I have felt demeaned by this experience at times, but I have recently come to regard even the crassest of these manoeuvres as attempts to overcome alienation. It is the one form of anintermediary human contact likely to occur in an urban setting. Conceding at the outset that the initiative clearly rests with the male, it is yet evidence of the possibility that persons with no prior connection, no normative obligation, no bureaucratic sponsors, might fall back on intuition for each rejoinder. There is a spiritual boldness about directly accosting a person and demanding to be shown mind – any cliché is a failure. Every random encounter is a koan. I would be delighted to see the elevation of this genre to an art form with women initiating such encounters with the same freedom men enjoy.

In order for this to be possible, not only women but all persons must be informed by an environment in which martial arts are cultivated. I may seem to be dictating a curriculum; I am indicating a precondition for non-fearful relations. No one acquainted with the habitual humiliations humans inflict upon each other in the ordinary course of events is going to bring high stakes to this gaming table unless he knows how to turn aside such intrusions imperturbably. The option not to engage must be protected: it is prior to involution. Artistry lies also in gentle refusal. When the put-down is truly developed, even the recipient will be gratified, just as a good line can be appreciated by one who bows out.

No more pressing matter for descaling can be construed. Delegated power must be recalled. Without going into a song and dance, let me emphasize that I am not endorsing the fostering of aggression, only the integral capacity to elude it. Failing that, to divert it. Failing that, to block it. It is not essential that each become adept, but each must modulate his outlandish fears so as not to contribute to the undertow of paranoia which makes such great political capital.

Another matter that is no more curricular than learning to walk is basic medicine, already implied in the preceding. To learn the possibilities of motion inherent in the musculature perforce entails knowledge of the treatment of bruises and swellings, of massage, of the setting of broken bones. Actually it implies a great deal more: knowledge of the pattern of nerves and blood vessels and of the properties of plants (assuming anything is piercing the concrete or failing to feed on a midnight dumping of toxic waste). Again, the individual should neither specialize in nor overlook anything. Familiarity unwittingly accrues merely by being drawn into the altercations and visceritudes of parallel lives. I am not suggesting that the medical establishment can be hoisted on its own stethoscope: my concern is that alienation with respect to one's own body be diminished.

The monolithic character of the immediate environment is conducive to racism, and I would add as an afterthought, to boredom. Sartre ventured that mediocrity is self-chosen and a source of pleasure to the anti-Semite. This suggests that boredom and racism may be related in a curious way. To refuse to acknowledge the interfusion of all particulars is to fall back on routine drudgery with a vengeance, and often to inflict this smothering atmosphere on contiguous persons, especially children who are powerless to uproot themselves. If one chooses mediocrity for oneself and others, one becomes virtually impenetrable. To approach such a one, move between politeness and subjectivity seamlessly. Abide with him until you find the ragged edge of his yearning and create a situation in which he may partially fulfil it. (Suppose Hitler hadn't been thrown out of art school in Vienna?) Hemingway noted that fascism is a fabrication of the disappointed.

I must insist that the personal is the viable scale. Michael Zwerin excuses the few faults he finds with the canton (and half-canton) system by dismissing them as world problems: dearth of ecological awareness, subhuman treatment of migrant workers, inadequate pensions. This seems like begging the question to me. Further, his advocacy of MOBs (the acronym being intended to signify 'mind your own business') seems dated in the light of the emergence of 'the discontented', who must surely be regarded as an indictment of the alienation and transactional mentality that plague even the small governing unit (not to mention failure to insure affordable housing). Max Frisch (the literary laureate to be?) has called for dialogue.

The irony is that small units of authority often impinge disproportionately. The petty tyrannies endemic to the family and the work situation alone bring on more agony than anything government can do short of imprisonment and mobilizing for war. The District of Columbia (Washington, DC) is zoned in such a way that white residents of Georgetown can enter and leave by freeway without passing through neighbourhoods of the 71 percent of the population which is black. Recently in Smithburg, West Virginia, the Klu Klux Klan impaled a butcher knife into the back of a chair belonging to the Revd Michael S. Curry with the message, 'you will be dead'; a retaliation for his having preached a sermon against racism. (Curry fled back to Harvard Divinity School; his replacement at the United Methodist Church, the Revd Gene Holt, is a former army MP, beardless, short-haired and as yet unthreatened.) Police in the thinly populated state of New Hampshire have been known to forcibly escort Romany ('gypsy') caravans across the Massachusetts state line. In the last few years, rumours have circulated in Orleans and Châlon-sur-Saône that young girls had disappeared from a Jewish shop and had been killed in a secret ritual.

These are just a few examples culled from my files that illustrate, as Zwerin readily concedes, that small is not beautiful per se. Yet I cannot let it rest there. Downscale institutions are institutions. Those who control them are as fiercely adamant about their power (and often more so) as heads of state.

I am not prone to making neat causal connections: too much is going on concurrently to zero in on two linked phenomena. That is to say it is better to think in terms of contributions toward a trend than to imagine that events can be forced. Bear in mind that whatever you do or say is irrevocably in play and may suddenly surface in an unpredictable manner. Be consistent in multiple perspectives, especially your own. Freedom lies in the unsame. Gently persist.

Deep in our psyche – the community of all living beings

'WANDERING OWL'

'WANDERING OWL' is an animal liberationist.

'It may be critical to relocate deep in our psyche the sense of community and integral relatedness to all life forms that was highly developed in our tribal parents but which has all but atrophied in modern individualism.'
(P. and G. Mische, *Toward a Human World Order* 1977)

Animal liberation is about: liberation from the deprival of natural conditions of living (uncaging and large scale habitat maintenance), from cruel usages, from arbitrary and often painful and panicked death at the hands (and machines) of now dominant humanity.

These 'humane' or 'humanitarian' concerns, and they *are* humane and humanitarian, are not separate from ecological concern, for ecology – although it may be treated mechanically as an 'environmental' systems science by those persons who choose to so treat it – is in fact an altruistic discipline having as its goal an enlargement of the effective domain of love. Ecology most emphatically is not only the discipline of the survival of the human species. We may say instead that ecology has to do with the survival of nature.

Dansereau (in *Inscape and Landscape,* 1973) suggests that images, inscapes, mindscapes – partly composed out of our knowledge of the natural world – profoundly affect the human instrumentalities which increasingly (as human power increases) condition the landscape. Management is one such instrumentality. Ecologically (and we may add, ethically) uninformed, its images increasingly model a devastated planet. Science, technology, and human populations follow suit, with the result that human life itself grows more precarious and – we may add (and this is outrageous!) – nature finds itself being phased out.

Marcuse arrives at the principles of liberated nature through an examination of the realm of aesthetics where alone the principles survive, suffering repression everywhere else at the hands of technological rationality. The images in art are those of Orpheus and Narcissus, with reality characterized by sexuality, sensuousness, pleasure, joy, luxury, fulfilment, peace, beauty, song, reciprocity, rest, timelessness, unity, and Eros and Thanatos reconciled. It is paradise, wherein there is 'a productivity that is sensuousness, play and song'.

Humanity and nature in mutuality and rapport are central to the vision. Humanity and nature are united, so that the 'fulfilment of man is at the same time the fulfilment, without violence, of nature'. If the 'play impulse' were to gain ascendency, Marcuse concludes, the experience of the objective world of nature would not be one in which humanity dominates nature or is dominated by nature, and nature would be released from its own brutality.

Vegetarianism

Vegetarianism is obviously not all there is to animal liberation. It is, however, an essential component of any arrangement for human living compatible with the continued existence of animal nature. Phrases like 'the community of living beings', 'kinship with all life', 'interspecies identity', and the like, mean precisely that – and at the level of the individual animal rather than only at the level of endangered species. If it is an issue for the individual members of the human species to learn to live together, then this issue is also literally a real one which applies to the relationships among individuals of different species in the interspecies community. Humanity must find new ways to live, new 'food', and the space for nature to exist must be reclaimed – meaning either that human population must be (democratically) reduced or that radically novel ways of coexistence must be discovered. Yet the 'old ways' of humanity too must be sustained, and allowed more impact upon the present. The only way I know to think about this issue is to recognize that it has to be the case that therefore there exist forms of human living, not yet chosen, which in a sense 'substitute' for aspects of the old ways (particularly the killing of animals) but which not only do not diminish or vitiate the ways of the tribe, but instead constitute the fuller realization of ancient realities.

A last word on class: to the extent that class attitudes and attitudes toward nature are similar, we are unable to get clear about class in society. I will go farther. To the extent that we refuse to participate in the liberation of nature, there continues to exist such restraints on our imaginations that ideas are not released into our consciousness that are critical for our solving seemingly more purely human problems.

Taking control of religion

JOHN HERON

JOHN HERON is Founder and Honorary Co-Director of the Human Potential Research Project, University of Surrey.

How can I really relate to God unless I am properly autonomous, and how can I be properly autonomous unless I really relate to God?

Autonomy and distinctness of personal being is not the same as separateness, alienation, selfishness and self-centredness of being. To become self-transcending, to enter a heritage of consciousness in which the sense of separateness and ego-centredness falls away, is also at the same time to experience autonomy and distinctness of personal being at its most subtle and potent. Experience of transcendent, unitive states of awareness is experience, *inter alia*, of the consummation of personhood. Encounter with God does not dissolve the sense of being a person; rather it transfigures that sense into its archetypal form.

A valid religion is world-affirmative, life-affirmative, person-affirmative. It does not negate the value and reality of the world, of life, of persons and their needs, capacities and concerns. It affirms that the brilliance of this composite, here-and-now reality becomes ever more manifest as it is transfigured by wider and deeper vision of other realities inter-related with it.

The art of enjoyment I see as part of the religious life and one of its primary features is sexual intimacy. Religion that has human authority is uncompromisingly sex-positive, in my view. The art of sexual enjoyment is seen as one of the sacraments in living. Religion that acknowledges Goddess as well as God, Shakti as well as Shiva, Kundalini as well as Sushumna or the Path of Brahma, Yin as well as Yang, archetypal femininity as well as archetypal masculinity, will see sexual union as a potential treasure house of cosmo-genetic ecstasy and awareness. Mysticism and sex can be desperately cast asunder; or sweetly, subtly and potently united.

Authentic power

Authentic personal power, developing personal autonomy, would mean taking charge of the many sources of stress in life by the use of appropriate resources and strategies. Some are personal growth strategies: to do with regression and catharsis; to do with integration and reprogramming of the personality; to do with interpersonal skills training; to do with life-planning and lifestyle management; to do with creative expression and expressive style. Some are transpersonal growth strategies: to do with consciousness training and consciousness expansion, with prayer, worship and meditation, with the cultivation of specific forms of access to the other reality. Some are general or job-related education and learning strategies. Some are change agent strategies: to do with organizational development, with creating alternative institutions, with political processes of decision-making wherever decisions are to be made, with social confrontation of the rigid society. Some are technological and ecological strategies. I believe an authentic religion can flourish when it is rooted in the sort of personal power and autonomy generated by this array of competencies.

Persons with charismatic gifts, who stand specially poised at the interface between the two worlds, between this reality and the other reality, need encouragement and training to fulfil a potent function in creating a multi-dimensional society familiar with several sorts or levels of reality. Yet apart from special gifts in some persons, every person has a more ultimate charismatic identity, in the sense of having simple access to that source when personhood emerges. And in a community within a self-generating culture, the role and ritual function of Transcendental Witness can be rotated among members, to remind everyone of their own fundamental source and heritage.

Particularly important for such authentic religion is the interaction between personal power and political power. Political power is to do with who makes decisions about what. Above all it is to do with whether these decisions are taken over persons and for persons with no consultation with those who are affected by them; or whether they are made with persons, in consultation and collaboration with those affected by them. Participation, cooperation, peer process in decision-making would seem to be the valid political model for a religious organisation rooted in the autonomy of persons.

Patriarchy, in which human distress acts out the myth of male supremacy through traditional theology and religious convention, through a whole range of political and social structures, is in my view an anti-religious stance. Androgyny in the psyche, equipotentiality of religious and other roles for both sexes, are further requirements for the religion that affirms personal autonomy. What is important is that there is no sex discrimination in relation to roles that carry charismatic power, political power or both.

Satyagraha – holding to the truth

ROBERT HART

ROBERT HART is a writer and organic farmer in Shropshire.

At this most crucial period of world history, those of us who are striving for the survival of human beings, human values and small communities can find inspiration in the writings of Gandhi.

In an article in *Harijan* in 1936 he wrote, 'Modern science is replete with illustrations of the seemingly impossible having become possible within living memory. But the victories of physical science would be nothing against the victory of the Science of Life, which is summed up in Love which is the Law of our Being'. And in an article in *Young*

India (1931), he wrote, 'Just as a scientist will work wonders out of various applications of the Laws of Nature, even so a man who applies the Law of Love with scientific precision can work greater wonders. For the force of Non-violence is infinitely more wonderful and subtle than the forces of Nature, like, for instance, electricity.'

Gandhi made tremendous claims for the power and effectiveness of Satyagraha ('Holding to the Truth') if correctly applied by a dedicated individual – claims which would be dismissed as gross exaggeration if made by almost anyone else, but which must be taken seriously in the case of Gandhi, who was a man of the utmost moral integrity. For example, in another article in *Harijan* (1935) he stated: 'Non-violence is the greatest force at the disposal of mankind. It is mightier than the mightiest weapon of destruction devised by the ingenuity of man.'

How, then, is Satyagraha applied? Needless to say, it is not an easy way – harder perhaps, for a Westerner than for someone brought up in the Orient, where the disciplines of yoga and Zen have been familiar knowledge for centuries. To the Christian the phrase that best sums up the basic requirements of Satyagraha is Paul's 'bringing into captivity every thought into the obedience of Christ'. The first necessity is to strive to fathom out God's design for the world and the laws that govern that design, then one should strive to bring one's every thought and action into tune with those laws. Gandhi accepted that there exists a plane of Reality, higher than any plane recognized by the material senses and not subject to the limitations of time and space, where the Divine Design can be known and experienced in all its essential perfection. Any individual can attain this plane by passing through a course of drastic self-training after which it is his duty to translate its ideas into practical humanly comprehensible projects.

In his autobiography, *My Experiments with Truth* Gandhi wrote,

> For me Truth is the sovereign principle...This Truth is not only truthfulness in word...but the Absolute Truth, the Eternal Principle, that is God...Often, in my progress, I have

had faint glimpses of the Absolute Truth, God, and daily the
conviction is growing upon me that He alone is real and all
else is unreal...The fleeting glimpses that I have been able to
have of Truth can hardly convey any idea of the indescribable
lustre of Truth, a million times more intense than that of the
sun.

To Truth there are no conflicts, no enmities. Upon its plane of
Reality 'all things work together for good'. Satyagraha,
which means 'holding to the truth', teaches man that to 'love
one's enemy' is a scientific process. It involves striving to see
him as he is in Truth, as God sees him; a unique divine idea
with divine vocation to fulfil.

Here then, is the supreme boon of Satyagraha: that it can
enable the individual, the small group or small nation, to
overcome fear and a sense of intolerable frustration when
faced with enormous concentrations of military, financial
or political might. 'One on God's side is a majority', it has
been said. This can be proved to be literally true by anyone
who resolves to take a stand uncompromisingly – and, if
necessary, alone – on the side of the Divine Design for a
multi-faceted universe.

Universal woman

GEORGINA ASHWORTH

GEORGINA ASHWORTH is Editor of World Minorities *and
Founder of* Change International Reports.

Women as a 'species' are often described and treated as a
minority themselves, in literature and in sociological
treatise. This analogy is based carefully on women as a
social minority – a disabled group, or an untouchable,
inferior class – rather than on a 'small nation' concept. It is
useful, in part, to describe the inferior status of women in
fact, figures and psychology. Thus, to describe the latter,

we have a poem, 'Buraku: Non-Person', where the analogy is drawn between a member of the Japanese outcaste group, the Burakumi, which means 'non-person', and a universal woman.

Buraku – Non-Person

If I have a name
It and I belong
To someone else.

If I am seen
It must be in the approved cast
Of the mind's eye.

If I am heard
My voice should be secret with
The velvet of approval.

If I am to Be,
I must be clothed in the
Ridicule of fashion.

If I seek to think,
Thought must be hidden in the
Pocket of convenience.

If I am prey to want
It must be within the
Boundaries of giving.

If I care to dream
I must defer to the
Responsibility of my womb.

If I will step out,
My strides must be in the cloying
Mud of isolation.

If I am hurt
The din of anonymity must drown
My shallow scream.

If I try the truth
It must not reflect the dim
Evidence of me.

When I strike out
It must only be at the shadows
Of humiliation.

If I draw life
It must be upon the reproduction
Of the image of my father

If I complain
It cannot be about the weather
Of my obligations.

If I can doubt
It must not steal conviction
From the status quo.

If I can choose
My arbitration is between brand and brand
Not bearing life
Or avoiding strategic death.

If I will laugh
It must be only at the stone joke
Of my own existence.

If I have a name
It is sibillant with insult
Or with fear ...

In a Fourth World movement geared to the breakdown of monoliths, the guarantee of future representation of women, true representation, in any future structure of state or enterprise, must be a priority. The basic Fourth World issue is empowering the powerless. Here we have a group, a universal category, who have no power other than reproductive power. Despite small steps – the Treaty of Rome guaranteeing equal pay, for example – the exclusion of women from decision-making, from being agents of change, has been an essential and developing effect of the evolution of monoliths. It is possible to argue that the injustice of non-representation has been increasing over the past thirty years.

Domination and vastness, the enemies of the Fourth World, are, I regret to point out, the products of a chiefly masculine economic world. The larger army, the greater land, the bigger market are both the end and the means of achieving status and identity. I will not assert that the male has no concern for fellow human beings, but that concern tends to be exercised *after* the acquisition of power or money, or *after* the disaster. Thus Human Rights are a cause after *gross violations* have occurred; minority problems are recognized *after* a riot or a signal of distress; preventive care is not a social priority, perhaps it is not a masculine trait, perhaps because it is not visible or glorious enough? Thus the social impact of much economic development has been overlooked; indeed economic development has not been seen as a *service* to a community, not an integral part of the guarantee of human rights, or of all other forms of social development.

Perhaps if women's voice and needs had been heeded, again we might have a more rational society. Technology might solve more basic problems – how to provide clean water to remote villages instead of nuclear fall-out; how to eliminate measles as a killer of millions instead of swapping hearts for a few; how to guarantee a better life for a few children rather than a short and painful one for many, while being labelled a 'population problem'. The possibilities are endless. The ingenuity of women, 'making do' with inferior technology, with smaller budgets, without reward is overlooked in development.

Perhaps there is a triangular relationship that has yet to be researched between the 'inclination to warfare' – the development of the Arms Industry – and family policies – which reinforce the female domestic role and the absence of a male domestic role – with monetarist economics which, in the guise of free enterprise and non-interference by governments, manipulate the workforce by all manner of means. Today, to avoid equal pay, those forbidden loads again fall on female shoulders, despite 'protection'. Thus, here in Britain, girl farm-workers lift the loads while their male colleagues drive the tractors to qualify for higher status and higher pay. Thus, in India, the majority of construction workers are women. Thus, in Africa, the woman carries home kilos of wood for the cooking, bowing her back forever, while the male tends a herd of perfect donkeys, or goes to train as a tractor driver. Thus, despite protection, in South East Asia the electronics industry clocks in young girls for three-year contracts and sends them home at the end, blind and aged. Others flock into towns for this dubious privilege because their families cannot or will not support them. Idle land, used for show rather than subsistence, prestige rather than agriculture, means hungry families. Hungry families sell their children in order to survive. Girls, whose worth in Buddhist terms is next only to a dog, can go into prostitution or into other such exploitative industries, there to earn just a little more than nothing and to survive just a little longer than with nothing. Their brothers may become monks, supported by the community but essentially unproductive. The circularity of low social image and low pay and low status is starkly evident in these conditions, but it will apply in different degrees everywhere else. She is 'worth' little (she cannot get to heaven as a woman; only by being reincarnated as a man as a reward for bearing other pious and unproductive monks) so she deserves little; she gets little, so she is worth little. She is also, incidentally, carefully 'protected' in her contract so she cannot join unions or collective action to enhance her pay, status, hours or conditions of work.

No state in the world has done more than tinker with equality; none has committed itself to the non-exploitation of half its people. Equality means equality of opportunity, but also equality of the 'right to work' – the right to paid employment. Equality means the blindness of justice in laws of property, inheritance, divorce, custody, and custom. Equality means the sharing of that domestic burden within the family unit. Sharing does not mean 'helping occasionally' but a genuine assumption of half the burden, now so artificially heaped onto 'motherhood'. Genuinely shared, child care might make the males less anxious to eliminate the next generation. Genuinely shared, a redefinition of 'work', 'productivity' and life purpose itself, might emerge. Genuinely shared, this industry or service might secure enhanced status, higher priority in governmental spending, and the development of more socially useful technology in lieu of prestige toys and consumer con-tricks. Genuinely represented, the female gender might be able to emerge from complaints of exploitation to become a positive force for good in the future.

Women and...

SCILLA MCLEAN

SCILLA McLEAN is involved with The Minority Rights Group.

The world has a serious minority problem – that is, most of the world's significant decisions are made by a tiny minority: white middle class men who are between forty and sixty years old.

Women are still chronically under-represented in international decision making: for example, of all the people on all the delegations to the General Assembly of the United Nations, all 2,539 of them, only 224 are women: 8.82 per cent.

In national legislative bodies, parliaments, congresses and assemblies, however, their position is even worse. In India, in 1984, in the Lok Sabha, 5.1 per cent of representatives are women. In our own country, only twenty-three Members of Parliament are women, 3.5 per cent. Even in those countries where equality has been one of the cornerstones of socialism, and where over 30 per cent of delegates to the national peoples congress are women, as in China or in the USSR, there is not one woman in either country to be found at the heart of power, in the Politburo.

Even in the much vaunted swing to the left in France, no-one mentioned that only one in every ten of those deputies returned was a woman.

Consider this against the background of the grim situation of women nationwide:

- 80 per cent of Asian and African women are illiterate;
- in India, one woman dies every ten minutes from a septic abortion;
- there are approximately sixteen million refugees in the world today: the overwhelming majority are women and children;
- over fifty million women in Africa and the Middle East have their genitals excised or infibulated;
- women represent one third of the *official* labour force of the world; but they perform nearly two-thirds of all working hours, and receive only one-tenth of world income;
- women own less then 1 per cent of world property.

And conditions overall for women are *deteriorating*:

- Water scarcity is becoming chronic in countries of West and Central Africa, and many women are now obliged to walk 15 miles or more daily for water.
- It is estimated that the number of soldiers in the world today is twice the number of teachers, doctors, and nurses.
- There are now about one hundred million children under the age of five always hungry
- Sexual exploitation of South East Asian women has reached the point where not only do West German package tours include the services of women, but Thai girls are being sold outright for life, to German, Dutch, and Danish businessmen clients, for 20,000 marks.
- As recession hits western countries, cuts in public expenditure and social services mean that it is women in the home who pick up the tab, in terms of child care, provision of extra meals, and caring for the sick, disabled and elderly.
- Multinational companies are increasingly buying up land in developing countries for the growth of cash crops, depriving women, who have traditionally been the agriculturalists, of the ability to feed their own families, and of the accompanying economic independence.

In 1975 the World Conference of the United Nations Decade for Women was held in Mexico – the first official international gathering about women. (I don't say *of* women, since a large proportion of the delegates were male). It established a World Plan of Action, with fourteen minimum governmental objectives to be implemented by 1980. At subsequent follow-up conferences it became clear that only a minority of Western women are anywhere near achieving even *three* of those objectives.

It would seem then, that the lumbering machinery of the United Nations will not be very useful in changing the situation in which women find themselves. (The Decade and the Conferences did perform one useful function: governments were requested to provide information about many aspects of women's lives, and for the first time in history a body of facts on women world wide is beginning to be assembled).

However, women are beginning to realise that they have to play an active part in changing their situations – and not only that they have to, but that they can. In small groups all over the world, they are getting together to act. Here are a few brief examples:

- In Kenya, the majority of Kikuyu women go through a clitoridectomy during their teens, but discussion of the subject is taboo. Groups of women have formed income-generating projects (making sanitary towels out of cotton, since the only ones at present available are imported and are too expensive for most women in Kenya), and are able to introduce health education talks during the hours of work, which include discussion of the grave physical dangers of excision.

- In the USSR, a group of women from different towns got together and published in December 1979 the first issue of *Almanac*, a Samizdat Journal in which women could express their feelings frankly and learn the facts about conditions of work, abortion, contraception, divorce, and property laws. The women were arrested, and Tatiana Momonorova has since been obliged to leave Russia, but further issues are apparently circulating.

SISTREN is a Jamaican all-women theatre collective whose members, former street cleaners turned teacher aides, are using improvizational theatre as a means to break the walls of isolation that frequently surround women who live in low income areas. The collective has three primary objectives: to take theatre to low income communities; to create theatre which analyses and comments on the role of Jamaican women; and to provide members with supplementary income and participation in a self-reliant organization. Formed in 1977 with the support of the Jamaican Women's Bureau, their productions deal with the experience of women forming a union in a factory, the encounters of three ghetto women with the law, with housing, education and childcare problems. The eleven women members of SISTREN, none of whom have a high-school education, and who have up to four children each, have received both national and international recognition.

Concluding that nuclear technology is the ultimate madness of a male-dominated world, women are organizing themselves, to show their outright opposition. Women from six Scandinavian countries presented a document signed by 500,000 women to Kurt Waldheim in July 1980, demanding immediate implementation of the Resolutions of the United Nations Special Session on Disarmament. The women of Mourouoa Island in the Pacific have tirelessly petitioned the governments of France to cease atomic testing. In November 1980, 2,000 women in the USA formed a human chain around the Pentagon in Washington, demonstrating the solidarity of a broad coalition of women's groups against the arms race. In England, women walked from Wales to Greenham Common, (proposed site for the new Cruise missiles), arriving on 5 September 1980 and proceeding to organize a series of very moving and effective demonstrations. In June 1980, Scandinavian women set out on foot from Copenhagen through Germany, Holland and Belgium, arriving in Paris on Hiroshima Day, 6 August. Now new groups are forming daily, of women intent on making people aware of the deadly danger surrounding us.

These are just a few out of hundreds of examples of spontaneous consensus effort to tackle problems of ill health, ignorance, poverty, childcare, militarism.

But so far I have avoided the central problem, and that is the problem of power itself. The inequities with which women have to struggle all have one thing in common – they are enacted and perpetuated by huge monoliths of power, whether it is the state, the church, the arms industry, or simply tradition. How do you attempt to change something which is very powerful, if you have no power? What if you do not *want* to have power, since power and the things you believe in are antithetical? These, for me, are the central issues which this forum, and all the other discussions of this assembly, must face.

The minority problem described at the start of this paper remains to be changed. We have to look at the different ways in which women do change things. Some do it by changing their own local situation, creating an alternative way of doing things. Some do it by organizing pressure groups to lobby and monitor legislation. Some do it by networking. Some take the path through the existing system, hoping to change it from the inside, taking the risk of becoming part of it.

Workshops of the Future

ROBERT JUNGK

ROBERT JUNGK is the author of Brighter than a thousand suns *and* The Nuclear State.

It has been recognized for a long time that social inventiveness will have to be intensified in order to cope with the effects of scientific and technical developments.

Below I describe a method for promoting 'social ideas' and 'social inventions' which has ben tested since 1964, and amended on the basis of experience (Vienna 1965, Turkey 1967, Berlin 1968–69, Helsingor 1970, Vienna, Viktring, Salzburg 1972). It concerns a group project which tries to realize the demands of Denis Gabor to 'invent the future', and of Hasan Ozbekhan to 'create the future'.

These attempts to greater democracy at the design stage in social and political planning were found to produce greater involvement of those taking part; the early involvement heightens the interest in collective activities. Through participating in 'workshops of the future', the acclaiming citizen who merely casts a vote becomes the 'creative citizen'.

Procedure

The Critical Phase
The director of the 'workshop of the future' aided by two secretaries, starts by asking the participants which social problems they find most interesting and worrying. These problems should be defined in slogans within a limited time (about 30 minutes). It increases interest when they are presented on large sheets of paper for everybody to see. A group of subjects is then selected (e.g. forms of work, adult education, the population explosion, urban traffic, environmental pollution). The participants are then asked to make a negative list, again in slogan form, of individual complaints related to the main subject. If time allows the inclusion of each item should be justified. The critical phase often produces up to 100 individual items, sometimes mutually contradictory, and no censorship of any sort should be exerted by the director.

The Creative Phase
This is introduced by selecting one problem of detail named in the critical phase for joint creative thinking. Once this has been determined, the question arises as to which of the other critical slogans are most closely related to it. In this way the preparatory phase already stimulates a joint procedure which will be particularly important in the next phase.

If the 'workshop' has not worked together before, it is recommended to introduce a brief preliminary exercise for practising creative behaviour on a neutral theme before the joint action of proposals and inventions. For instance, the participants may be asked to propose imaginative and 'crazy' ways of using a sheet of white paper.

Before starting on the subsequent development of ideas which is the main purpose of the work, it is laid down as the main rule that any criticism of the conjectures, thoughts, concepts, visions uttered should be temporarily suspended and delayed, or used only as a preliminary to another idea ('not in this way, but that way...'). From the flood of ideas the director of the workshop selects single, specially promising ones and stimulates the others to extend, enhance and complete them. At this stage, the enthusiasm of the director is of decisive importance. During this phase too, it is advisable to provide a record that can be seen by everybody and give an experience of success. The filled sheets of paper are taken off from the blackboard and the course of the 'flight of ideas' put up on the walls. Three to five particularly promising ideas should now be selected and handed over to small groups for more detailed elaboration and for presentation at the next meeting.

The Examination Phase

During this phase, the developed proposals are presented to other participants, experts in the field, and people involved in political and social decision making.

The examination should be held less in a spirit of a realistic evaluation, governed largely by evaluation of past and present constraints, but rather of inquiry into the possible circumstances which might allow realization of the proposal, or prevent it, and how to overcome the obstacles. This leads directly to the next phase.

The Tactical Phase

This should concern the possibility of realizing the developed proposal. As in the creative phase, the imagination should be used to devise new and unusual, not previously tried, methods to realize 'social inventions'.

In this area of struggle against reactionary forces new ways are particularly important.

Possible Effects

In the long run, lack of success or echo would be very frustrating for the members of the 'workshop of the future'. It is therefore necessary to think of ways to influence public opinion and decision making.

This is most easily done in societies with high freedom of expression, by publishing the results of such democratic inquiries in leaflets, journals and newspapers. The expected increase in television channels and the resulting technical possibility of reaching a wider audience could provide further publicity for presenting and discussing such proposals. In addition, attempts should be made to invite the participation of politicians involved in decision making at all levels; from the community to the region to national and international bodies, in the trade unions and the government sector; and the earlier the better!

All the 'workshops of the future' may be assured of one kind of success (as hinted above); the increased involvement in social problems, which are no longer thought of as alien demands of an outside authority. However, it would be a mistake to withdraw to this educational effect: this would be counterproductive, as the project draws strength from the idea that the common man may be able to contribute to large social decision making.

Criticism and Development

Experiences to date with 'workshops of the future' show that proposals of above-average originality are obtained only after prolonged cooperation. The effects of anti-creative education and of an upbringing largely aimed at social conformity cannot be quickly discarded. The mistrust of one's own creativity is deep-rooted. That is why a large majority of the proposals emanating from all the 'workshops of the future' is but a repetition of earlier ideas. Hence it is imperative that the director of the 'workshop of the future' should be able to arouse the self-confidence of the participants. He will achieve that by deliberately diminishing and relinquishing his own guiding role.

The experience outlined here must be complemented, examined and extended by means of systematic studies. It is quite astonishing that research on creativity has been very little concerned with 'social inventions and proposals' and has concentrated largely on technical innovations and consumer products.

The application and development of methods of group creativity (brain storming, synectics, etc.) for social innovation provide unexplored possibilities. The results of research into group dynamics could also find interesting new applications.

The following aspects also require further thought: it is progressively more difficult to be informed about current developments. This partial lack of information which affects all of us has hitherto been felt to be purely negative. However, research on creativity has shown that a high state of information in any field tends to reduce rather than increase the possibility of creative action. In such cases lack of knowledge may be, for a short time, a positive factor.

The effects could be important politically, because it would put an end to the disqualification of most citizens from decision making due to insufficient technical qualifications. In the 'workshop of the future' they can voice opinions and make important contributions, precisely because they are not too strongly bound to the 'reality' of experts by up-to-date knowledge.

A loathing of the world

JEFF NUTTALL

JEFF NUTTALL is a sculptor, poet and author of Bomb Culture.

First I want to consider three lines of development in the culture of recent decades and the art from which it springs.

One: Painting

In the early years of the century some painters ceased to depict recognizable objects in their work. While this was often done to throw focus on the painting as an object in its own right it was also done in a transcendental spirit. Melevitch and Mondrian wished painting to be pure in the same way that pure mathematics is pure. In pure mathematics one does not have one, two, three objects. One simply has one, two, three.

In abstract painting one does not have geometry and colour describing an object, one simply has geometry and colour. In both cases the word pure implies that the world of material experiences is impure, that the mind has some unfettered area free from extraneous entities. Purity and freedom, meaning freedom from the world, are paramount ideals.

So purified painting began to comment on itself, it having foregone the possibility of commenting on anything else. Paintings reduced their components in order to ask what are the minimal definitive requirements of a painting, painting being held to possess some Platonic essence. The fact that painting is a collection of artifacts made with paint was missed because such a fact belonged to the world of experience and not the world of ideas. Consequently the pleasure-giving, life-enhancing properties of the artifacts reduced until artists in vast numbers, in all seriousness, were displaying blank canvasses.

The next stage was the substitution on gallery walls of typed statements for paintings, an explanation of the possibility of a painting being held to be *purer* than all that dabbling in turps and coloured clay. The painter *free at last* of the necessity to paint.

Two: Sexuality

The difficulty twenty odd years ago arose from a sexual deadlock in which we were all trapped, composed of the residue of Judeo-Christian prudery, rendering sex undiscussable and, therefore, preserving a disastrous ignorance about sex; of fear of pregnancy holding women back from their own orgasm, thus robbing humanity of its most illuminating experience, forcing women to use sex as a bargaining point; of the fear, guilt and violence arising from all this. Sex was clearly the healthy natural appetite whereby we reproduce our kind so any rational society was going to bring it into the open and rid it of guilt and fear. Once brought into the open with safe birth control and the withdrawal of censorship, however, the society addressed itself to a sexuality in which reproduction was not so much controlled as despised. Eroticism then developed, which is sex without function, and homosexuality was extolled as the superior form at some levels of society.

Homosexuality can be nothing but erotic. *Purely* erotic one may say. Completely *free* of any moral contracts or lasting liaisons arising from reproduction. Ultimately we have a thriving pornography which is sex without even a partner, sex *unsullied* by contact with any element of the outside world, but a glossy photograph, a sex of the mind just as conceptual painting is art of the mind.

Three: Rock Culture
Rock music began to lay claims to being more than Saturday night hop music, began to claim an oracular function, around the mid-sixties. As a mouthpiece of protest and spontaneous ecstasy it quickly moved on, either to rabid commercialism or to transcendentalism along with the move to the use of delusory drugs. In its transcendental mood it assured a range of pure experience free of the impediments of the world.

Around the mid-seventies it changed, eschewing the pleasure, hedonism and escapism of the hippy forms, espousing a style in which ostentatious lack of talent fused with a dress-style of caricatured cruelty and ugliness. It did this in a spirit of puritan zeal, declaring the society and its inhabitants to be fouled, lionising murderers and suicides, posing in an hysterically casual writing-off of the world.

Now I've described a fairly broad range of recent cultural forms because I want to stress the element they all hold in common, which is a loathing of the world and its inhabitants, including the self. Pleasure-orientated movements have attempted to create pleasure areas alternative to (purified of, free of) the world. Puritanical movements have criticized the world in a way in which splenetic hatred of the world cancels out the possibility of therapeutic effect.

One thing we know about all these cultural forays is that they have failed and I would suggest that the reason why they have failed is because they all refuse the world as material with which to work.

What must be worked for now in this devastating era of defeat is the cultivation of a love of the world and a culture which inflames it. This isn't going to be easy because the world at the present time is disgusting in all its aspects. There is scarcely a group, a cause, a creed or a nation which has found anything to espouse but loathing expressed in cruelty. We have experience of ourselves which is difficult to come to terms with because we have no honour left and no honourable place in which to locate ourselves, not even the Fourth World movement. However, we must love somehow and we can only do that effectively if we get it into our heads that, even in disgrace, we and our world are all we have to love. I advocate a powerful antic sensuality which is big enough to enfuel that love, which may take pleasure in a completely discredited world and which may then provide the basis for a beneficial creative manipulation of that world, self, and species from which we can never be free.

Free sexuality

WENCKE MÜHLEISEN

WENCKE MÜHLEISEN is a Norwegian performance artist in charge of the visitors' centre at Friederichshof commune near Vienna.

Replacing the Nuclear Family
Friederichshof is situated in the Austrian province of Burgenland, close to the Neusiedler See, and not far from

the Hungarian border. Here, in the ruins of a former royal estate, a cultural centre has developed which has come to serve as a model for more than twenty groups that have developed in Europe. There are about seventy grown-ups living at Friederichshof (roughly equal numbers of men and women), twelve children, and a varying number of guests.

The basic question which directed the development of this model was: how can people live together in such a way that the creative self-development of the individual is optimally combined with the demands of a community which functions well? The question was not to be answered through an ideological programme, but through continuous experimentation.

The development of the model moved away from current ideas and approached a new concept of community. Social consciousness should no longer be rooted in moral traditions, but in a liberation of the human organism from all fears and suggestions caused by our upbringing. Only when the emotional and sexual relations between people can be formed without guilt can they develop free of obsessions and compensation, free of the destructive remains of hatred, jealousy and secret competition.

At Friederichshof a model society is developing which enables so many emotional relationships and creative activities to arise, that the individual is no longer dependent on the relationship to one single partner. When we speak of free sexuality here, it is not a question of indiscriminate promiscuity, but of evolving new forms to replace the nuclear family, not through exterior norms, but from within. In these new forms the old norms should not be totally negated but preserved in Hegel's sense of the word. Love, warmth, trust, stability and clear orientation for the children should get a freer and at the same time more solid foundation.

The Ecology of Human Relationships
The social organization of sexuality is a central question for society. In the past, however, this question has seldom or never been posed consciously. The full extent of its

importance first became apparent through the clarifying work of psychoanalysis, which especially uncovered the concealed workings of suppressed sexual energy in all human relations and social processes. This resulted in a new fundamental insight for the understanding of human history and society – for example, in opposition to the philosophy of Marxism. What was meant by this was that the crucial points were no longer in the economic area, but one level deeper, in the biological–sexual sphere. As part of the so-called 'societal basis' we have not only the economic organisation, but also of more encompassing importance – the sexual organization of the society. This means the way in which the society has organized its sexual life and how it has channelled its sexual energies. If we see sexual energy as a fundamental component of our life energy, we immediately realize the importance of this question. The system of channels for sexual energy interlaces the body of society like a secret nervous system which transmits and processes the sexual impulses of attraction and repulsion. It is of course of the utmost importance whether this sexual nervous system of society lies in darkness, or if it is consciously integrated in the social life. In the first case it influences human life from a region which lies outside of social control, and it is therefore not susceptible to conscious social transformation. Also, repressed sexual energies are almost always of a destructive nature. It is only in the most rare cases that they can be sublimated into truly positive cultural achievements. As a rule, every sexually repressed society develops in its belly such an explosive mixture of dammed up sexuality and aggression, that the brutality with which it discharges knows no limits. Crusades, inquisitions, wars, and concentration camps, are the psychological consequences of a culture that has been falsely programmed in the sexual area. The connection between suppressed sexuality and cruelty has characterized our whole history up until today. Morals served as a bulwark against the asocial character of these suppressed energies. Thus the suppression was not overcome but was internalized. In this way a vicious circle was set going that no religion and no peace ideology could handle. It no longer suffices to recognize the ecological interactions, or the dangers of nuclear energy — one must recognize the root of the evil: the destroyed ecology of human relationships with its virulent point of focus: blocked, degenerated and mystified sexuality. So long as mankind does not succeed in transforming the forces of suppressed sexuality into forces of communication, love and creative life, man cannot be a free citizen of this earth. The liberation of sexuality is a biological prerequisite for a free and social development of human beings.

Free Sexuality

Which kind of sexual freedom was intended? First of all, freedom from the limitations of the couple relationship. The group agreed that everyone could enter into sexual relationships with anyone else, regardless of the existing partner relationships. This was the external solution. It was however not immediately the inner solution. Sexuality should also be set free internally. This meant being free from fear of guilt, free from the fear of losing someone, free from jealousy, free from obstructed biological energies and fantasies that inundate the conscious mind. Then sexuality becomes an immediate expression of emotional contact and of joy of life. It is based not on any ideology or any sexual morals, but on the emotional suppleness and resonance that exists in a body that is free from fear.

On 1 May 1973, free sexuality began at Friederichshof. Methods had to be developed quickly so that the process that was set rolling was not reversed. The new ground that was being trod was not to be abandoned when the first resistances appeared. In order not to fall back into the old structures out of complacency or fear, it was agreed that each night everybody should sleep with a different partner. The search for a partner which took place every evening took the form of a game in front of the group where everyone stated his wishes. Emotional tensions were worked out in the so-called 'actions analysis', (a combination of Reich's vegetotherapy psychodrama and Primal therapy), for bringing the blocked emotions in the body to controlled outbursts. The emotional drama which centred around the themes of love, hatred, competition and fear should no longer remain in the intimate sphere of the individual but should find an open and communicative expression. This kind of 'catharsis' was a stabilizing element in the group life. It was supplemented by the group's sitting together and talking every evening. Out of these two elements, the actions analysis and the evening discussions, evolved a specific form of evening gathering which was later called 'selbstdarstellung'. One person went into the middle of group and tried to articulate, in as expressive a way as possible, his emotional situation, through dancing, through theatre, words and singing. Behind this was the concept of changing and forming one's own situation and oneself by applying an artistic perspective. The emotional illness, the fear, the sexual resistance, the repressed aggressions etc., these things that blocked life, were to become a conscious element in the presentation. Thus began the crucial developments which today above all characterize the cultural work at Friederichshof: the internal synthesis of art and therapy. Nietzsche's high praise of art and the artist 'because it mobilizes people and carries all their biological energies into culture' was here being realized in a both serious and playful way. The more playful, humorous and artistic the methods, the more 'forbidden' and embarrassing things could be brought into the presentation. Working on taboos was always a characteristic of artistic progress, but now the human being himself had become the object of this work. Especially the forbidden and pornographic contents of sexuality were to be treated with humour in order to transform them into positive social forces. By liberating sexuality from its asocial elements, from projections and from mystification, the group members become much more sexually communicative. The capacity for emotional and sexual contact with as many people as possible is an indication of a person's social maturity. The art of 'selbstdarstellung' rendered subconscious things conscious through a playful process of regression. By giving the 'shadow' concrete form, it is integrated into the 'persona'. It went beyond the forms of theory to date by letting these processes of regression and 'individuation' be carried out in reality, not just in fantasy. Thus an example was set which was decisive for the growth of awareness which underlies this whole model: true development and true awareness can only result from the transformation of ideas into practice. The building blocks for a new culture result from the practice of constant experimentation.

As for the liberation of sexuality, it is not only a question of quantitative increase of satisfaction, but of a transformation of the sexual quality itself. Sexuality contains its own value. This unabashed sexuality is in no way directed exclusively towards the needs of the man. Experience up till now has shown that women, once they have disengaged themselves from the hypnosis of the couple relationships, generally use their new possibilities faster, more enthusiastically and with more pleasure than men. Open emotional and sexual relations are not compatible with patriarchal role patterns. A new culture could actually develop based on these foundations, a culture where women stand truly equal to men. There was probably no social experiment in the western world where women have had such a strong position as at Friederichshof and in the groups oriented towards Friederichshof.

At first glance it may not be apparent how the system of free sexuality can solve the problems of fear of losing someone, of jealousy and of competition. Would one not rather expect that these problems would worsen? In contrast to the monopoly of marriage, there is now some kind of free market system, but without private property. Although there is compensation, there is no property that one could lose. The fear of losing someone and jealousy sometimes remain as emotional clichés from the nuclear family, but in time they fall off because one notices that they no longer have any relevance. As for competition, one finds here quite a different attitude towards it than in other alternative groups. Acting competitively should not be discouraged, it should be learnt. Competition, seen as a positive contest, is a natural driving force behind development and perfection. But since we have not learnt to compete openly, at least not within the framework of a positive society, we know competition mostly in its indirect, intrigue-making, asocial forms. The feelings of inferiority which usually underline exaggerated humility and withdrawal should slowly give way to the feeling of one's own potency. The whole group consists today of small sub-groups in which a homely atmosphere arises by doing things together in one's spare time and in the evenings.

Free sexuality is more than only an interesting subject of sexual psychology, it is an abbreviation for a new form of human community. It is not just a question of individual therapy, but of societal planning. We believe that the model of Friederichshof can result in some concrete general perspectives for international peace and future research. Here we mean especially the problems of overpopulation, of growing criminality, of the increase in psychosomatic illnesses, and of ecology. It can hardly be denied that a community with a lively communication, with fulfilled sexuality, and creative work, no longer is forced to seek substitute satisfaction and therefore is not dependent on consumption and its associated environmental and energy wastefulness that we have today. The ecological crisis is partly the result of the industrial production of wasteful consumer goods. This production, however, can only be maintained so long as people keep demanding substitute satisfaction, because the elementary need for contact remains unfulfilled. The ecological movement of today should also be concerned with developing a new model for consumption. However, if such a model is not to be implemented with force, it must be part of a new model for inner human satisfaction and fulfilment. The ecological movement will therefore in the long run be able to promote its cause only if it decidedly transforms itself into a 'psychological' and social movement. The ecological models of living that are aimed at in several countries must at the same time be models for a new type of culture, character formation, community and liveliness, love and research. They must become models for changing the way of life from 'having' to 'being'. We have tried to show that at the heart of this transformation lies the development of new social forms for love and sexuality. The old forms of marriage and of the nuclear family belong to a cultural age which, due to these forms, was incapable of solving its problems from within, and which therefore was constantly driven into greater and more dangerous contradictions. The biological 'recultivation' demanded by ecologists must necessarily include a recultivation of our deformed emotions and our suppressed sexuality.

(Information on Friederichshof and their courses can be obtained from: Friederichshof commune, A-2424 Zurndorf/bgld., Austria.)

Barefoot doctors — Decentralizing health care for the New Age

MARCUS McCAUSLAND

MARCUS McCAUSLAND has investigated how complementary therapies can improve the quality of life for cancer patients and their families.

To remove the intolerable burden from UK doctors' shoulders of lists of up to 3,650 patients, a new category of helpers is required. This is the Medical Assistant, the 'Barefoot Doctor', or 'Feldscher' recommended by the World Health Organisation, but with much greater use of the abilities of the individual concerned. These individuals we have named 'Local Counsellors', whose responsibilities for the promotion of health and self-healing, we outline here:

- They become natural leaders in their small community. Good health is catching, therefore they must be whole, healthy beings themselves so that others may follow their example.
- They have *time* to listen to problems and understand the role that problems play in the personal growth of each

individual. They have the sensitivity necessary to discuss these problems, while 'tuning-in' to the emotions and feelings of the person concerned.

- Local counsellors will have a direct link to a specific General Practitioner at a 'Caring Community Centre'. Thus, one GP and five Local Counsellors may form a health team responsible for 2,000 individuals – if the GP's list is larger, more Local Counsellors will be required.

- Local Counsellors are given sole authority to take any reasonable action which they consider necessary to help those who come to them for assistance. They are solely responsible for a flock of 400 individuals of all ages, both sexes and varying degrees of health and ill-health, who are selected on a geographical basis, so that it is possible for Local Counsellors to know them all personally and to understand the particular problems faced by each family and individual. This knowledge can be immensely helpful when the time comes to discuss a personal problem with someone who is seeking advice.

- There are approximately 10,000 Health Visitors in the UK at the moment (apart from large numbers of Social Workers, midwives, trained hospital nurses, etc.), who could provide the ideal nucleus on which to build the army of 140,000 Local Counsellors who will be required. Morale will be high because they will have a common objective, a strong commitment and a clear identity. They are in a unique position to improve the quality of life in this country.

—Each class of person recruited will need a somewhat different form of training. In general, however, for beginners training should be simplified and reduced from that presently demanded of Health Visitors, who have to possess three qualifications: State Registered Nurse; midwifery; and a Health Visitors' certificate.

- A one year course in Positive Health Education would give the newly-fledged Local Counsellor the confidence to start work in the field and to learn by experience.

- The objective of Local Counsellors will be to introduce Positive Health into homes, schools, industry and into every 'hole and corner' of our society, and to take a lead in eliminating health hazards wherever they manifest – whether as pollution, accidents, child bashing, loneliness, tension, vandalism, unemployment, etc.

- Group work with families, and people with common interests, will be the Local Counsellor's normal method of teaching and helping individuals. This will involve the use of Altered States of Consciousness, tuning and harmonizing the group and using the group energy for self-development and some forms of simple healing.

- The Local Counsellor will advise on: home helps; day nursing; child care (day centres, day nurseries, registered nurseries, and child minders); the meals service; ante-natal and post-natal care; families in temporary accommodation; handicapped children and adults.

- Local Counsellors will be individuals who have come to terms with life and with themselves, who have learned to follow their own inner guidance and use true discernment. They will help their small community to find an identity so that it gradually becomes self-motivated within the large Community of which it forms a part, ˛and to which they are closely linked. The Community members will remind individuals when they stray from inner harmony and integrity, so that self-discipline will grow naturally within the Community, based on the highest values.

- Local Counsellors will help individuals to heal themselves by building with them a continuing one-to-one creative and healing relationship. The methods they use will depend on the natural abilities which they have themselves developed – e.g., counselling; relaxation with guided imagery; prayer; healing; touch; massage; natural therapies; placebos; simple drugs; first aid, etc. They will also give instruction in self-help in the home. But at all times, it should be remembered that the Local Counsellor, as a person, provides the major therapy — and *is* a form of therapy.

(The above article is extracted from a pamphlet entitled 'Trends in Health Care', available from Health for the New Age, 1a Addison Crescent, London W14.)

6 Right Livelihood

Right livelihood

GUY DAUNCEY

GUY DAUNCEY is author of The Unemployment Handbook.

The existing economic order is exploitative of the South of the world; there is a direct chain of responsibility from our wealth to their refugees and death by famine. The 'New Economic Order' cannot be built without changes in the North and has no hope of emerging *until* the countries of the North undergo this inner economic transformation, and discover their own sources of economic stability within their own local communities, instead of seeking it in unfair terms of world trade and finance (trying to dig their heels in deeper into the backs of the South). Hence the direct connection between the emergence of the new local economy and the global issues of the North–South debate.

This crisis of era–change brings two very real personal crises to individuals – (a) a crisis of no-work (unemployment), caused by the advance of new technologies, and (b) a crisis of meaning within work, experienced by people who have jobs, but who obtain no nourishment from their work any more, and who feel increasingly starved of meaning and purpose.

There is a desire to move away from total dependence on paid work, and to find ways to integrate together various kinds of work and activity into one coherent and meaningful lifestyle:

Paid work for others
Paid work for oneself (self-employment)
Subsistence activities
Local (unpaid) community activities

Activity in the home economy (beer, chickens, DIY etc.)
Personal activity (crafts, study, meditation).

We need to develop explicit structural changes that will
enable the desire for this change to take on real and
legitimate expression – setting up job-sharing registers,
skills-exchanges, local cooperatives, schemes to pay rates
in kind instead of in cash (via commitment to local
community activities), changes to the benefits system, to
allow and encourage people to earn money while
unemployed (currently very difficult or impossible).

Local *self-help groups* will have a very important role to
play in this transformation to the economic basis for the
new era. Self-help groups for people who are
unemployed, enabling people to make quite major steps
towards a redefinition of personal identity and
activity–work; and self-help groups for people becoming
self-employed in various ways, bringing support from
others in a similar situation.

Since the late 1970s, there has been a marked upsurge of
interest in local community-based economic initiatives,
such as *Community Business Ventures, Local Enterprise Trusts,
Small Industry Groups, Job-Sharing Registers, Neighbourhood
Trusts*, etc. The recent riots in Britain's cities will have a
very marked effect on national acceptance of these
initiatives, and will probably result in support and finance
being made available to them. There is a clear sense afoot
that at the national level, leaders are holding their hands
up in despair, saying 'What can we do ?', and openly
asking for suggestions.

The pilot work that has been done in small communities
over the last few years now has an opportunity to be taken
seriously, and to take its place as a major contribution to
the evolution of the next era, as expressed economically.
We are witnessing the reappearance of the local, or
indigenous economy, which could become the mainstay of
the new economic order in the coming era.

(Guy Dauncey has founded the 'British Unemployment
Resource Network' to further these ideas. A sample copy of
the BURN newsletter may be obtained from BURN, 318

Summer Lane, Birmingham, UK; current prices on application to BURN.)

Small businesses and social change

DAVID SIMMONS

DAVID SIMMONS is the author of Ideals and Dogma *and* Economic Power.

To understand what is wrong with society, we must first understand how the whole system works. The economic structure influences the political system, and politics controls society. What is wrong, and how our society functions, is very much dependent on the type of economic system we have.

The system in Britain, as in America, Japan, and other countries, is monopoly capitalism, a structure based on big business giant corporations, each one controlled by a mere handful of people. The top 100 of these companies account for half the output of the British economy.

Let us assume that each corporation is controlled by just two people – although there are many cases where major companies are dominated by just one man – then just 200 people make the decisions which directly control half of the British economy.

But because of the size of their companies, they have political influence as well, and this gives them control of virtually the entire economy. The political friends of the corporate leaders may be relatives, old public school friends, ex-business partners, members of the same club, or just brothers under the wallet. And when these friends are elected into power, they listen to the opinions of the businessmen, and propose and promote legislation which aids the big company; laws which allow the big firm to ignore the health of their workers and their customers, to exploit citizens of the Third World, to buy up smaller companies which threaten them, and to evade tax.

According to a recent survey, half of our big corporations, with profits running into hundreds, even thousands of millions of pounds a year, pay no corporation tax at all.

Those same political allies support defence expenditure, which is highly profitable for the businesses involved, and cut back funds for an education system that is already aimed at producing factory fodder, at churning out a school-leaving electorate which has been given the minimum necessary education to perform its production line assembly work. Our schools are a conveyor belt, geared to producing employees who will serve the system; they are not taught to think for themselves, or to question the validity of the system. They are simply the victims of the system.

What is wrong is the scale of business, and the fact that our political system serves companies instead of people.

The solution is two-fold: reduce the size of the companies, and demand that politicians serve the people. So what we need instead of big business is small business.

Small businesses may have anything from one to five hundred workers; and if five hundred sounds a lot, consider that the Morgan car company has just over a hundred workers, while the typical corporation may have 50,000 employees.

An economy based on small firms is utterly unlike the big business economy. There are too many small firms for them to be able to form a close-knit group, to lobby MPs, to demand biased laws, to press for special treatment for their particular company.

The people who run small firms usually base them in the area in which they live. Their concern for the quality of local health, housing, education, and leisure facilities will be the same as their employees. So there is no reason for them to evade local taxes, or campaign for a reduction in civic amenities. The town in which the company is based is as much the home of the boss as it is for the shop-floor worker, whereas the big corporation does not have any concern even for the country in which it is nominally based.

The small firm does not have the same division between employer and employee. The owner lives in the same town, works in the same building, goes to the same pub, and sends his – or her – children to the same school. Even with 500 workers, the firm would still be small enough for the boss to know everyone personally, and in co-ops, the employer/employee division would be non-existant.

A person who starts a small business chooses what the firm will do. So usually it will be something the person is interested in, not just a way of making money. And when people are interested in what they are doing, they are more likely to try and do it well. So small firms will tend towards quality products, and goods that are worth making.

Because of their number, small firms have to compete for business. They cannot simply fix their prices with the market leader, because high prices mean lost sales; and the small firm needs every sale it can get. The big company has various sources of income; in addition, it often has some control over the distribution and sale of its goods. So it can afford to lose a little if price-fixing harms sales; and it can use its influence to ensure that its products are prominently in front of the customer.

The small firm has no such power; it must keep prices as low as possible and the quality of the goods as high as possible. It must be more efficient, or make better products; but it must be sure of its survival.

And none of this is just theory or speculation. Studies comparing small business towns with big business towns have shown that where small firms predominate, there is more equality, standards of living are higher, health is better, local amenities are better, and even the towns themselves are more attractively laid out.

The comparison is just as valid for nations. Small firms create a different type of economic structure, one in which business operates in a different way, and company goals are conditioned by social needs. Small firms allow the political system to develop independently, influenced only by the wishes of the voters. So political and social organisations are controlled by the electorate, and work for the benefit of the people.

Governments tax those who can afford to pay, not those who are unable to evade taxation; housing is built as it is needed, not as an extra when there is money left over from defence expenditure. Government does what is necessary for society's well-being, not what it can manage with the minimum amount of tax it has been forced to raise.

What is the next step? Once we accept that the small business economy is utterly unlike monopoly capitalism, and better in nearly every way, the automatic response must be to get rid of big business. The only question is how?

The main ways to achieve this aim are by starting up new small firms to compete with the big companies, and by pressuring the government to remove legislation that benefits the big corporations or harms small firms.

Other methods include not buying the products of the big firms; forcing them to live up to their legal obligations at home and abroad; increasing public awareness of the relative merits of large and small firms; assisting and buying from small firms whenever possible; and encouraging better education *now*, so that more of tomorrow's citizens will be able to decide for themselves what sort of society they want, instead of just accepting what the politicians give them, as most people do now.

Big firms are powerful, but at the same time, vulnerable. They are always capital intensive, often in debt, and rarely able to operate their plant at full capacity. They can usually break even at about 75 per cent capacity, but this means that a one per cent drop in sales moves them from profit to loss. This means that they are vulnerable to change in public opinion.

In the last few years there has been growing awareness of the importance of small businesses. Politicians were made slightly more aware of this by the Bolton Report in 1971. But for most people, the turning point was Schumacher's *Small is Beautiful*. Since then, concern for small firms has snowballed. *The Guardian* and *The Observer* have regular columns on small business affairs, many new groups campaigning for small firms have been started, and a lot of useful legislation has been introduced.

All this in an economy that is still dominated by big corporations, and where anyone learning economics is taught that big firms are more efficient, and are therefore better for the economy. And where most politicians still preach – or practice – that same bigger-is-better message.

Yet this is only the beginning. Support for small firms is still growing, and will continue to grow. And all the time, more and more people are setting up their own businesses. Some have worked for big firms, and been stifled by their bureaucracy. Others are looking for independence, or their own lifestyle. And some people simply believe that small firms are the key to a better future.

Starting a small company is not easy, even if the person knows exactly what type of business he or she wants to engage in. This can be a difficult decision, but it is not essential to make the right choice first time. Sometimes the first choice turns out to be a dead end, but the experience gained from learning about it leads naturally to a more suitable career.

But when the decision has been made, it is necessary to acquire the money and the knowledge needed to run the company, and one good way to get both at the same time is to get a job with an established company in the same line of business. After a year or two the person would have a good understanding of the chosen trade, and a reasonable quantity of savings. The best way to learn any job is by actually doing it; that way, you get experience, practice, *and* all the background knowledge related to the job.

Then it is time to start the business, perhaps as a second job to begin with. That way, there is a steady supply of money from employment to support the business in its early years, and the founder is still able to draw on the experience of fellow employees.

Employment is also a good way to find partners whom one can go into business with. This is very important if the chosen trade involves so many skills that no one person could master them all. And sometimes it is not a matter of learning; in artistic or creative fields a person either has the talent, or doesn't. If the company has a number of founders, each one can specialise in jobs that he or she is best suited to.

There are many businesses that require a variety of skills, and it would be wrong to give up on a chosen trade merely because one did not have *all* the necessary skills. With a selection of the right partners, or some carefully chosen friends, plus the advice that small business organisations and professional bodies can give, almost any trade is possible.

It is also a good idea to study the trade, reading any books that are available, and any of the trade papers or journals. That way, one learns about the whole of the business, and not just the part that one is engaged in, which may be a relatively minor part. So you would be continually picking up new ideas, learning about different techniques, different facets of the business, and new possibilities for expansion.

It should not be thought that anyone going into the motor trade will be causing ulcers in Dagenham by next Thursday. Building up a new business is a slow process, and changing society is even slower. But depending on the type of business, it is usually possible to build up a thriving company within five years.

And five years is not such a long time for a person working in a business which they have chosen as being the most interesting. Sometimes it is just like turning a favourite hobby into a paying enterprise; and it is usually a lot more fun than working for a living.

As soon as the company is self-supporting, any excess cash can be used to assist other companies, or for donations to charities. Income tax should be kept to the minimum, as there is no point in paying more tax than is legally necessary, to a government that spends the money on defence contracts for big business. This can be avoided by paying modest wages, but generous fringe benefits. This gives the workers an acceptable real wage, and gives the company a good surplus of cash, to be used for investment, or any other suitable purpose. Company donations to charity are no longer tax deductible, but if this can be reversed, then people can use their business to finance free schools, housing charities, Oxfam, or whatever they believe does the most good.

By building up a small business, one can weaken the economic power base that supports the existing system. The precise way you choose to create change must be decided by each individual, according to personal preference. But some things can be stated with certainty; it is essential that we change the existing social system, and it is possible to do so.

(Useful contacts:

The Business Network, 'aims to channel energies into progressive social change', F. Kinsman, 2 Langton St, London SW10.

Burklyn Humanistic Business School 'is an experiment in combining instruction in fundamental business skills with "new age consciousness" techniques, 1700 Montgomery Street, Ste. 230, San Francisco, Calif. 94111, USA.

School for New Age Entrepreneurs, 'the ultimate agents of change in making the transition to a new way of living', Tarrytown House, E. Sunnyside Lane, Tarrytown, N.Y. 10591, USA.)

A human-scale business

NICHOLAS SAUNDERS

NICHOLAS SAUNDERS the original Editor of Alternative London *and* Alternative England and Wales *and founder of a wholefood warehouse in London.*

The following is a brief outline of ideas explored during my first three years in Neals Yard (Covent Garden, London).

The *wholefood warehouse* was the first retail business I set up. The idea was to provide the cheapest possible goods in 'mid-bulk' sizes – between retail and wholesale – and to provide worthwhile jobs.

I decided on a pricing system that ignored the usual percentage mark-up. Instead I put on charges for each factor involving cost: a handling charge based on weight; a packing charge based on stickiness; a charge per item for selling, and extra charges if we collected goods or they were perishable. The overall result was that our mark-up varied from about 16 per cent for largest sizes of easy-to-handle expensive items to 100 per cent for smallest packs of

sticky cheap food. For success in a small business I think
such a novel and rational approach to costing is important
– in our case it made it clear that we could not compete
with supermarkets selling small machine-packed sizes or
wholesalers selling whole sacks, but for in-between we
were the cheapest in town.

I also kept the choice reduced to some 150 items. This is
less than usual but is a number that most people can easily
get to know well – the supplier, quality, uses, country of
origin, position on shelves and in the storeroom. This
again I feel is important – to tailor the number of items
carried not only to the building but to the organization,
and without specialist office staff or stock control systems
then you must have a small choice of goods or be
inefficient.

The work was labour intensive, but arranged efficiently.
In particular I spent great care on designing and building a
packing trough which was convenient for all sizes of
people to work at and was sociable in that two people
worked side by side with a third behind. But other factors
which I feel were very important were that the height and
position of the trough allowed people using it to see the
whole room – 'feels like being on the bridge of a ship'. And
that the room itself should be pleasant with unobstructed
windows, space to walk around and its corbelled brick
work left exposed even though this meant keeping the
stock level lower than convenient.

I did not believe in labour-saving machines, which
involve noise or limitations on the way people work – in
fact I believe that physical work can be enjoyable when
there is variety and the need to use one's brain. The work
consisted of driving; loading the truck, unloading using a
hoist by the 'jump out of the window' method; packing;
cleaning; stocking the shelves and selling. No noisy
machines were used.

The organization went through many stages. I was keen
to try a 'work credit system' in which each job was
awarded credits but the value of the credits was decided by
those doing the jobs – based on 'Walden 2'. In theory each
person could work at his or her own pace and be paid
according to the real value of his or her efforts. I believe it's

important for people to see and feel the value of their efforts, otherwise some people go through each day feeling exhausted, but without contributing much at all. But this idea wasn't acceptable at all and after the first day's trial I abandoned it!

The most accepted system was based on two teams each working three days a week, plus a 'duty manager'. The team of five people worked as long as necessary to keep the shop running well and were paid a percentage of the takings, so that if the shop was busy they had to work more but got paid more, but if it was slack they could take it easy or go home early.

The duty manager was rotated every two weeks – he or she did ordering, pricing, banking, and general management. People had the opportunity of running a high pressure and large turnover business after only three months without qualifications or references. I believe that learning responsibility is very important; to see what needs doing and to do it and to be able to tell someone else to do things – and to sort out the problems resulting from one's own mistakes.

However, all these systems relied on someone to supervise. At times things ran freely by themselves, but it wasn't a stable set-up – it needed someone to act as quality controller and ready to step in when things went badly wrong.

As a future structure, I was keen on making the shop into a customer co-op – giving them overall control of policy yet keeping the workers in control of week-to-week running and policy; however this was completely unacceptable to the workers. I think that a combination of workers' co-op and customers' co-op is a worthwhile direction to go in, even if it implies bringing together opposite interests.

Economies of scale?

BRUCE LLOYD

BRUCE LLOYD is an independent business consultant 'concerned with organizational innovation and creativity'.

All firms begin small and grow either through internal expansion, acquisition or, more usually, a combination of both. It is popularly accepted that a primary underlying justification for corporate growth in general, and merger activity in particular, is that of realizing economies of scale unavailable to a small firm.

Despite the overwhelming theoretical evidence supporting the existence of economies of scale, it is not easy to find practical evidence that these benefits are in fact significant. One researcher noted that, 'While most active acquirers do not obtain an attractive return, a few do. The relatively few successful acquirers obtain very large returns, and the prospects of these large returns tempt other firms to engage in merger activity.'

This article is not concerned with the debate over whether small or large firms are more efficient, productive and profitable. The answer is invariably 'It depends'. The whole problem of correlating size with performance begins with the question, 'relative to what?' To other firms in general? To other firms in the same industry? Is it plant size, rather than that of the firm, which is important? Or is it the level of concentration in the industry? In this article many of these problems have been ignored. Suffice it to say that size is an ambiguous concept.

The increasing emphasis on the humanization of work activity has invariably been associated with reduction in size of the work unit. However, this article argues that large size, of itself, is neither good nor bad, but depends entirely on whether the size is appropriate to the circumstances of a particular situation.

Some inventions favour large size, while others have precisely the opposite effect. Developments such as the steel stripmill, the railway or the conveyor-assembly system in automobile manufacture, can only be fully exploited by the relatively large firm; and they will normally tend to raise the average size of the firm in the industry as a whole.

Other inventions have had the effect of reducing the advantages of large size. In the days when steam was the only form of industrial power, the engine with its boiler and shafting were the major cost elements and the ones in which economies of scale were most marked. The invention of the electric motor provided a much more flexible source of power, where the small unit could be used just as effectively as a large unit. Again, trucking, as opposed to the railway, moved the balance towards small firms in the transport industry, as well as encouraging small firms in other industries by reducing the cost of collecting and delivering goods in small quantities.

The difficulty in considering any particular industry arises because remarks only apply to it at a specific point in time. Railways began as small local companies and gradually grew into regional systems before nationalization (in the UK) brought them into one huge concern. Centralization pressures arise at one point in time, while decentralization tendencies occur at another. Leaving the political arguments aside, there is a sound technical/economic case for arguing that certain industries at certain points in time are most appropriately managed as national (publicly owned?) concerns, but implicit in this argument is the existence of a point in time for certain industries where a movement in the reverse direction would be more appropriate.

The dangers of building industrial dinosaurs can only be overcome by modular construction methods, multi-purpose buildings and concentrating on the construction of plants of the minimum economic size. It appears that in many industries small firms do not suffer a great disadvantage in operating sub-optimal sized plants.

Diseconomies of Scale

A number of factors result in diseconomies of scale:

Law of diminishing returns

The Law of Diminishing Returns states that if the amount of one or more factors used in a particular form of production is fixed, and increasing amounts of other factors are combined with the fixed factor (or factors), then both the average output in relation to the variable factor, and successive additions to total output, will eventually diminish. For every doubling in size of a unit or system, there will be a lower rate of decline in the unit cost than at the previous stage.

Effect of ideal capacity

Large plants not only take longer to build than small ones, they also require more accurate demand forecasts because of the high cost of below-capacity operation.

Technical risks

With large plants, greater costs arise from technical obsolescence. This applies to any other factor that results in the loss of profitable markets. While the damage is often not great when small plants become obsolete, it can be crippling to large ones (although, of course, a firm with a single plant will be vulnerable irrespective of the plant size.) What is important in these cases is to spread the risks across a number of products, with each plant as close as possible to the minimum economic size. This also minimizes the cost of providing for a breakdown of the plant, either through the cost of a standby plant or stocks or the costs of disruption if there is a breakdown and no alternative plant or stock is available.

As the scale of production increases, so do the risks. The greater the output, the greater will be the loss from an error of judgement. It can be argued that this supports the case for large firms since they are the only ones that can survive such mistakes! But this only applies to a diversified group, as Rolls-Royce found out to its cost.

There are other technical constraints as well. It is often more difficult to control conditions in a large plant; for example, controlling the temperature in a large furnace.

Other risks

Damage from fire can similarly be a major tragedy in a large plant. The reliability of a $5,000 pump is of paramount importance when it can result in downtime on a $10,000,000 plant. Extra component reliability, or more maintenance, cost money. It has even been reported that big plant losses have made some insurance underwriters withdraw from the market.

Bureaucracy

There is no doubt that the larger the firm the more bureaucratic its organization becomes. For effective operation, more rules and regulations are needed to ensure that the organization's activities are consistent and coordinated. This can require stricter discipline and more impersonal relationships. There are also many special organizational and motivational problems associated with large companies. A few of these can be briefly mentioned:

- Change tends to be much more difficult in a large firm.
- As the size of a firm increases, so does the proportion of time any individual in it will spend on 'internal' contact within the firm. Yet in the long run, the survival of the company will depend on a continual and sensitive awareness of changes that are taking place in the external environment.
- The scope for developing internal objectives increases as the organizational size grows. This can range from corporate status symbols to playing internal 'power politics'. Large companies are more likely to become involved in non-profit-making prestige projects.
- Labour relations problems tend to be greater, particularly where rapid changes are taking place or are required.
- It can also be argued that large companies tend to have a greater sense of social responsibility, doing more research, providing more employee fringe benefits, and giving greater attention to activities such as exporting. (There is, however, no empirical evidence to suggest that larger companies do, in fact, export a higher proportion of their output.)

Another rarely considered diseconomy is 'the diversion of scarce managerial time and energy into making the merger or acquisition succeed'.

Individuality
As mass-production techniques are able to satisfy man's basic material needs, the emphasis switches from standardized products to those reflecting a greater individuality. This characteristic is more prevalent in the higher income bracket and reflects itself in the demand for a wide range of products, from cars to clothes. Although the mass market is extremely important in terms of volume (and, of course, in terms of social priorities), it is the more individualistic higher-income market where the profit margins are usually the greatest.

Price changes
In some circumstances large plants can put extra demand on scarce input resources, thereby forcing up the price of these factors. In other situations, where the proposed unit is large in relation to the total market, the increased level of output can also reduce the price of the product. When this effect occurs, it has to be allowed for in any calculation of optimal size.

If significant economies of scale do exist, any firm wishing to enter the market will have to do so with a relatively large plant. Should many firms pursue the same policy, over-supply conditions can quickly develop. Where this involves capital-intensive plants, a vicious price war can easily arise since the marginal cost of production will be low.

Interest charges
High interest charges mitigate against large projects in two ways: first, because of the extra cost involved in capitalizing the interest charges during construction; and, second, because of the additional loss of revenue and profits during the longer period before the plant is completed and reaches profitable operation.

A detailed analysis of economies and diseconomies of scale is invariably missing from any acquisition programme. This is one reason why so many mergers are ultimately classified as failures. The lack of understanding of the forces involved is also why there is little correlation between size and efficiency/profitability.

Multinationals must go!

DAVID MELLOR

DAVID MELLOR was coordinator of the Eco Third World Working Party.

It is very important to recognize that Multi-National Corporations are a rapidly expanding phenomenon at present, being largely a post-war development. In 1977, 100 companies controlled between them 50 per cent total manufacturing output in the UK. In 1980 the estimate was 66 per cent.

There are arguments in defence of MNCs on the grounds that some of their activities are beneficial. This may be true, but I hope it will be accepted that as a whole they are incompatible with the aims of self reliance, and honourable behaviour between countries. The good elements in their activities can be continued by other means.

The inevitable conclusion of 'MNCs must go' is perhaps not the only one. I couldn't see any others.

If you can learn to live with MNCs you can live with anything, nuclear weapons, junk food, authoritarianism, overcrowding, vanishing wildlife, resource shortages.

Damage to the Less Developed Countries by MNC Activities

In relation to many LDCs' economic strength, MNCs have considerable financial, technical and negotiating powers. The statistic that in 1972 the top twelve MNCs had greater incomes than the thirty-five poorest states of the world is only the tip of the iceberg as far as manipulative power is concerned.

Of critical importance is the power of the MNCs in dominating the Agri-business, siphoning agricultural resources and high profits out of LDCs. In this case it seems that the USA is the source of most trouble.

MNCs have been shown to export, and hard-sell, goods which are sophisticated, expensive and inappropriate to local needs. There are cases of goods banned or withdrawn in the west being dumped on LDCs:

- DDT in Guatemala used indiscriminately – grain, meat, milk have dangerous concentrations.
- Medicinal supplies are frequently sold without the safeguards which are required in the parent country, e.g. *Boots* the chemist sell Aspirin, Phenacetin, Caffeine APC over the counter (counter sales were banned in the UK in 1974).
- Unsafe electrical goods withdrawn in the west – sold off in Asia
- Banned fireproof pyjamas (carcinogenic) sold off in Asia
- Toxic waste and polluting industries 'exported' to LDCs
- Tobacco marketed intensively and without warnings in Africa
- Powdered milk marketed intensively in areas where its proper use is impractical
- Western junk foods sold with high-power advertising in competition with local, healthier, cheaper foods.

Many profound ecological crises with consequent human suffering are being promoted by MNC activities either directly or by setting behaviour models which are followed by the LDCs themselves. Soil erosion, salination of ground water, deforestation, desertification, are some of the effects of imposing unsustainable practices on a large scale in areas where adequate political controls and assessment capabilities are absent.

Defensive arguments are often raised that developing countries welcome investment by the MNCs and that governments of the countries concerned are the best judges of the impact of particular activities. We should be clear that the governments or ruling elites are not necessarily the best arbiters of the social or environmental effects of MNC activity and that our international conduct should discriminate in favour of the best interests of the broad mass of the people in line with the philosophy of our ecological politics.

Damage to Industrialized Countries by MNC Activities

In this context the damage generally discussed is economic and, to a lesser degree social (e.g. consumerism). Environmental damage is more easily recognized in less developed countries where the contrast between indigenous activity and the activity of outside business is much greater.

The abilities of MNCs to transfer tax liability, investment, manufacturing capability and employment between countries introduces a competitive struggle between countries and has a destabilizing effect on the performance of each country. Existing controls seem largely inadequate (Vesteys !).

Exploiting differences between countries in health and safety legislation, environmental controls, labour organization, puts pressure on to restrict advances in those areas for fear of losing out to a competing country.

Within industrialized countries there is a large degree of internal trading between various parts of MNCs. 66 per cent of all foreign direct investment is in other industrialized countries and a fifth of all world trade is between various parts of MNCs. There is a considerable proportion of economic activity open to manipulation by MNCs.

The ability of MNCs to concentrate finance, technical, marketing and other resources, permits market manipulations of many products, particularly consumer items. A surprisingly large proportion of products are, in fact, owned by only a few major companies. Domination of markets can stifle innovation and lead to reduced variety both in choice of manufacturing techniques and in products. MNCs have rapid economic growth as their 'personal' philosophies and so may be fairly described as chief agents of growthist, capital, politics.

They can force along, by virtue of their concentrations of technological research power, the pace of high-technology, accelerating the introduction of, e.g., automation, micro-processing capability, new military equipment at a pace faster than society can assimilate it.

The Growing Political Power of MNCs Relative to Governmental or Community Authority

The growth of large and powerful organizations (including, but not exclusively MNCs) which begin to approach the power and negotiating strength of developing countries and become significant forces compared with governments of developed countries, presents an increasing challenge to the independence of action and decision making of the government. MNCs have already been identified in a number of cases where the authority of governments has been denied. ITT conspired to overthrow Allende in Chile. BP broke UK sanctions against Rhodesia, Rio Tinto Zinc are in breach of UK sanctions in exporting Uranium from Namibia.

1973 – US Senate Finance Committee said 'International Financial dealings give MNCs the power to promote international monetary crises'.

Global Reach by Barnet and Miller describes an evolving clique of world managers set to impose a commercial order on the entire world which by its nature can conflict with local aspirations.

It is a recognized problem that internal data on finances, managerial decisions and international relationships are difficult to obtain from MNCs and so effective control over them seems elusive. It therefore seems that future rapid growth of MNCs threaten to supplant government by election with government by commercial managers.

7 Agriculture

Woe and doom to the agricultural empires!

JOHN SEYMOUR

JOHN SEYMOUR is the author of Self-Sufficiency.

Before we start getting hot under our collars about the deplorable state of agriculture we should just consider the whole matter from the point of view of the *farmers*. I happen to have been a farmer for a large part of my life and so I have a certain fellow-feeling for these sometimes maligned individuals.

The word *farmer*, in Britain now, has come to cover such a diverse collection of beasts that it has ceased really to mean much at all. Much of the best arable land in England is either owned or managed now by huge companies, financed from the City of London. I suppose these companies can be called 'farmers' – what else can they be called? Much more of the land is owned and farmed by old farming families who have swallowed up their neighbours' land and now operate as limited companies. Most of the members of such families take their holidays in places like Kenya. They seem a far cry from old Farmer Giles jogging along on his chestnut cob mare. Much of the land, particularly in the poorer north and west — the upland areas — is farmed by hard-working poor men in units of thirty or forty acres or so. It seems ironical that the rich land is held in huge units while the poor land is held in small ones. It should of course be the other way round. But big capital is not drawn into the poorer parts of the country.

The company farmers, or agribusinessmen as we should really call them, will tell you that they have got so big because they are efficient. So they are, because they are in a marvellous position to tap government subsidies and are very efficient at it. Government subsidies make up an enormous part of the income of these huge enterprises, and they tend very much towards amalgamation of holdings into bigger and bigger units.

The enormous disparity between large and small farmers makes it difficult to consider farmers as of the same species really. There is nothing like it, so far as I know, in any other industry. You can say 'poor hard-working farmers' and you will be accurately describing quite a large group of people. They are damned poor and extremely hard working. I know many a small farmer in Wales who has never had a holiday — even on Christmas Day — in his life and never expects to have one. If the farmer is ill for a day it is a major crisis. And yet the big corn growers of East Anglia and the Midlands and the South are among the wealthiest people in the country. There are very many thousand acre farms and after all the *land alone* of one of them has got to be worth a cool one to two million pounds. And there are not a few ten thousand acre holdings. Many a small farmer has to drive to the pub on an old banger of a tractor because he cannot afford an old banger of a car.

Lest anybody should think I am blaming the big farmers for being rich let me hasten to say I am not. The big farmers, like everybody else in this country, are told when they are young what the rules of the business game are, and what the goal is. The goal of course is money. By sticking to the rules they have reached the goal.

And, they can argue, they grow quite a lot of food, and they grow it with a minimum amount of labour. They (and the government) have made enormous investments in the most powerful and sophisticated machinery, and their annual expenditure on chemicals is astronomical. For, you see, it is the chemicals that do the work that the workers used to do. Herbicides take the place of the old horse hoe and hand hoe, nitrogen fixed with oxygen to form nitrates and nitrites with enormous expenditure of power take the place of the old dung cart and yard full of fattening bullocks, and uncounted fungicides, bacteriocides, insecticides and other poisons take the place of good husbandry.

Thus with practically no labour, some of these huge

agribusinesses produce colossal crops of wheat, barley, potatoes and sugar beet. I worked on a hundred acre farm in Essex when I was a boy. Besides the farmer and his wife there were six men and a boy, five horses, six breeding sows, a hundred hens, and we fattened a hundred bullocks every winter. No chemicals at all were used and there was no tractor. Now the same farm is part of a three thousand acre holding and the whole three thousand acres employs four people, there is no four-footed animal on it but the manager's dog, and no poultry. True, what had been a beautiful piece of country – one that Constable would have loved to paint – has become a featureless barley-prairie, like so much of Essex is now, but that cannot be blamed on the farmers. They are only playing the game according to the rules they have been given for the goal which is what we know it is, money. If the English people want other answers – they must ask different questions.

Now the long-term future of these giant agribusinesses is hardly in dispute. They are for the chop. For they are entirely dependent on cheap petrochemicals. There is absolutely no doubt about that. The land owned by these organisations is as completely sterile now as land can possibly be. For decades they have been practising monoculture (one crop farming), guarding against the inevitable pests and diseases that this invites by dousing the land with poisons (most wheat crops on such establishments now get sprayed six or seven times), putting no natural manure on their land (the animals have been divorced from the arable land in most cases so there is no manure), burning all straw which is, of course, fertility, and yet growing very large crops of corn. And how they have been doing it of course is simple: by huge annual applications of fixed nitrogen. Without the latter there is no way that they could grow anything. And weeds of course – they are suppressed by other petrochemicals. Amazingly weeds still persist – even after three decades of annual poisoning. Life is very resilient.

But who is to say that this form of agriculture could not be sustained to the end of time – *provided* the NPK supplies and – even more important – the supplies of herbicides and pesticides hold out? Remember though the supplies of the latter have to be now *enormous*. A great many of the ships that ply nowadays between England and other countries carry little else.

When people claim that Britain is fifty per cent, or this or that per cent, self sufficient in food they are talking nonsense. She would be – *if* the vast imports of fertilizer, chemicals and – perhaps above all – high protein livestock food – were free. They are not. Only in the tropics can you grow really economically high protein vegetable produce. The old mixed farms, with their high labour component, used to be able to get their animal protein from the land itself, in the form of very young hay, field beans, fodder beet, things like that. The modern agribusiness cannot do it. It has to fix on one cash crop – generally barley or wheat – or at the most two or three, and high protein crops don't come into it. So the animal farmers, who more and more tend to be specialist animal farmers and not arable farmers as well, buy English barley but get their high protein component from the tropics – or from the sea.

Owing to the exponential increase in Japanese and Russian fishing fleets right over the world the fish are nearly finished. It is hard to believe that the mighty oceans that cover this planet could ever be fished out but they will be, at the present rate of fishing, in a decade. Bang goes fishmeal – whalemeal also. The Third World are not going to go on giving over seventy per cent of their arable land (as they do now) to growing high protein crops to send to us lot. As this century wears on *famine* is becoming more and more widespread in the hot countries, galloping soil erosion, desertification, salination, deforestation, are ruining the capacity of tropical soils to continue to supply us.

Surely the writing is on the wall – written up in letters of a size and brilliance that nobody can overlook? The Editor of the *Farmer's Weekly* hasn't seen it yet and nor, apparently, have the big chemical combines. Or maybe they don't *want* to see it – there's none so blind as those who don't want to see.

It's fun to be a Jeremiah and cry woe! and doom! But apart from being fun, in this particular instance it is quite right. The implications for Western Europe – and for Russia – are portentous. Russia, which has gone further with amalgamation, mechanization and chemicalization of agriculture than any other country, is now completely hooked on North American wheat. If that *really* were cut off, the Russian empire would collapse like a pricked balloon. Northern Europe is hooked on petrochemicals.

Trees for salvation

ROBERT HART

ROBERT HART is the co-author of Forest Farming, *prefaced by E.F. Schumacher.*

If small nations and other communities are to work out their own salvation as independent units, without submitting to exploitation and oppression by the vast power-structures of the modern world, it is essential that they should strive to achieve the highest possible degree of self-sufficiency in the basic necessities of life.

At this most crucial epoch in history, many far-sighted people have come to the conclusion that, if humanity is to survive under tolerable conditions into the next millennium, a new 'post-industrial' way of life must be evolved. It must be a way of life capable of satisfying the basic physical and spiritual needs of every man, woman and child on earth, without excessive reliance on limited and expensive mineral resources and without causing irreparable harm to the environment, but – on the contrary – enhancing it. All these requirements can be met by Agroforestry.

By means of this new-old technology, it would be possible to supply fully balanced diets for everyone, mostly from locally grown crops; fibres for clothes and curtains, carpets and ropes, baskets and brushes; oils for soaps and paints, lubrication and lighting; timbers for building and tools, furniture and fencing; medicines; glues; waxes and dyes; fuels for cooking and heating, and raw materials for paper-making and many other industries. In particular, research has been undertaken ever since the last war to find plant-products that can be used as equivalents of fossil-fuels and petrochemicals, for the supply of energy and the manufacture of detergents, plastics and many other sophisticated items.

Research now being undertaken in several countries is revealing the fact that there exist vast, untapped, renewable plant resources, which, if fully developed, could enable rural-based communities to supply most, if not all, of their own needs without excessive toil.

The new-old science of Agroforestry is studying many neglected plant species with tremendous economic potential, while developing organic techniques of cultivation and utilization which give rise to higher levels of productivity than under existing systems, and which do not in general demand skills beyond the capacity of the average man and woman. The majority of the plants being studied are trees and other hardy perennials, whose cultivation does not involve the labour, uncertainties and costly use of machinery and chemicals associated with conventional annual crops.

Thus agroforestry should not only supply the basic physical needs of a local community but should also be the means of supplying full-time occupations for all its members, not only in managing the plantations but also through employment in local workshops, factories and research laboratories. The rural areas – often hardest hit by economic depression – could be re-vitalised, and the present worldwide drift of rural populations to the towns reversed. Traditional communities could be re-formed, traditional cultures recreated and broken families reunited. At the same time the beauty of the natural environment, so often destroyed by deforestation, erosion, mineral working and ill-planned building, would be restored and even enhanced by widespread tree planting. All this would help to get to the root of problems of unrest, tension and violence. For harmonious, truly peaceful living, men and women need the soul-food of natural beauty as much as they need fresh, natural foods to build their bodies.

Systems are being devised which are carefully adapted to the ecological conditions of the regions in which they are designed to function, including many inhospitable areas such as deserts, marshes and rocky hillsides which are at present regarded as unsuitable for agriculture. Moreover, in contrast to the monocultural practices which are conventionally followed, agroforestry systems comprise carefully worked out combinations of mutually beneficial species. So, from every standpoint, agroforestry is a profoundly ecological technique.

I shall now deal with the agroforestry potential of six types of area or ecosystem involving special problems.

Deserts

These cover about a third of the world's land surface and many are rapidly spreading, due to wind erosion caused by over-grazing and deforestation. Almost all, however, could be reclaimed – even without irrigation – by the use of hardy, drought-resistant, deep-rooting plants capable of tapping any groundwater resources that may be available. Once these are established, they can often be used to 'nurse' more tender crops, including fruit and nut trees. During the last thirty years the Chinese have demonstrated the feasibility of these techniques over thousands of square kilometres of desert, which they have transformed into forests and orchards, gardens and croplands. Desert soils are often very rich in minerals and, once regenerated, can attain a high degree of fertility.

Bill Mollison, founder of a system of agroforestry which he named Permaculture, has been taking a sympathetic interest in the problems of Australian aborigines, for whom he feels deep respect. After careful study of the area in which many are settling, he has come to the conclusion that the concept of Australia's 'dead centre' is a myth. In a book called *Arid Land Permaculture*, which must be an inspiration to anyone concerned with desert reclamation, he has detailed a number of techniques by which agroforestry could be brought to the aborigines in their new homes, including even 'ecological houses' protected by economic climbing plants. By utilizing a variety of systems for drawing and conserving every drop of water in, under or over the environment, he shows that a large number of trees and other perennial plants can be induced to grow in areas which most white Australians regard as irredeemable. These include figs, olives, grapes (the three staples of arid lands in the ancient Mediterranean), as well as bamboos, mulberries, date palms, oranges, lemons, cumquats, walnuts, pistachios, avocados, guavas, pomegranates and apricots.

Rainforest

The incessant heat, humidity and gloom of the tropical rainforest constitute an environment in which conventional annual crops find difficulty in thriving or even surviving. There is a constant build-up of pests, diseases and weeds, while nutrients are leached out of the soil by the torrential rains. When the forest is destroyed by fire and bulldozer, conditions tend to become worse still. Soils become compacted and impoverished and lose their structure by the triple effect of tropical rain, tropical sun and heavy machinery; they become lateritic, that is, as hard as concrete. Then all attempts at agriculture and horticulture have to be abandoned.

If, therefore, rainforest areas are to be made suitable for human settlement – and one of the excuses put forward by the Brazilian government for the devastation of parts of Amazonia is the need to find new homes for the population of the arid north-east – then certain procedures are indispensable:

- A careful study should be made of the ecology of the region to be settled, and plant species similar or identical to those adapted to that ecology should alone be grown.
- The forest should not be clear-felled, but wide strips of natural woodland should be left to shelter the new growing areas and protect them from erosion.
- All areas of bare soil should be protected as quickly as possible from leaching and the spread of weeds, by mulching and the planting of groundcover crops.

If these conditions are fulfilled, then it should be possible to establish agroforestry schemes of unprecedented productivity, as the Chinese have clearly demonstrated in their own rainforest area.

Wetlands
Though to the average Westerner areas of lake, river, canal and marsh would not seem suitable for agroforestry, in the East a number of water plants have long been cultivated for food; these include the lotus, water-chestnut and water-spinach. In the state of Chad in Africa and in Mexico a prolific tropical alga called *spirulina* is grown in alkaline lakes and consumed, after being dried, as a source of cheap protein; it produces eighty times more protein per hectare than the soya bean and constituted the main marching ration of the Aztec warrior. The largest wetland project in the world is the highly efficient and highly mechanized harvesting by Rumania of reeds in the Danube delta for pulp. These few examples indicate that it would be possible to establish multi-purpose agroforestry schemes in many wetland areas, with trees such as the willow and alder to stabilize banks and provide shelter.

Maritime areas
The main problem with these is to provide shelter from gales and to find plants that will tolerate a saline atmosphere. The Chinese have planted hundreds of kilometres of sandy beaches with trees, above all the most famous of tropical maritime plants, the multi-purpose coconut palm. The Seri Indians of Lower California, on the west coast of Mexico, harvest a curious cereal called eelgrass or *zostera marina* which actually grows beneath the surface of the sea, and have developed a herbal method of the desalination of seawater.

Cold uplands
There exist vast stretches of peaty moorland and mountain slopes in northern Europe, not least Britain, as well as Canada and Siberia, which could be abundantly planted with the acid-tolerant berries which flourish under such conditions. Many of these belong to *vaccinium* species and include bilberries, blueberries, cranberries and huckleberries. Blueberries, some varieties of which have

fruit as large and sweet as grapes, could have a great future as plants of infertile moorland and heathland soils. The cloudberry, another plant of the far North which is popular in Scandinavia for its sweet berries, could also be cultivated on a large scale, as could several edible fungi, notably the honey fungus. Shelterbelts of trees and bushes would, of course, be essential.

Industrial wastelands
In these, which can often be found near the centre of large cities, the special problem is to find plants tolerant of polluted soils and polluted atmospheres. Richard St Barbe Baker, founder of the 'Men of the Trees', gave a great deal of thought to the possibility of planting up slag heaps in mining areas, not only to beautify the environment but also to stabilize the dumps and thus prevent disasters like that at Aberfan. Among trees he found suitable for the purpose were: the alder, ash, beech, birch, sweet chestnut, sycamore, field maple and evergreen oak. The London plane and honey locust are also tolerant of urban smog.

If agroforestry projects were launched in urban areas, just as 'city farms' are springing up all over Britain, while ecologically minded town dwellers established mini-projects in their gardens, this 'greening' of the cities might in time counteract the serious loss to the world's oxygen supplies caused by the wholesale destruction of the tropical forests.

The new-old science of agroforestry could, in fact, sponsor the development of a comprehensive new technology – the life-technology of the post-industrial era.

Food sense

PATRICK RIVERS

PATRICK RIVERS is a farmer in Gloucestershire. His book Diet for a Small Island (Turnstone, 1981) *is summarized below.*

Paradoxically, most of us in Britain are suffering from *malnutrition* – not under-nutrition, but over-nutrition – from a diet that is unsuited to the mid-twentieth century. Either we have drifted into it or we are being 'programmed' to eat this way to suit the profitability of the food industry... or both; but, whatever the cause, the way we eat is patently extravagant, wasteful, unbalanced and potentially dangerous. Our diet is over-rich in meat, fat, sugar (and other refined carbohydrates), over-processed and adulterated with additives and the contaminants of agribusiness. We should not be eating such a diet. Instead, we and others should be eating more food which comes fresh from our own gardens and allotments, more produce *direct* from Britain's farms, less through food-processing factories and less from distant places.

If enough of us were to go some way to putting our diet right, not only would we all be better off in health, pocket and enjoyment, but Britain as a nation would no longer be dependent on others for nearly half her food – in a world facing overall food shortage.

In other words, *the diet best for the people of Britain is the one Britain herself is best able to grow.*

The Malnutrition of Affluence
Most of us who live in the rich North eat far more than we need for an age when machines do so much of the work. The result is that nearly half the people in Britain are overweight and a fifth are obese – 20 per cent heavier than the recognized average weight for average height. The more obese you are, the shorter your expectation of life.

Most of the rest of the world's people, in the South, suffer the malnutrition of poverty – under-nutrition – but ironically we all share the same chief consequences: less enjoyment of life, more disease and an earlier death.

In Britain we have become increasingly addicted to the over-packaged, over-refined and processed, over-advertised convenience foods which dominate the supermarket shelves and earn for themselves the nickname 'junk food'. What they lack in roughage they make up in chemical additives: artificial colouring agents, preservatives, stabilizers, emulsifiers, bulking agents, and even artificial flavourings. The giant food industry has not introduced these chemicals to nourish us, but to persuade us to buy, and to help it market its wares more profitably.

Successive food and health ministries have shown little or no concern over the nation's 'industrial' diet. On the contrary, the Ministry of Agriculture, Food and Fisheries puts up a spirited defence of modern food technology and the industrial colossus it has spawned. If, as they imply, Britons eat healthily, then what is the nation's 'track record' on health? The more sugar we eat, the more prevalent is tooth decay – now costing the country well over £300 million a year. Coronary thrombosis, unknown to nineteenth-century physicians, now kills some 100,000 people a year. The death rate from cancer is rising, and it is now suspected that as many as half of all cancers may be related to food and drink. Doctors write more than fifty million prescriptions in a year for sleeping pills, tranquillizers, anti-depressants and stimulants, while food additives have now been shown to cause mental disorders. We spend over £8,000 million a year on the National Health Service, yet it can barely cope, and private health care has become a rapidly growing business. Social indicators of ill-health are almost limitless.

Food for Profit

As corner shops close down in the face of supermarket competition, as small firms succumb to takeovers, and 'big names' spend millions on advertising their brands, while most fresh food is unadvertised, true choice – as compared with spurious choice between almost identical brands – virually disappears. A mere thirty firms now control over half Britain's food manufacturing industry, and just fifty firms control over half the market in distribution.

On the land the same trend exists. Family farming as a way of life has given way to the huge farms of 'agribusiness' – inexorably linked with the petrochemical companies and the banks, with balance sheets as their guides. The criterion throughout is 'food for profit, not for people'.

A Countryside Revived

A more self-sufficient Britain will need more families living on the land – a development capable of solving more problems than it might create. In Britain now, a mere 2.7 per cent of the workforce is in agriculture – the lowest in the EEC, where the average is 9.7 per cent, where Eire has 24.3 per cent on the land and Germany 7.3 per cent. So even if we substantially increased our agricultural workforce we wouldn't exactly be returning to a pre-industrial way of life! On the contrary, any increase would provide work which city-based industry is patently failing to offer.

Decentralization would be stimulated as industry tended to follow the new farm families, in order to provide for local needs. We would witness a dying countryside revived.

Won't the Poor Get Poorer?

At present the world is neither short of food, nor land on which to grow it. Poverty is the cause of hunger. Food 'flows' not to where there is most need, but to where there is most money. In consequence, while many eat too much, even more eat too little. If food were more equably distributed, and waste reduced, there would be more than enough for everyone, even for many years to come.

In very many countries of the South, where hunger is widespread, the most fertile land is farmed, not by small farmers, but by wealthy local landowners and the multi-national corporations of the North. This land grows little, if any, food for local consumption. Instead, most of its produce is exported to Britain and other countries in the North; a high proportion as food for farm livestock, rather than for people of the North to eat directly. The same land also grows non-food export crops, such as cotton, rubber, jute, coffee, tea and tobacco.

Countries in the South retain only a small share of the profits made by multi-national companies from all these exports. Most of this is used to benefit the countries' small ruling élite, landowners and middle-class, and to build and try to maintain modern cities and industrial projects, inappropriately modelled on the North.

At present the Good Earth grows enough food as *grain alone* to feed everyone on it 2 lb (4 kg) a head each day, which, though monotonous, is a diet as nourishing as that of any well-fed Northerner – and far better balanced. In practice, much of that grain is wasted. Over one third of it is fed to livestock for meat destined for Northern tables. Why wasted? Because livestock 'shrink' 1,800 lb (816 kg) of grain to produce 250 lb (113 kg) of meat. More sensibly, the hungry eat grain as it is!

As we can see, then, there is no shortage of food. The poor simply cannot afford the prices which British farmers can afford to pay. In monetary terms it is more attractive to feed farm livestock than people; more attractive to grow luxury tropical crops for export than staple food crops for indigenous people; more attractive to grow *non-food* crops, even though the land could grow food equally well. In consequence the governments of many Southern countries, are forced to import food! The South today is a *net importer* of food from the North.

The Alternative Diet Summarized

What We Should Eat

MORE	LESS
	Total food intake (unless underweight)
Food grown in Britain	Imported foods (especially from countries where people are hungry)
Food grown near your home	Food grown or processed the other side of Britain
Natural flavours, texture and colour	Synthetic flavouring and colouring

MORE	*LESS*
'Energy' from cereals (especially wholemeal bread), vegetables and fruit (fresh or naturally stored)	'Energy' from oil and fat (especially of animal origin) and from highly refined foods (especially sugar and white bread)
Proteins from vegetables and cereals	Proteins from meat, fish, milk, cheese and eggs
Vegetables and fruit in season when cheaper	Vegetables and fruit out of season when expensive
Naturally grown food (from organic farms and from gardens and allotments where possible)	Vegetables and fruit, bred for appearance etc. rather than flavour, grown with chemicals and sprayed with poisons
	Food from factory 'farms' (especially veal, bacon, pork and non-free-range poultry and eggs)
Fresh food generally Wholefood (with roughage intact)	'Convenience' and other processed foods (especially ones containing chemical additives)
Herbs and spices	Salt

MORE	LESS
Home-grown beverages and plain water	Tea, coffee and alcohol

How You Benefit

MORE	LESS
Varied fare	Unimaginative uniformity
Pride in cooking and serving	Conditioning to advertising
Appreciation of 'feast days'	Taking treats for granted
Well-being (especially better health, slimmer appearance and clearer conscience – over world hunger and animal exploitation)	Disease (especially coronary heart disease, diabetes, cancer and tooth decay) Depression and unexplained fatigue
Money saved in household (especially by eating less, growing your own and eating more nutritious unprocessed food)	Cost (especially due to needless transportation, processing, packaging and advertising)
Money saved by nation (especially imports, NHS costs, transportation, packaging and advertising)	Balance of payments problem

MORE	_LESS_
Certainty of future food supplies	Interrupted food supplies (especially through war, drought and famine)
FOOD GROWN FOR PEOPLE	FOOD GROWN FOR PROFIT

8   The third world

Can the rich help the poor?

JOHN PAPWORTH

JOHN PAPWORTH was previously Personal Assistant to the President of Zambia.

Can the rich help the poor?

When they try, the dangers they run into are:

- That the self-help capacities of the recipients are undermined.
- That 'aid' is focused on non-sustainable targets.
- That even unconsciously, aid given is in urban rather than rural-orientated terms.
- That indigenous cultural and social patterns are disrupted and distorted.
- That aid becomes an integer of government budgeting, from which it is an easy step to deploying more of other governmental funds for non-productive purposes such as armaments.
- That side effects of aid will exacerbate other social and economic problems.
- That aid becomes an endorsement of the prevailing political ideology structure.

Some more general considerations also need to be reviewed.

First, aid programmes have failed, despite much help and an increasing sophistication in the mode of giving, especially by private agencies; the poverty gap is becoming wider, not narrower. Even the oft-heard counter-assertion that the gap would be wider still but for the aid given is subject to considerable qualification in terms of the seven points listed above.

Second, there is growing evidence that it is impossible for the poverty gap to be closed by methods so far employed or envisaged. In overall terms, given the current economic depression in the rich countries, and the possibility at least that some of the factors promoting it may prove to be permanent, it is highly probable that in real terms aid may be reduced even from its present niggardly levels.

And, third, we need to ask whether it is a valid objective to give aid at all in terms which presuppose a need to make poor countries carbon copies of rich ones, especially when the rich countries have generated multiple forms of crisis for themselves and the world at large from the methods of self-enrichment they have pursued.

The problems of the effects of aid upon the morale of recipients is one which has surfaced repeatedly through a long period of history. It is, in fact, very difficult to give aid without making the dependants more, rather than less, dependent on it, and modern attempts to solve this problem, where they have been made, have rarely been successful.

This is true of forms of economic development introduced from outside a country even when seen as investment rather than aid. Dr. Schumacher used to argue, for example, that the introduction of railways into India in the nineteenth century had been far too rapid, since this enabled the Indian Government to move large quantities of food in times of dearth and this led peasants to be less concerned with growing a sufficiency in normal times.

It would not, in fact, be difficult to make a list of the kinds of aid which weaken the spirit of self-reliance and another of those forms which strengthen it, and the list of the former category would surely be very much longer. It would include, for example, most forms of finished goods, most forms of capital goods, arms (of course) and education perhaps? Large complex city hospitals? Tractors, inorganic fertilizers, pesticides, herbicides and fungicides, milk processing plants, large dams and hydro-electric schemes, monster state farms, birth control pills, TV stations, and so on.

On the positive side might be listed some specific forms

of training, especially at the professional level, advisory and information services, short-term technical assistance, and the location or initial provision of some essential component for the needs of a complex localized development scheme. (I have in mind here how one Indian village was enabled to 'take off' when a suitable supply of caustic soda was located and which enabled it to start a soap-making enterprise entirely from local resources).

Since third-world poverty is basically *rural* poverty, and more specifically *village* poverty, it is to the village economy that aid efforts should be directed.

Even with this focus we need to make a clear distinction between aid which is palliative (and fully justified as such, as, for example, when the crops fail and thousands are faced with hunger or starvation) and that which tackles the roots of rural poverty.

These may be summed up as being the lack of village employment and village incomes. These factors really are paramount and need to be seen as such. We have no evidence at all that if a village is generating sufficient wealth for its own needs that it will not proceed to service its own needs for schooling through the primary levels, and to provide for a clinic and a visiting doctor service and other social needs.

Hence, to focus on sending aid for schools and clinics, to make no mention of other forms of social need, is largely gratuitous, and is helping to *create* dependence and missing the real development needs of the people.

Giving aid, especially on a long-term basis, is in fact, an exceedingly difficult thing to do. The lesson to be learned is that to be effective both the giving and the receiving of aid should be on a non-centralized basis. Centralized aid agencies, except for emergency measures, are always at risk that they will themselves become part of the problem they are supposed to be alleviating.

It is this which prompts the prospect of channelling aid through a process of village or parish twinning, a scheme which enables a rich Northern village to 'adopt' one in the poor South, to get to know its people and its problems and to generate the kinds of help which will enable it to establish self-generating incomes and jobs creation.

The problem then becomes: how to start a process which generates both jobs and incomes on a self-sustaining basis?

In a large Zambian village near the Malawi border called Mtowe a primary school headmaster spotted this need and went on to organize something which could have major and beneficial repercussions around the world.

He was alarmed at the way in which his school-leavers could find no work in the village and were drifting off to the cities. (They could find no work there either, but that is another story). So he called some of them together and formed a school-leaver's club. Their first (unpaid) task was to cut some poles from the forest and to erect a structure with a grass-thatched roof which became their workshop. At the same time the headmaster secured the help of the local White Fathers' Mission. These far-seeing priests secured the services of a young couple from Austria: he was a very capable carpenter, plumber and potter, she knew all about sewing and dressmaking. The White Fathers augmented the small stocks of simple handtools already in the village and the club was in business.

In no time at all the boys had more orders for furniture and for doors and window-frames than they could handle and the girls found the same with their dressmaking service. Even people from the nearby town of Chipata came to place their orders, so that, for the first time in its history, instead of the wealth of the village being drained away to the urban areas it was the urbanites who were contributing to the wealth of the village.

The young people branched out; they built a shed for chickens and another for pigs; the village headman gave them the use of a large area of land on which, after clearing, they planted cotton, groundnuts, maize and sunflower. A shift system developed so that the youngsters spent about one-third of their time in the club workshop and one-third in the club field. And the last third? The parents of most of the youngsters were farmers, and when their older children gave a third of their time to helping them with their traditional farming, their support for the club (a very important factor indeed) was assured.

After a couple of years the youngsters found that they

were earning much more money than their parents! But what to do with it? How to care for it so that daddy did not drink the lot? A branch of the National Credit Union was formed which held the savings and paid interest. This led to another development of major importance. The Credit Union was able to make loans available to local farmers to buy seed or stock, or to improve their farms. For the first time the local peasant-farmers had an assured source of local credit – something which the big city banks had never been able to provide.

The youngsters bought a pair of oxen for ploughing; and this led to another spark-off: scotch carts – simple wooden structures mounted on the axle and pneumatic wheels of an abandoned car and as important to the villager, both as a means of transport and as a status symbol, as a tractor is to a big farmer. The club's scotch carts soon earned local fame both for their workmanship and for their cheapness – less than half the price of those from an urban factory.

The points to be noted about this success story are that it was the result of a local initiative; it relied almost entirely on local resources; it was designed to meet local needs; it created both jobs and incomes on a self-sustaining and expanding basis; it had the full backing of local people; and perhaps most important of all, it stopped the drift of young people away from the village. Not a single youngster has left the village since the club was formed.

The major 'aid' input was, of course, the services of the young Austrian couple (who were not only technically competent but had the kind of personalities which made for confidence and respect and which enabled them, in the dubious American phrase, to win friends and influence people).

This is the kind of groundwork on which the Village Development Trust is seeking to build – to encourage village and parish people in the developed world to recruit young people to go out to a village of their adoption to impart their skills.

'To give money' said the late Dr E.F.Schumacher 'is to imprison people in their poverty, to impart knowledge is to give them the means to be free.'

Unity – the only hope for the poor

KAMLA BHASIN

KAMLA BHASIN is the author of Training for Participatory Development.

S.F.D.P. Project, Nuwakot, Nepal.

The first few steps were the toughest.
The initial cautious attitude of the peasants towards the project was expressed thus by a group leader:

> When Adhikariji came to us for the first time we were a little sceptical. We were not quite sure how these groups would work. We were afraid to take loans from the government thinking it would get us into unnecessary trouble. But we decided to give this idea a trial anyway.

Once the first few groups were organized, the idea lost much of its original vagueness. Small groups of seven to twenty persons, all small and marginal farmers, came to be forged around an economic activity. With outside help the groups began to formulate production plans and to apply for loans from the local branch of the Agriculture Development Bank through the local cooperative society. Because of group guarantees the small farmers and landless peasants were not required to furnish any collateral to become entitled to receiving loans.

Some statistics about the groups
There are now thirty-seven groups in Tupche with 658 members. The repayment of loans is almost 100 per cent, thanks mainly to group responsibility and group pressure. With no default in repayment the small farmers have proved to be better loanees than rich farmers whose default rates are quite high.

Joint production activities
Here are two examples: the twenty-five members of one group have taken a joint loan of 7,200 rupees to start a

common poultry farm. To house the birds the group members have jointly constructed a shed on a piece of land bought by the group out of group savings. A young boy, the son of one of the group members, has been employed on a salary of 100 rupees a month to take care of the poultry farm.

Members of another group told us that to become more cohesive they decided to start a community orchard. They bought some land next to a piece of barren land and gradually occupied the barren land also, extending their orchard to an area of 1.5 hectares. The bigger farmers of the area wanted to discourage this 'audacity'. (They were obviously not happy to lose their 'monopoly' through audacious acts like illegal occupation of land, etc.) 'But due to group strength they were not able to disturb us', was the proud boast of one of the members.

Why Is Group Formation Catching On

...especially in view of so many past failures of programmes such as this one. The main reasons would appear to be the following:

- The fact that 'the village' has not been seen in this project as a homogenous whole. It was decided to include only the small farmers in the project and in spite of pressures from the better off sections to 'gatecrash', this decision has been strictly enforced. Thus there are no divergent class interests within the groups.

- The fact that the groups have been deliberately kept small, making intensive and open discussion possible between the members on a basis of equality.

- The fact that the programmes have not been imposed from above. The group members decide which activities they want to start first and they plan these with outside help. Because of this planning from below the group plans have been need-based and realistic.

- The fact that the group leaders are not nominated but elected by the members.

- Because unity and cohesion in the groups has been built up through specific functions like repaying loans, managing the saving fund and regular monthly meetings.

– Continuous guidance and support from governmental departments and other institutions has also helped.

Evaluation has been built into the project. The small farmers were as active in these evaluation sessions as they have been in running their groups. In 1982 there were over 800 groups of small farmers and landless labourers. This small experimental programme has now become a national programme and it is going to be expanded further to cover more areas and more women and men.

The Global Supermarket is not the solution

JACOB VON UEXKULL

JACOB VON UEXKULL is the Founder of the Right Livelihood Award (the 'Alternative Nobel Prize') for those working on practical solutions to the real problems in the world today.

For decades the path and goal of development remained unquestioned: via 'free' trade to a worldwide standard of living comparable to that of the USA. Some years ago developing countries began to realize that they had been tricked. 'Free' trade was not the path which had made the rich rich, but a system which they had introduced in order to preserve and expand their advantages. India and other colonies were forced open to British imports while Britain retained her protectionist tariffs until she was so much stronger that she could proclaim the virtues of global free trade.

But if the free trade myth has been exposed, others persist. The belief that 'science and technology offer the hope for managing and ameliorating'* the problems of the Third World is based on the assumption that the rich countries arrived at their present privileged position because they started out with a larger reservoir of scientific and technological knowledge. But the development of

European science was based on knowledge originating in Asia and Africa. Without the opportunity to exploit a major portion of the earth's accumulated irreplaceable raw materials this knowledge would not have led to the present imbalance.

The UNCSTD/ACAST symposium claimed that it is 'vital' for economic growth to spend 9500 billion dollars(!) in the next twenty years on modernizing the world transport system. These 'experts' seriously believe that malnutrition is caused by the problems of transporting food to the countryside 'where starvation is more common than in the cities'. But transport problems did not prevent the Sahel zone from being a nett exporter of food during the recent famine. The poor countries EXPORT four million tons of high-quality protein foods (fish, oil cakes, peas, beans, lentils, etc.) per annum while IMPORTING three million tons of cheaper, mainly gross grain-based protein.

The Global Supermarket is not the solution, but the cause, of hunger. Endemic malnutrition is most common in those areas most influenced by Western expertise, where traditional crop combinations have been replaced by cash cropping and the basis of traditional meal systems destroyed. The poor are the losers in a worldwide competitive bidding for the food grown in their own countries – the losers often against the superior purchasing power of Western pets and livestock!

Where 'interdependence' has become a smokescreen for the usurpation of resources by a small minority, selective disengagement from – rather than total integration into – the Global Supermarket is a more sensible course. Trade is after all a necessary cost and not an automatic addition to human well-being! It is absurd to see the Global Supermarket as a mere extension of traditional markets which were integrated into a system of social values and responsibilities. Today's commodity markets, in which some participants have access to satellite information which can predict harvests in advance, is hardly comparable to a 'meeting-place of equals'.

Instead of trying to weight the market scales in their favour and imitate the West, the developing nations would do better to 'modernize their subsistence activities and thus outwit developed nations' (Ivan Illich).

The developing nations today still have a choice. The villages of the world can survive without the rich man's market draining their resources. The metropolises of the rich are only days away from starvation if the Global Supermarket is closed. Will the developing nations continue to fulfil the task begun by colonialism: the enforced marketization of humanity? Or will they realize that the only NEW ORDER worth working for is one in which human knowledge and experience is freely shared, in which the global village has regained its soul!

Instead of exhorting the rich to consume more in order that a few more crumbs may trickle down to the poor, is it not time to admit that the 'trickle-down' theory has failed and is absurd anyway in a world of limited resources of which the industrialized nations have already consumed much more than their share? Is it not time to try the 'trickle-up' theory, based on a minimum income, generosity and sharing? It is estimated that four million US Americans have already 'unplugged themselves from the commodity circuit' (Ivan Illich), having seen through the mirage of the consumers' paradise. They live in communities of many kinds and credos but with the common aims of consuming no more than their share of the earth's resources and finding fulfilment in non-material growth, which is truly limitless. This is not the ascetic poverty of joyless fanatics, but the joyous frugality of those who have outgrown the tyranny of infinite wants. Material abundance is available now to those who know the meaning of plenitude and sufficiency. Those who do not will forever find the world too poor for the millennium.

Behind the minority who have already left the rat race stands a majority who have not yet found a way out. Inside a system which recognizes only material choices they can often only express their dissatisfaction in material terms. But the change may be sudden. The walls of Jericho appeared as massive forty seconds before they collapsed as they had done forty days previously. 'In every domain, when anything exceeds a certain measurement, it suddenly changes its aspect, condition and nature. The curve doubles back..., the solid disintegrates, the liquid boils, intuition suddenly bursts on the piled-up facts (and) another world is born' (Teilhard de Chardin).

*UNCSTD (UN Conference on Science and Technology for Development), Vienna 1979, Final Document.

The world trade roller coaster

HAZEL HENDERSON

An 'independent futurist', HAZEL HENDERSON is the author of The Politics of the Solar Age *and* Creating Alternative Futures.

The case of Jamaica is a bellwether, whereby we can re-examine all theories in the light of new forces at work. For almost a decade, Michael Manley's socialist government was mocked by the structural dependencies of Jamaica's cash-crop, raw material export-based economy, hooked in typical neo-colonial patterns to the world trade roller coaster. These vulnerabilities of excessive inter-linkage to a global system well beyond Manley's control reflect the pathologies of small, weak countries still addicted to such trade patterns, requiring continual 'fixes' of external capital infusions and increasing indebtedness, whether to the IMF or to other Northern Hemisphere-controlled financial institutions. Breaking such cycles of dependency would mean many years of painful withdrawal and the reorienting of these economies toward more domestic agricultural self-reliance and local manufacturing to add value to their raw materials, revival of indigenous crafts and culture rather than Westernized consumerism, the retraining of workers, while restructuring and forging links based on regional trade, bartering and monetary agreements. Generally re-integrating such economies into shorter-loop, more localized patterns better fitted to local cultures and ecosystems could gradually replace the vagaries and long-loops of the world trade system.

But Jamaica ran out of time. Mr Manley's valiant attempts to confront the IMF while trying to explain its inequitable workings to his impoverished people did help to create a new framework for rethinking and debate in such 1980 documents as the Terra Nova Statement, signed in Kingston and the Arusha Declaration issued in Tanzania. But Manley's efforts were overwhelmed by events and the very destabilizations he sought to explain and mitigate. Mr Seaga's even less-workable formulas hark back to the obsolete comparative advantage model and will only exacerbate Jamaica's dependencies in the world trade arena. Indeed, one could put Adam Smith himself in charge of Jamaica and it would make little difference. Similarly, Karl Marx might do little better, since these structural dependencies cannot be mitigated by 'economic development' policies alone, but must include social, cultural and regional issues and fit more closely with local resources.

The key issues must be discussed in plain language. To what extent should any country be inter-linked on the world trade roller coaster; and to what extent does this increase or decrease domestic vulnerability and destabilization? At what rates can various sectors of a domestic economy adjust to global monetary flows and events, and what are the social and ecological costs of such adjustments? What are the political, economic and technological consequences of world trade dependence, *vis-à-vis* domestic self-reliance? None of these issues lend themselves to old economic formulas.

The human population explosion: the need for small self-reliant communities.

PROFESSOR RICHARD SCORER

RICHARD SCORER is Emeritus Professor at Imperial College, London.

There are regulatory mechanisms within the lion species which prevent their numbers from becoming so large that they eat up all the zebras. Although it is of great interest to speculate what these mechanisms may be, and likewise to examine human history to see what has caused periods of steady human population, of rapid growth, and of terrible losses, throughout history, we have to recognize that the greatest disturbance to any balance there may have been in the past has come in our own time.

Up until the eighteenth century, the mechanisms which restrained population growth were familiar to everyone. Disease and famine most particularly, but also the occasional destruction and disorganization of war, were all dreaded. But there were also social pressures which we find it hard now to visualize. When a society lives near to the limit of its resources, everyone knows that extravagance both in consumption and in family size can lead to personal unpopularity.

The dominance of Western values today

But let us not be idyllic about these mechanisms; they are features of life which we in the West, particularly in the last two generations, have gone to considerable expense deliberately to avoid or make ineffective. The societies which have maintained high population densities close to the limits of resources, have done so only by a high degree of conformity which has, according to western standards, smothered enterprise, inventiveness, heresy, experiment, and even respect for those of other cultures.

With a population held down mainly by disease for which no aspect of the culture was regarded as to blame, it was possible to live with a reserve of material resources without the fierce social discipline practiced in Asia and in Central and South America before the conquest of them by Europeans. Even today the traditional Tibetan culture assigns almost all males but the first-born to the monasteries, to celibacy, and to a study of the static wisdom of centuries ago. This would be impossible to impose on any European community.

Human race near to collapse and anarchy

We know we are threatened by what Shaw called the 'diabolical efficiency' of a mechanized, and now computerized, culture; for its power in terms of money, energy and information is so great. Not only does it surround us with its products to such an extent that Nature is being driven into reserves, but it takes charge of our senses, and tells us that the world is what it shows us on the box and in its books and papers.

The consequence of this is that as the great contradictions of our age become more obvious, and the need for remedies more urgent, the remedies themselves are thought of as being of the same kind, imposed by 'the system' from the centre.

No one realizes more than the energy tycoons of the West how near to collapse we, the human race, have come. This collapse is not extinction as is often implied in simple-minded scenarios, but anarchy. Unfortunately the mechanical revolution has been hurriedly followed by a biological revolution in which the constraints on population through disease have almost completely been abolished in little over a human generation. While the fuel lasts, this newly exploding population is being supported on non-renewable resources; and if we do not grow fully aware of the consequences of the exhaustion of the fuel very soon, the collapse of society when the fuel runs out will be as bewildering as the day after a nuclear war which wrecked the machine and the trust in the governments we had all depended upon.

The fallacy that population growth ceases with a certain standard of living

If we examine the population profiles of nations which became industrialized early on, we see that it took about six human generations for the proportion of children first to grow, the population to 'explode', and finally to stabilize. If India were to follow the same path its population would be about 5,000 million (25 per cent greater than the present world total) by the middle of the twenty-first century when a steady population would be achieved, with a low birth-rate to match the modern low death-rate. This evolution simply cannot happen because it would be impossible to support that number of people even at the present low average level of consumption of India. Still less, therefore, could they be supported in affluence.

The population explosion we are now experiencing is quite unnatural by any standards. It is produced by the science of the affluent industrialized countries which have chosen to dominate the world and interfere in the life-style of the rest without a thought for the consequences except that 'it must be good for them to become like us because we don't want to be like them'. Although the proportion of people undernourished in the world has decreased, the West's intention to decrease the total number of such people has failed.

Transition to variety

The real transition of our time is the growing gigantic financial indebtedness of the third world. This indebtedness will soon increase no further because it is not a good investment by any criteria. Consequently the third world will begin to jump off the Western bandwagon as its cost becomes more evident every day: and what else is left but the disintegration of giantism?

Our task is to present a credible scenario in which devolution is the order of the day, and small communities take upon themselves responsibility for their own demographic future.

Our Western lifestyle is, in one very scientific sense, the most inefficient ever seen on earth, for it takes far more resources to get one individual through a day than any other lifestyle ever tried out by mankind.

There is good evidence that the leaders of the most successful energy industry, oil, appreciate the situation. They know that oil is wonderful and valuable, and that it is a shame that will hang over their generation that it was unnecessarily squandered. They see that our economic and political system cannot share it fairly between the generations, nor within any generation, and they have no heart for spreading to the whole world a dependence which must shortly come to an end. Seeing that only by the accumulation of debts impossible to repay can the poor have access to oil on a significant scale, they find themselves becoming energy technologists of a more general nature. Seeking to help the poor, not by gifts, but by self-reliance, they are turning to biomass, animal and vegetable wastes (or even production) as a future sustainable source of energy for mankind's primary and basic needs.

For without such a lead from the poor of today into self-reliance, what will the West and its successors do when they too become poor? The choice is between a stifling uniformity, and a dazzling variety which stretches over the horizon to lands where unknown cultures flourish in the place of today's gigantic world airport, and where a man will not need to explore the heavens to find new things.

Within such a dream lies the solution of the population problem for a species which treasures the qualities of the individual. If the West cannot give that to the world then we are lost indeed in ungovernability.

Ladakh – a global model

HELENA NORBERG-HODGE

HELENA NORBERG-HODGE has worked among the Ladakhis in Kashmir, on the borders of Tibet, for the last nine years.

When Margaret Mead first visited Samoa in the 1920s, she

found a traditional society untouched by Western influence. She found a people living in harmony with the land, a society in which cooperation, rather than competition, prevailed. Recently, her account of Samoan life has come under attack. She exaggerated what she saw, she was duped, she was positively deceitful. Samoa was never the Paradise she described. Or so it is claimed.

I have never been to Samoa. But I have spent nine years in Ladakh, living closely with the Ladakhi people and speaking their language fluently. *What I see in Ladakh mirrors almost precisely what Margaret Mead saw in Samoa.*

From all accounts, Samoa is now a pitiful place. Crime and violence are rampant, unemployment high, pollution widespread. Gone is the Samoans' self-respect; gone too, their self-reliance. The fish which the Samoan people themselves once caught with their own nets are now taken to America, Taiwan and Korea.... only to be sent back to Samoa in cans. The all-too-familiar pattern of passive dependence is firmly established; a dependence that generally leads to irreversible cultural – and environmental – degradation.

Ladakh is one of the very last traditional cultures still essentially intact. And, like Margaret Mead's Samoa of sixty years ago, it is a model of social and environmental harmony. There is virtually no crime, hardly even a trace of aggression. The environment is preserved and protected, never abused.

We often talk these days of 'sustainability': sustainable societies, sustainable futures. The Western way of life, as it is today, is *not* sustainable: in a finite world, life cannot be lived as if there were no limits. By contrast, the Ladakhi culture could survive for ever. There, the limits are acknowledged, and respected. A population of 100,000 provides for itself from the scarce resources of its own ecosystem.

Margaret Mead believed that Samoa was important as an example of a happy, harmonious society in an increasingly divisive world – as living proof of our ability to structure society so as to encourage, rather than positively deny, such qualities as cooperation and love.

As ecological destruction piles up on ever-greater social friction, an example of the way things *could* be becomes ever more crucial. Today, Samoa can no longer provide that example. But Ladakh *can*.

The Ladakh project

Modern influences now threaten to undermine traditional Ladakhi life, in much the same way that they undermined the Samoan culture a few decades ago. Conventional development – catalyzed by an uncontrolled tourist industry – threatens to destroy Ladakh for ever. But there are alternatives: alternatives that are not only viable now, but which will continue to be equally viable – in other words, *sustainable* – in the years ahead.

The overall concern of the Ladakh Project is to put the Ladakhi people in the position of being able to help themselves: encouraging solutions that preserve, rather than destroy, their traditional values and the independence of individuals and communities. For this goal to be realized, we need to follow two broad paths. First we have to encourage young Ladakhis to maintain respect for their own culture, to encourage them to see the value of their own ways. And second, we need to show that there are means of 'updating' these traditional ways without totally rejecting them.

The attitude of Western visitors to Ladakh is almost always the same: 'What a wonderful place! What a pity it has to change!'. Yes, it does have to change. But is it absolutely inevitable that it must change *for the worse*? Does development have to mean destruction?

A principal focus of the Project has been, and will continue to be, an *educational programme* designed to encourage a *long-term view of development*. Working in particular with the young people of Ladakh, we are trying to encourage a more *ecological* perspective.

The picture most Ladakhis have of life in the West is a very distorted one. Having seen it only in its seemingly attractive form of digital watches and camera-laden tourists (who spend – in the Ladakhi context – the equivalent of $150,000 *a day*!), they have the impression that modern technology provides infinite wealth and leisure, and requires only very occasional work. By contrast – and this is a crucially important point – their own lives seem slow, primitive and inefficient. They are made to feel stupid for being farmers, and for getting their hands dirty.

Our educational programme is helping to correct some of these misconceptions. We are bringing the Ladakhis a more balanced picture of the West, and thereby of themselves. And we are telling them how more and more groups and individuals in the West are now seeking to create a saner, healthier world. We are showing them the parallels between the new 'post-industrial' age of which these people speak and what they – the Ladakhis – *already have*.

The question of *energy* is of over-riding importance. No single factor has been more decisive in the decline of traditional cultures the world over than a dependence on imported fossil fuels. In Ladakh's case, such a dependence could arise all too easily. With temperatures dropping to as low as −40°C, the cold of winter is undoubtedly the biggest problem the people have to face, and is responsible, directly or indirectly, for the high infant mortality rate and for a large proportion of the more serious diseases.

Over the last four years, the Project has been demonstrating simple, low-cost methods of *passive solar space and water heating*, as an alternative to the recent practice in the 'modern' sector of using imported kerosene and coal (traditionally, animal dung is the principal fuel). In particular, we have concentrated on the Trombe wall-space heating system: a technology which makes possible a dramatic increase in living standards, while allowing traditional socio-economic and environmental patterns to be maintained.

Local interest has been enormous. As a direct result of our work, the State government has this year donated a magnificent plot of land (the *last* remaining plot in the capital, Leh), for us to build a *Centre for Ecological Development*.

The construction of the Centre will be the main activity of the Project for the next two years. The building will incorporate a wide range of energy-saving technologies: from the Trombe wall system to simple handpumps, from composting toilets to insulated cooking stoves. It will also include meeting rooms for the *Ladakh Development Group* (a local organisation that was established in 1981), a restaurant (to attract people to the Centre, and to help support it in the years ahead), and a library of environmental literature (about 200 books have already been assigned to the Project).

The Centre will also be home to a new drama group. Last year, we produced a series of village plays (written by a Ladakhi monk) concerned with important development issues. They created an extremely positive response, and proved a very effective way of delivering the ecological message. This summer, we will produce more plays, for presentation in both Leh and outlying villages.

A small Medical Centre will be established in Nurla, a village forty miles West of Leh. Traditional Ladakhi medicine is a blend of the Chinese and Indian systems, and dates back to the eighth century. It is a form of medicine that is gaining increasing respect in the West. The Centre will give local 'amchis' (doctors) support in their work and research.

We will also be initiating a major programme of tourist participation. Every year, 10,000 tourists visit Ladakh. We will establish regular forums in which Ladakhis and Westerners will be able to discuss the region's development.

Finally, we will continue to test, develop and demonstrate a wide range of appropriate technologies. The dissemination of the Trombe system will continue to be a priority, and will be actively pursued. In addition, the various technologies to be included in the Centre will be taken out into the villages, and offered as alternatives to the more expensive and energy-intensive methods currently being introduced as part of the process of modernisation.

Ladakh can go one of two ways:

EITHER It can follow in the footsteps of the Hopis, the Eskimos and the Samoans, and be totally decimated;

OR it can build on the wisdom of its traditional past, to become a *model* – a global model – *of controlled ecological development.*

The people of Ladakh know which path they want to follow....

9 Green Cities

The cause of giantism in cities

RICHARD HUNT

*RICHARD HUNT is a television designer turned jobbing
gardener, and author of the pamphlet* The Natural Society.

A hundred years ago a corner shop could make a living on,
say, 200 customers. As more railways, hospitals and
prisons were built, and as the costs had to be recouped
from the workers in taxation, so the cost of living
increased. So the corner shop needed 300 customers
instead of 200 to make a living, to maintain its buying
power not to increase it. And as the infrastructure and the
externality costs, the motorways, the ambulances, the
game reserves, increase, so a shop will need still more
customers and fewer staff and a higher mark-up. (The
mark-up in the rag trade has increased from 30 per cent to
100 per cent in the last twenty years.) That is the reason for
the growth of Macfisheries or Woolworths. And the same
applies to factories. One factory needs more and more
customers and fewer staff to make a living and they are
forced to buy more and more machinery. If the local
council opens an old peoples' home, the rates go up, the
cost of living goes up and Timothy Whites needs another
1000 customers.

So giantism is caused by the increasing infrastructure
and externality costs and by the transfer of activities from
the unpaid-labour activities of the small community (the
Informal Economy) to the paid-labour economy of the
government.

The growth of towns and cities started when peasants
lost their land to big landowners and were forced to go to
where the food had been taken, the garrisons, castles,

abbeys or palaces, and earn back the food by labour.

After that, London, for example, grew as a major port, not because of its geographical situation, but because the powers of the livery companies (powers granted by the government, for a consideration) were able to forbid most trade to all other ports. In the sixteenth century nearly all our exports were of cloth. Not only was trade thus narrowly based; it was also heavily concentrated in a single port, London... by the end of Henry VIII's reign as much as 88 per cent of the cloth was shipped at London, by a deliberately exclusive policy that the rich London merchants adopted to their less fortunate rivals, a policy made possible by the government grant of powers to the livery companies. Every livery company was given powers, for a consideration, to restrict provincial trade and production.

And as the capital controlled the provincial towns, the towns controlled the villages. They received a charter to hold a market from the government, for a consideration. This 'charter' forbade any surrounding villages to hold a market. The town had a monopoly of all wholesale and most retail trade.

The *Cambridge Economic History of Europe* writes:

> Towns became economic and social units just when and because certain places were set apart and defended by laws and privileges making them market and production centres and denying some or all such rights to the countryside around. In origin and essence the early towns depended on such segregation of economic functions and so, in a definitive though particular sense, on the existence of monopoly. They *were* because other places were not: they *had* because other places had not. They grew when and where lords restricted trade to a centre, granted special protection and privileges to those who settled or did their business at a defined place, gave a legal market to some locality and so denied economic activity to somewhere else.

This sort of implies that this situation is no longer so. But it is indeed still so. In Reading a local functionary told us: 'Reading jealously guards its monopoly'. There is one market, still. No other is allowed in the area. Two attempts have just been forbidden. Farmers are still forced to bring their livestock to Reading, because of the slaughter-house laws. Until very recently, all farm produce had to come into Reading and except for a few farms shops which are now permitted, it still does. Manufacturing and commerce outside Reading is all but forbidden by the zoning laws.

Towns and cities also grow when the government (the government again) takes taxation from the periphery and, as it always does, spends it at the core. Jobs are created in the towns and cities. The countryside gets unemployment. Nowadays the only job which their taxation creates within the village is one schoolteacher.

Towns are the product of monopoly rights granted by government, of restrictive laws passed by government and of taxation spent at the core, by government.

Thus the cause of giantism can be traced back to governments who, for a consideration, give monopolies to multi-nationals, give government contracts to multi-nationals, give land grants and mining concessions to multi-nationals, give trading monopolies to towns and cities, and governments who spend taxation on the infrastructure and externalities and spend it in the towns.

Governments cause giantism. In theory perhaps they can also end it. But this is unlikely, considering the considerations.

Neighbourhood land nationalization

NICHOLAS ALBERY

NICHOLAS ALBERY is a member of the Green Town project for a 'New Village' in Milton Keynes, UK.

With something like 84 per cent of the land in the UK in the hands of 7 per cent of the people, it is as if we were living in some third world dictatorship.

I believe that a New Communities policy is a temporary expedient inadequately substituting for a policy of land reform.

Nationalization of land by central government would be a nightmare, but various forms of neighbourhood control of land might work.

In my preferred gentle and gradual scheme for neighbourhood land reform, a group of eight or so immediately neighbouring households would have the first option on land or property and the right to dismantle large estates, when an owner dies or transfers ownership; and would be able to select a purchaser subject to veto and at a price approved by open meeting of the surrounding neighbourhood (up to 1,000 inhabitants).

This wider neighbourhood, with the assistance of suggestions from central government, would set their own criteria for nationalization – such as the maximum size of holdings according to quality of land, the quota of disadvantaged city people to be settled, proof of skills and training required from applicants for smallholdings, and degree of priority to be given to sons and daughters of the previous owner.

Land liberation

SHIRLEY-ANNE HARDY

SHIRLEY-ANNE HARDY is a Scottish author who has been promoting Henry George's teachings about land reform and community land rent for over twenty years.

Any discussion of land reform has centred on land nationalization – a measure with a safe and obvious repugnance. For by that indiscriminate procedure the *use*-value of all land would, of course, pass into the State's hands along with its rental value, which would not only give the State inordinate powers over land use, but would take with it, as well, the private title to houses, etc., which would then all be held on lease from the State, and so, on the State's terms.

Fortunately, as Henry George pointed out, for justice to be done between men – 'it is not necessary for the State to take land, it is only necessary for it to take rent'; and it should be emphasized at this point that the collection of that rent may be made as local a matter as society decides.

With the collection of the rental value of land, the private title to the house, workshop, or whatever the fruits of human labour be, would not only be in no way invalidated, but rather would be affirmed, by the establishing of this clear and definite distinction between community-created and privately-created wealth. Thus the buildings on land would be bought and sold on the market, exchanged privately, bequeathed, or whatever the individual desires, just as now. Only there would be no capital cost of land to pay in buying these – the real millstone of mortgages, etc. Instead the buildings, upon exchanging hands, would bear with them, as it were, an invisible ticket stating the rental value owed annually to the community for the land which they occupy – a valuation which the community would, of course, see it kept up-to-date.

In this way: (i) Land would cease to be an investment proposition, (for anything except investing your energy in). (ii) No more would foreigners buy up our homeland – and we would set the tide against the reverse horror of Westerners buying up the rain-forests of Brazil, etc.; and reveal the paper feet upon which apartheid stands. (iii) Land speculation would be ended at a stroke, for there would be nothing to speculate upon (provided the community kept its valuations up-to-date). (iv) A powerful and ever-tightening monopoly at the base of all productive effort would likewise be obliterated – a monopoly with effect through the entire economic system, and the 'robber that takes all that is left' to the wage labourer beyond a virtual subsistence wage. (v) As land would become a liability to hold instead of an asset, vast unsuspected resources of land would be released, under this reform, for people's use, as individuals, corporations, banks, pension and trust funds, etc., hastened to disburse themselves of superfluous land in an economy where it would no longer be possible to reap rental benefit – present or speculative –

merely from land-holding. (vi) Landowners, as such, would cease to be; all men would be equally placed as land-users. (vii) What Henry George called the greatest waste in society – the waste of human beings – would cease, as work opportunity became available to all and people resumed the choice of whether or not to be their own bosses.

'Small is beautiful': the urban and industrial scene

Because unused and derelict land goes untaxed and unrated under our present system, fears are expressed by some that when such land is made to bear its share of rental payment, development upon it will take the form of tower-blocks, etc.

This is a grand misconception! It is the *present* system that produces this kind of landscape.

Think! When monopoly power over land can overnight multiply ground rents in a city street between 400 per cent and 900 per cent (just one randon example), the land rentier has as good as served multiple notice on the small businesses there to quit. 'Small' may be 'beautiful', but small is not the portion that goes to the land rentier under land monopoly! And as this is the first part in the production equation, the rest remains helplessly hooked to it. These properties amalgamate, a suitable 'developer' is brought in, and the 'big is beautiful' highway rushes before us. It is speculation in rental values which is the primary land speculation and goes on all the time – and sits laughing at legislation directed against speculation merely at point of sale.

Make no mistake! The reason that big business, as chain and superstore, can undercut the prices of small businesses every time, is that the former are the ones who have cut through the land rent barrier, and turned it to their advantage by investing in land.

As for the fears expressed by some that small local communities could not be trusted to act from ecological and long-term interests: where is the State doing that, we would like to ask – in agriculture or anywhere else? But where local communities seem to lack this true incentive, it is the dispossessed who have understandably lost interest in what they do not see any more as their inheritance. First restore *that* to them with the collection of land rent – then discover that caring is natural for those who have a real stake in their environment. 'We are made for cooperation – like feet, like hands, like eyelids, like the rows of the upper and lower teeth' – a cooperation that has its natural span through time as well as space. These words of Henry George seem to me to harmonize with all that is best and soundest in ecological thinking.

(Two pamphlets available from Shirley-Anne Hardy (address: The Rocks, Pitlochry, Perthshire, Scotland), are: 'The Land Question', (from which the above article is extracted), and 'Britain's Biggest Growth Industry: Creating Derelict Land' by Alice Coleman. Current prices available on application to Shirley-Anne Hardy.)

The transport trap

ALICE COLEMAN

ALICE COLEMAN is reader in Geography at King's College, London, and Director of the Second Land Utilization Survey of Britain.

Maximizing transport facilities

One of the first planning fashions in Britain was a drive to relieve overcrowding in inner city areas by forcing vast numbers of people to leave. They were evicted from their homes, and their homes were demolished. The option of remaining in the inner city no longer existed. Many inner cities have lost two-thirds or even three-quarters of their former population, and the present round of structure plans state an intention of removing five million more people. Whether they want to or not, most of these people are forced to move further out from the centre, to suburbs or new towns or to villages round the major cities.

As a result of these large-scale migrations, commuting has become a great growth industry. Places of residence have been divorced from places of work by ever-increasing distances, at ever greater cost in money, time and fatigue. Some commuters seek to escape the tyranny of the railway by using cars, but this sets up a vicious circle. The roads become clogged; they have to be widened; more property is demolished; more people are displaced outward, where they swell the throng of commuters, and help to clog up the widened roads.

The massive migration of people has meant a massive loss of rates. The remaining inhabitants have to pay more, so some of them move out. The still smaller remainder have to pay still more, which triggers off a further exodus. Rates rise in a vicious circle and every twist produces more displaced people to fuel the vicious transport circle.

Minimizing transport need

It is time to take a serious look at the radically different alternative: *minimization of transport need*. This is a rarely practised policy which aims to reduce dependence upon transport facilities. It arranges a diversity of land uses so that common destinations such as shops, jobs, schools, etc., are within easy walking distances from homes. Low-cost accessibility is fostered, without enforced expenditure on daily transport, although the option to commute is left open for those who genuinely prefer it.

Jane Jacobs demonstrated that there are also important social benefits when habitats are designed to permit walking as the normal mode of transport. People see each other on the streets and can build up mutual public acquaintanceship in a gradual stable way. They can fulfil public roles at street scale without having premature private and committed relationship thrust upon them, and consequently a sound social structure, based upon mutual trust, can develop. Such communities engage in many forms of neighbourliness and mutual help on an informal basis, which provides a good, integrative model for children as they grow up. The neighbourhood is also self-policing. Where people are known to many passers by, they do not feel they can commit crimes undetected, and crime rates are generally rather low.

Recolonizing the inner city

Planning develops an artificial model of what is good for people and sets out to restrict the choice of habitat and location to these preconceived ideas. Because some people were leaving the inner city it was assumed that virtually all people should leave the inner city, and because such large numbers have been made to leave it is now assumed that they wanted to leave, and that the decentralization must therefore continue.

Quite apart from whether or not people really want to move further out, what of the people who would like to live further in? Until very recently it was not good form in planning circles even to mention them. But now they are beginning to make their wishes known. They want to live in the inner city, and they do not want the regimented council flats which have monopolized the dwelling stock.

Very few modern houses for sale have been bult in inner city areas, but those few have been snapped up immediately by eager buyers. Behind the few that have been able to acquire an inner city house, there must be thousands more unwilling commuters who want to shed the burdens of daily travel, especially as fares escalate.

There are many building firms that would be only too glad to construct houses on vacant sites if the land were made available instead of being hoarded in a dog-in-the-mangerish way by its public owners. It is sometimes argued that recolonization of the inner city would be setting the clock back, but is this not an excellent thing to do in a declining society? There are many former benefits to be regained: relief from the burden of commuter fares and reduction of railway losses; fewer commuter cars, and more economical journeys for commercial traffic; a saving of road improvement costs; a great saving in the energy now wasted on unnecessary transport, less time spent on daily travel, more time spent with the children, better child-rearing and family relationships; improved physical and mental health as a result of more daily walking; a better local social structure and a gradually reduced crime rate, a broader rates base and hope for relief of the rates burden; the conservation of green-field sites that would otherwise be taken for still more decentralized housing and new roads and motorways.

The smallest nation in Europe

NICHOLAS ALBERY

NICHOLAS ALBERY is Minister of State for the Environment of the Free and Independent Republic of Frestonia.

I am Minister of State for the Environment for a small country called Frestonia. I used to be its Minister of State for Industry and, before that, British Ambassador. On 31 October 1984, the Free and Independent Republic of Frestonia celebrates its seventh anniversary of independence.

Frestonia is situated to the North of the Shepherds Bush roundabout, London W11, and consists of thirty-two semi-derelict houses on 1.8 acres, a triangle of three roads enclosing a long thin communal garden, the whole inhabited by ninety-seven ex-squatters, including half a dozen children, and surrounded by tower block estates.

The terraced houses used to be owned by the Greater London Council and were first squatted eight years ago when the GLC plan was to demolish the whole area and build a giant industrial estate. There was a great deal of local opposition to the plan, as the nearby estates feared it would result in increased heavy traffic. A council 'consultation' meeting attended by 200 locals resulted in a unanimous vote against the plan. But the council pressed on regardless.

Independence

So in October 1977, stimulated by a visit to Christiania, the 'free city' squatted army camp in Copenhagen, I suggested we declare independence from Great Britain. We issued a referendum and there was a 94 per cent vote in favour (with only 73 per cent in favour of applying to join the EEC). Our Garter of Arms, Richard Adams of Open Head Press, designed a fine coat of arms (the motto was 'Nos Sumus Una Familia' – we are all one family), and we sent our declaration to the British queen and we applied to join the United Nations, while warning them we might need a UN peacekeeping force, to keep the imperialistic GLC from invading our country.

It turned out to be a tactic worth recommending to any neighbourhood threatened by bureaucracy. The GLC suddenly started to sit up and take notice. Their spokesman told the press they had a lot of sympathy for us – which was certainly news to us – and that they would talk to us 'in the United Nations or wherever'. The GLC leader, Sir Horace Cutler, wrote a typically quirky letter ending 'if you didn't exist it would be necessary to invent you' (to which we replied 'since we do exist, why is it necessary to destroy us?'). And even Sir Geoffrey Howe got in on the act, writing that G.K. Chesterton's 'Napoleon of Notting Hill' had inspired him as a child, and that he would follow up our cause with the GLC.

Media

The media went mad, with 'our foreign correspondent in Frestonia' reporting in British newspapers, an editorial in the *Daily Mail*, and CBS Television filming Australian Television filming Japanese Television trying to get into one of our houses.

The first year of independence was quite enjoyable. We founded the Frestonian National Theatre (which ran the London premiere of Heathcote William's *The Immortalist*) and the Frestonian National Film Institute (the first performance was the unlikely combination of *Passport to Pimlico* and the Sex Pistols). We issued postage stamps, which worked worldwide, using one stamp for foreign mail to Britain and two for overseas (only once did the British GPO bring back a sack-full of undelivered Frestonian mail, which got through on second posting). We also had a very posh visa stamp, to deal with the increasing tourism – particularly coachloads of school-children from Denmark who came for a five-minute tour round the borders.

By Christmas 1978, the GLC must have thought that all was reasonably quiet again and they sent us eviction notices. We lobbied every councillor at home and the decision was reversed. We also forced a public enquiry into the Hammersmith Council structure plan for the industrial estate, proposing instead our own plan for a 'craft village' of houses with workshops attached. The inspector recommended our plan.

Respectability

We became respectable, forming a limited company, the Bramleys Housing Cooperative Ltd., but gradually the spirit of Frestonia has somewhat faded – the National Theatre and Film Institute were evicted, Independence Day is no longer such a glittering occasion, and a new crop of leaders has arisen, doing great work in the name, not of Frestonia, but of Bramleys Housing Co-op – building a sauna bath, establishing a Law Centre – and now, seven years after independence, the end is in sight.

The GLC have sold the land to the Hammersmith Council, and the British Housing Corporation has allocated millions of pounds for 1984/1985 to knock down our lovely terrace of houses to build again from scratch, since our architect's plans for 'gradual renewal' were long ago defeated.

There will still be a craft village of sorts, with a row of pricey new workshops facing a row of pricey new houses, into which surviving Frestonians will be rehoused, but it won't be Frestonia any more. Gone will be the enclosed communal gardens where people wander naked in summer, gone will be a great deal of control over our own destinies, since the Housing Corporation are giving the money to the Notting Hill Housing Trust, who were supposedly acting on our behalf, but seem more and more to be running the show themselves.

Victory
It smacks to me of the sort of thing that happens to third world countries, when they are overwhelmed with inappropriate third-world aid, but nevertheless it will represent a tremendous advance over the original plans for an industrial wasteland, and a small victory for David versus Goliath – ninety-seven ex-squatters working in unison with the local estates will have defeated the giantist GLC and Hammersmith Council, and saved a small part of Shepherds Bush from a bleak future.

Readers tempted to declare their neighbourhood an independent state and wanting copies of our documentation, please write to the Minister of State for the Environment, 108 Freston Road, Frestonia, (via London W11, UK), enclosing £1 sterling, or the equivalent in other foreign banknotes (no cheques).

10 War and Peace

The cause of war
– the Law of Critical Power
in recent history

PROFESSOR LEOPOLD KOHR

(The following extract is taken from Leopold Kohr's book, The Breakdown of Nations.*)*

Whenever a nation becomes large enough to accumulate a critical mass of power, it will in the end accumulate it. And when it has acquired it, it will become an aggressor, its previous record and intentions to the contrary notwithstanding.

Because of the significance of these causal relationships, let us define the nature of the critical volume of power and the role of its underlying social size with the focus turned on external aggression. In contrast to the sharply defined mass of power necessary to set off an atomic explosion, the critical mass of power necessary to produce war is somewhat relative. As in the case of internal criminal outbursts, it varies with the sum of power available to any possible combination of opponents. But the moment it is greater than this sum *in the estimate* of those holding it, aggression seems to result automatically. Inversely, the moment the power of a nation declines to below the critical point, that nation will automatically become, not peace-*loving*, which no nation is likely to be, but peace*ful*, which is just as good.

Moreover, the same law that causes an atom bomb to go off *spontaneously* when the fissionable material reaches the critical size, seems also to cause a nation to become *spontaneously* aggressive when its power reaches the critical volume. No determination of its leaders, no ideology, not even the Christian ideology of love and peace itself, can prevent it from exploding into warfare. By the same token, no aggressive desire and no ideology, not even the ideology of Nazism or communism, can drive a nation into attack as long as its power remains below the critical volume. It is always this physical element of power, dependent in its magnitude on the size of the community from which it flows, and generating at a given volume as its inevitable consequence aggression. It seems the cause of any and all wars, the only cause of wars, and always the cause of wars.

Even the most superficial historic survey confirms this relationship. There could be no gentler peoples on earth today than the Portuguese, the Swedes, the Norwegians, or the Danes. Yet, when they found themselves in possession of power, they lashed out against any and all comers with such fury that they conquered the world from horizon to horizon. This was not because, at the period of their national expansion, they were more aggressive than others. They were more powerful. At other times, the British and the French were the world's principal aggressors. When *they* had the critical volume of power that allowed them to get away with aggression, they too drove everything in front of them with fire and sword until a vast part of the earth's surface was theirs. The only thing that stopped them in the end was their inablity, their lack of power, to go any further. At still other times, peoples such as the Dutch were peaceful in Europe where their power was sub-critical, and aggressive in remote regions where their relative power was critical. More recently, and this is their only distinction and difference, Germany and Russia emerged as the champion aggressors. But the reason for their belligerence was still the same. Not their philosophy drove them to war but their suddenly acquired great power with which they did what every nation in similar condition had done previously – they used it for aggression.

However, as powerful Germany was as aggressive as others, weak Germany was as harmless. The same people that overran the world with the formidable soldiers of Hitler's formidable Reich, formed externally the most inoffensive societies as long as they lived divided into jealous and independent small principalities such as

Anhalt-Bernburg, Schwarzburg-Sondershausen, Saxe-Weimar, or Hohenzollern-Sigmaringen. They had their little wars of course, but none that would have stamped them as different from the Italians of Parma, the French of Picardy, the English of Devonshire or the Celts of Cornwall. Where they escaped the power-breeding unification of Bismark, they remained peaceful even through the periods of the two world wars as was demonstrated by the inhabitants of Liechtenstein and Switzerland. The Germans of the Reich itself, stripped of all power as they were after World War II, threatened to become again as peaceful in the nineteen-fifties as the Anhalters were a hundred years ago. Hence the extraordinary string of socialist election victories which were so puzzling to so many of our commentators who were unable to understand how a party in a *war-loving* country could win on an almost cantankerously anti-militarist platform. Clearly, deprived of power, even the aggressive Germans see no charm in a military destiny just as, endowed with power, even the saintly Indians have demonstrated in their bullying campaigns against Hyderabad, Kashmir, and Nepal, that they are not averse to the pleasures of warfare.

We thus see that the phenomenon seems invariable as well as universal according to which the danger of aggression arises spontaneously, irrespective of nationality or disposition, the moment the power of a nation becomes so great that, in the *estimate* of its leaders, it has outgrown the power of its prospective adversaries.

Their quarrel not ours

JOHN SEYMOUR

JOHN SEYMOUR is an author, and trustee of the Fourth World Trust.

One geriatric succeeds another in Moscow and a third holds his finger with difficulty off the trigger in Washington DC. The latter spent most of his life as a young man riding about on a horse in front of a camera pretending to shoot people.

What has happened in this our age to reverse the traditional roles of the old and the young in our societies? All down the ages the old were considered to be the wise ones, the peacemakers, the restrainers of the hot rash heads of youth. Now it is the other way round. The old press on to greater and greater armaments – force us nearer and nearer to the brink of the final holocaust – while it is the young, and middle-aged, and at least the young in spirit, who urge restraint.

Tweedledee in Moscow says he will withdraw some of his rockets if Tweedledum does the same. He knows, of course, that there is not the slightest possibility of Tweedledum agreeing to this, otherwise he would never have made the suggestion. Tweedledum of course laughs the idea to scorn and says he cannot possibly withdraw one rocket – until he has *more* rockets than he believes Tweedledee has. But Tweedledee is never going to let such a thing happen. For every time Tweedledum instals some more of these lovely shiny toys Tweedledee is going to instal some more too. Given the intellectual level of the dialogue which is going on between these two aged heroes there is no possible way in which this difficulty is going to be resolved.

If only one of the heroes had the true courage to say: 'I will scrap one rocket. Then, if you want to do the same – you scrap one rocket too!' If it worked they could each scrap one more. At least it would be a start. But then each must have *more* rockets than the other one before such a thing could be and that, of course, is mathematically impossible.

The Russians have learnt, in Afghanistan and other places, that imperialism doesn't pay in this modern world. The United States learnt that very convincingly in Viet Nam. Neither side is disputing territory. Neither side has any real quarrel at all. They have just got themselves into the same stupid impasse as two of those unutterably stupid people – the Wild West gunfighters that Tweedledum was once so good at acting, who start staring each other out in a saloon bar with their hands hovering above their six shooters.

Well we in Europe can probably do nothing to influence these two cowboys – but surely we *could* – and *should* – simply get out of the silly quarrel altogether? Surely non-alignment is the only sensible policy? Surely it is sensible to say – if you want to nuke us there is nothing we can do about it. True, if we had nukes too we could nuke you as well but what would that help us? We will trust in conventional armaments backed up by an *armed citizenry* to try to deter either of you from occupying us, but meanwhile we will take no sides in what is a childish and groundless quarrel; we will not threaten anybody, we will simply get on with the business of living peaceably and developing the only true civilization that has ever come out of the Western World.

There is not the slightest doubt that if we hold our present course Western Europe will be completely destroyed. Russia and America may survive, for they are huge enough to absorb the shocks, but Western Europe – the cradle of all that is fine and creative and sublime that has come out of the white section of the worlds' peoples – will be reduced to cinders and ashes. The Americans have long admitted that their best policy is to fight their wars on European soil. The Russians, if pushed to go to war, would quite rightly and sensibly eliminate the American forward bases first.

But if we said to Tweedledum 'Take your filthy rockets off our sacred European soil' and to Tweedledee: 'If you invade one civilized country you will have to face an armed citizen behind every hedge and in every ditch, so that your present experiences in Afghanistan will seem like a summer idyll in comparison!' we might not prevent those two senile heroes from destroying each other but at least civilization would have *some* small chance of survival.

Of course, as John Papworth, our noble mentor, reiterates, the only final solution to the impasse, short of the ultimate solution of death for all, is for those two obscene monstrosities – the USSR and the USA – to be

broken into their component parts again. Idaho would
never want to go to war against the Russians, nor would
Azerbaijan wish to invade America. We should, of course,
exert all our influence to achieving such a result. And, in
order that our influence should carry the weight of
example too, we should set about setting free our Welsh,
and Scots, and Basques, and Bretons and all the rest of
them. And us.

The Nation-State has proved a disaster.

I have been reading John Papworth's book, *New Politics*,
and have found completely convincing, if I ever needed
convincing, his contention that it was the City States – the
small countries – that produced everything of value in our
civilization. Of *course* we must labour for decentralism, for
until we achieve it our civilization will continue to decay
and will be at risk.

But, I submit, and here I know I differ from John
Papworth, we *cannot wait* to achieve decentralism before
we disengage from this stupid and disgusting quarrel
between the two barbarisms of the East and the West. We
must disengage *now*! We must have nothing to do with
either of them. What? We are too scared to take on Russia,
should her barbarian hordes invade us, without help
from America? When the wild mountain tribesmen of
Afghanistan, who have to make their own rifles in
primitive hidden workshops, are holding a huge Russian
army without any help from anybody? We – the Western
Europeans – the most civilized people on Earth?

Let us by all means flood Russia and America with anti-
nuke propaganda, and propaganda for regionalism and
decentralism. Those countries derived what little scraps of
civilization they have from us in the first place. Maybe they
will have the humility to learn from us again. If we could
take those two senile-puerile heroes and bang their heads
together – that would be fine. As we can't, let them get on
with it. It is their quarrel not ours.

Saving the giants from themselves

PROFESSOR E.P. THOMPSON

E.P. THOMPSON is involved with the European Nuclear Disarmament movement, and author of Protest and Survive *and* Writing by Candlelight.

Europeans in increasing numbers are despairing of the logic of deterrence. They are looking outside the old parameters of 'balance' to the long-neglected processes of political discourse and cultural expression.

Weapons do not, as yet, invent and make themselves. There is a human decision to make them. Who takes such decisions? How?

This is a question more important than those of throw-weight or circular error probable, yet it is assumed unanalyzed in deterrence theory. From the time of Eisenhower and Khrushchev, the leaders of the superpowers have shrugged off personal responsibility. But so also have some of the highest scientific and even military advisers to these leaders. I need not mention the distinguished line of arms control, scientific and defence advisers to US administrations who have candidly signalled their profound disagreements with the decisions of government. In the Soviet Union, blanket official secrecy makes the record less clear: we must go back as far as Khrushchev's memoirs for a similar account of the rejection of prime scientific advice, in the encounters between Khrushchev and Andrei Sakharov.

In Britain the Official Secrets Acts are so heavy that we learn a little of the process only some years after the event, and then only from advisers so eminent that they are immune from prosecution. Three notable cases can be cited from 1979 to 1980: Lord Louis Mountbatten, Lord Zuckerman, and Field Marshal Lord Carver. Mountbatten, in a concise and humane speech delivered at Strasbourg two months before his murder, signalled his extreme anxiety at the nuclear arms race and indicated that specific advice he had given, when Commander-in-Chief of the

British General Staff, against any strategy which entertained the possibility of limited or theatre nuclear war. Carver, another outgoing Commander-in-Chief, and a conventional proponent of NATO deterrence theory, has signalled in a succession of interviews and letters to *The Times* his long-standing opposition to an independent British nuclear weapons system. Zuckerman, who was Chief Scientific Adviser to the British Government from 1964 to 1971, has surveyed, in a lecture of outstanding importance, the record of two decades in which 'the views of the Killians, the Wiesners, the Kistiakowkys, the Yorks' – and (by implication) the Zuckermans – were consistently overruled.

We are faced here with an extra-ordinary situation, although not a situation for which a historian is altogether unprepared. Not only the nominal leaders of states, but also their chief scientific advisers and chiefs of general staff disclaim responsibility for the most central decisions of state policy – all gesture toward an ulterior process to which they themselves became captive. It was Eisenhower who warned of the 'danger that public policy could itself become the captive of a scientific-technological elite.' Zuckerman, the scientist, passes the buck down the line to technology. The 'military chiefs, who by convention are the official advisers on national security, merely serve as a channel through which the men in the laboratories transmit their views' and 'chief scientific advisers have proved to be no match for the laboratory technicians':

> The men in the nuclear weapons laboratories of both sides have succeeded in creating a world with an irrational foundation, on which a new set of political realities has in turn had to be built. They have become the alchemists of our times, working in secret ways which cannot be divulged, casting spells which embrace us all.

We have at last identified the human agent of our doom, concealed within a secret laboratory, casting malevolent spells. And this brings us close to the findings of experts on arms control who have identified the ulterior thrust towards weapons innovation in such terms as 'technology creep.' Undoubtedly this directs us to a significant moment of process, which appears to its own actors in this way. Yet there is still something unexplained. For this traces the most significant tendency of our times to a source, either in a laboratory conspiracy, or in an inexorable technological determinism of a kind for which historians (or, I should say, historians whom I consider to be reputable) do not find any historical precedent. That is, some vulgar practitioners of determinism apart, historians do not find that technology (or inventors), unaided, created industrialization or capitalism or imperialism. Nor can technology creep, unaided, bring us to extermination. Historians find, rather, a collocation of mutually supportive forces – political, ideological, institutional, economic – which give rise to process, or to the event. And each of these forces exists only within the medium of human agency.

I see no reason why this historical finding must now, in the 80s, undergo drastic revision. But this need not lead us toward any optimistic conclusions. We may be led to an even more pessimistic finding: that technology creep is indeed supplemented by a host of collateral and mutually supportive forces which, taken as a set, constitute the process which has led us to 'this present unhappy day'. And if we read Zuckerman with care, we find that the men in the laboratories did not do all this alone. They also 'knew how to respond to the mood of the country, how to capture the attention of the media, how to stir the hearts of generals. They have been adept ... in creating the climate within which political chiefs have to operate.'

The cast has now become larger: it takes in public opinion, the media, the military, the politicians. In sum:

- the weapons systems — and their 'laboratory' techniques, lobbyists and public relations operators – attract a large concentration of the resources and scientific skills of the host society and are then transformed into huge inertial forces within that society, whether bureaucratic or private in expression;
- they are interlocked with the government bureaucracy (exchange of personnel with Defence ministries and with Party bureaucracy, and so forth), and become adept at lobbying in the media and in the organs of the state;

– there is generated around them a large supportive and
protective security and policing apparatus, which, in its
turn, enhances the control of information and the
inhibition of opposition, and which actively furthers the
crystallization of a supportive ideology.

Politicians then rise in influence from the weapons
system and security apparatus themselves (Brezhnev,
Bush). As in all long-term historical processes – and
imperialisms provide clear examples – now one and now
another of the collateral forces may attain dominance: now
the 'alchemists in the laboratories', now the generals, now
the media, now the politicians, may appear to be calling
the tune. But this is only as it seems to the actors at a
particular moment within the process, for in truth
alchemists, politicians, generals and ideologists are all part
of one set. Technology can creep only because ideology is
creeping alongside it and because politicians are creeping
away from any decisive control. And behind the politicians
is the pressure of those hundreds of thousands of electors
who 'are making their living doing things which were
promoted years before by their political predecessors. It is
the past which imbues the arms race with its inner
momentum.'

That is a pessimistic conclusion indeed. It leads reflective
persons within the system to suppose that there may be
only one remote possibility of staving off the end. By some
wizardry at the highest level of diplomatic engineering
between the superpowers – SALT XIII? – the plug will at
the last moment be pulled, and the waters of nuclear
menace will drain out of the rival baths just before they
overflow onto the floors of the world. This most
momentous political action will be taken by the leaders of
states and their advisers, without any of the normal
preliminaries of general political agitation and discourse. It
is supposed that the very same political forces which have
made these insane structures will suddenly unmake them:
the weapon systems and their political and security
support systems will de-weaponize themselves.

This will not happen. And what this analysis should
indicate is that it is precisely at the top of both opposed
societies that agreement to de-escalate is most impossible.

It is here that inertia and 'creep' have their uncontested reign. It is here that the advice of scientists and even of rational military minds is jammed by a concatenation of competing interests and bureaucracies. It is here that the maintenance of cold war becomes an actual interest, and an instrument of policy in the subjection and control of client states, the legitimation of other kinds of adventure, and the suppression of dissent. It is here that the futile exercises of 'balance', of contests for 'face', of 'posture', of endlessly protracted negotiations about minutiae, and of worst case hypotheses, govern every encounter.

The conclusion is evident. If we are to develop a counterthrust to the inertia of the weapons systems, then we must do this first of all, not at the top, but at the bottom, in the middle, and on the margins of both opposed state structures. Only here is there space for the insertion of any rationality. We can destabilize the weapons systems only from below. The means must include those of political discourse and agitation: of lateral exchanges of many kinds between the middle ranges of society in the opposed blocs; of detaching client states from their dependency on either bloc and adding to the sum of influence of non-aligned powers; of pressing measures of conversion to peaceful production within the weapons system itself; and of contesting, with every surviving resource of our culture, the enforcement of security and of information control. Our strategy is neither against the USA or the USSR. It might help to save both giants from themselves.

Peace is a way of life

IVAN ILLICH

IVAN ILLICH is the author of Deschooling Society, Limits to Medicine *and* Celebration of Awareness.

This is my thesis: under the cover of 'development', a worldwide war has been waged against people's peace. In developed areas today, not much is left of people's peace. I believe that limits to economic development, originating at the grassroots, are the principle condition for people to recover their peace.

The assumption of scarcity is fundamental to economics, and formal economics is the study of values under this assumption. But scarcity, and therefore all which can be meaningfully analyzed by formal economics, has been of marginal importance in the lives of most people through most of history. The spread of scarcity into all aspects of life can be chronicled; it has occurred in European civilization since the Middle Ages. Under the expanding assumption of scarcity, peace acquired a new meaning without precedent anywhere in Europe. Peace came to mean *pax economica*. *Pax economica* is a balance between formally 'economic' powers.

The history of this new reality deserves our attention. And the process through which *pax economica* monopolized the meaning of peace is especially important. This is the first meaning of peace to achieve worldwide acceptance. And such a monopoly ought to be deeply worrisome. Therefore, I want to contrast *pax economica* with its opposite and complement, popular peace.

Since the establishment of the United Nations, peace has been progressively linked with development. Previously this linkage had been unthinkable. The novelty of it can hardly be understood by people under forty. The curious situation is more easily intelligible for those who were, like myself, adults on 10 January 1949, the day President Truman announced the Point Four Programme. On that day most of us met the term 'development' for the first time in its present meaning. Until then we had used development to refer to species, to real estate and to moves in chess. But since then it can refer to people, to countries and to economic strategies. And in less than a generation we were flooded with conflicting development theories. By now, however, most of them are merely curiosities for collectors. You may remember, with some embarrassment, how generous people were urged to make sacrifices for a succession of programmes aimed at 'raising per capita income', 'catching up with the advanced countries',

'overcoming dependencies'. And you now wonder at the
many things once deemed worthy of export: 'achievement
orientation', 'atoms for peace', 'jobs', 'windmills' and,
currently, 'alternative lifestyles' and professionally
supervised 'self-help'. Each of these theoretical incursions
came in waves. One brought the self-styled pragmatists
who emphasized enterprise, the other would-be politicians
who relied on 'conscientizing' people into foreign
ideology. Both camps agreed on growth. Both advocated
rising production and increased dependence on
consumption. And each camp with its sect of experts, each
assembly of saviours, always linked its own scheme for
development to peace. Concrete peace, by thus being
linked to development, became a partisan goal. And the
pursuit of peace through development became the over-
arching unexaminable axiom. Anyone who opposed
economic growth, not this kind or that, but economic
growth as such, could be denounced as an enemy of peace.
Even Gandhi was cast into the role of the fool, the
romantic or the psychopath. And worse, his teachings
were perverted into so-called non-violent strategies for
development. His peace too was linked to growth. Khadi
was redefined as a 'commodity', and non-violence as an
economic weapon. The assumption of the economist, that
values are not worth protecting unless they are scarce, has
turned *pax economica* into a threat to people's peace.

The linkage of peace to development has made it difficult
to challenge the latter. Let me suggest that such a
challenge should now be the main task of peace research.
And the fact that development means different things to
different people is no obstacle. It means one thing to TNC
executives, another to ministers of the Warsaw pact, and
something other again to the architects of the New
International Economic Order. But the convergence of all
parties on the need for development has given the notion a
new status. This agreement has made of development the
condition for the pursuit of the nineteenth-century ideals
of equality and democracy, with the proviso that these be
restricted within the assumptions of scarcity. Under the
disputes around the issue of 'who gets what' the
unavoidable costs inherent in all development have been

buried. But during the seventies one part of these costs has come to light. Some obvious 'truths' suddenly became controversial. Under the ecology label, the limits of resources, of tolerable poison and stress became political issues. But the violent aggression against the environment's utilization value has so far not been sufficiently disinterred. To expose the violence against subsistence which is implicit in all further growth, and which is veiled by *pax economica*, seems to me a prime task of radical peace research.

In both theory and practice all development means the transformation of subsistence-oriented cultures and their integration into an economic system. Development always entails the expansion of a formally economic sphere at the cost of subsistence-orientated activities. It means the progressive 'disembedding' of a sphere in which exchange takes place under the assumption of a zero sum game. And this expansion proceeds at the cost of all other traditional forms of exchange. Thus development always implies the propagation of scarcity – dependence on goods and services perceived as scarce. Development necessarily creates a milieu from which the conditions for subsistence activities have been eliminated in the process of making the milieu over into a resource for the production and circulation of commodities. Development thus inevitably means the imposition of *pax economica* at the cost of every form of popular peace.

To illustrate the opposition between people's peace and *pax economica*, let me turn to the European Middle Ages. In so doing, I emphatically do not advocate a return to the past. I look at the past only to illustrate the dynamic opposition between two complementary forms of peace, both formally recognized. I explore the past rather than some social science theory to avoid utopian thinking and a planning mentality. The past is not, like plans and ideas, something which might possibly come about. It is not something which ought to be. The past has been. It allows me to stand on fact when I look at the present. I turn toward the European Middle Ages because it was near their end that a violent *pax economica* assumed its shape. And the replacement of people's peace by its engineered counterfeit, *pax economica*, is one of Europe's exports.

In the twelfth century, *pax* did not mean the absence of war between lords. The *pax* that Church or Emperor wanted to guarantee was not primarily the absence of armed encounters between knights. *Pax*, or peace, meant to protect the poor and their means of subsistence from the violence of war. Peace protected the peasant and the monk. This was the meaning of *Gottesfrieden*, of *Landfrieden*. It protected specific times and places. No matter how bloody the conflict among lords, peace protected the oxen and grain on the stem. It safeguarded the emergency granary, the seed and the time of harvest. Generally speaking, the 'peace of the land' shielded the utilization of values of the common environment from violent interference. It ensured access to water and pasture, to woods and lifestock, for those who had nothing else from which to draw their subsistence. The 'peace of the land' was thus distinct from the truce between warring parties. This primarily subsistence-oriented significance of peace was lost with the Renaissance.

With the rise of the nation-state, an entirely new world began to emerge. This world ushered in a new kind of peace and a new kind of violence. Both its peace and its violence are equally distant from all the forms of peace and violence which had previously existed. Whereas peace had formerly meant the protection of that minimal subsistence on which the wars among lords had to be fed, henceforth subsistence itself became the victim of an aggression, supposedly peaceful. Subsistence itself became the prey of expanding markets in services and goods. This new kind of peace entailed the pursuit of a utopia. Popular peace had protected precarious but real communities from total extinction. But the new peace was built around an abstraction. The new peace is cut to the measure of *homo economicus*, universal man, made by nature to live on the consumption of commodities produced elsewhere by others. While the *pax populi* had protected vernacular autonomy, the environment in which this could thrive and the variety of patterns for its reproduction, the new *pax economica* protected production. It ensured aggression against popular culture, the commons and women.

First, *pax economica* cloaks the assumption that people have become incapable of providing for themselves. It empowers a new elite to make all people's survival dependent on their access to education, health care, police protection, apartments and supermarkets. In ways previously unknown, it exalts the producer and degrades the consumer. *Pax economica* labels the subsistent as 'unproductive', the autonomous as 'asocial', the traditional as 'underdeveloped'. It spells violence against all local customs which do not fit a zero sum game.

Second, *pax economica* promotes violence against the environment. The new peace guarantees impunity – the environment may be used as a resource to be mined for the production of commodities, and a space reserved for their circulation. It does not just permit, but encourages the destruction of the commons. People's peace had protected the commons. It guarded the poor man's access to pastures and wood; it safeguarded the use of the road and the river by people; it reserved to widows and beggars exceptional rights for utilizing the environment. *Pax economica* defines the environment as a scarce resource which it reserves for optimal use in the production of goods and the provision of professional care. Historically, this is what development has meant: starting from the enclosure of the lord's sheep and reaching to the enclosure of the streets for the use of cars and to the restriction of desirable jobs to those with more than twelve years of schooling. Development has always signified a violent exclusion of those who wanted to survive without dependence on consumption from the environment's utilization values. *Pax economica* bespeaks war against the commons.

Third, the new peace promotes a new kind of war between the sexes. The transition from the traditional battle for dominance to this new all-out war between men and women is probably the least analyzed of economic growth's side effects. This war, too, is a necessary outcome of the so-called growth of productive forces, a process implying an increasingly complete monopoly of wage labour over all other forms of work. And this too, is aggression. The monopoly of wage-related work entails aggression against a feature common to all subsistence-oriented societies. Though these societies be as different from each other as those of Japan, France and Fiji, one central characteristic is common to all of them: all tasks relevant to subsistence are assigned in a gender-specific way, to either men or women. The set of specific tasks which are necessary and culturally defined, vary from society to society. But each society distributes the various possible tasks to either men or women, and does so according to its own unique pattern. In no two cultures is the distribution of tasks within a society the same. In each culture, 'growing up' means to grow into the activities characteristic there, and only there, of either man or woman. To be a man or a woman in pre-industrial societies is not a secondary trait added on to genderless humans. It is the most fundamental characteristic in every single action. To grow up does not mean to be 'educated', but to grow into life by acting as a woman or as a man. Dynamic peace between men and women consists precisely in this division of concrete tasks. And this does not signify equality; it establishes limits to mutual oppression. Even in this intimate domain, people's peace limits both war and the extent of domination. Wage labour destroys this pattern.

Industrial work, productive work, is conceived as neutral and often experienced as such. It is defined as genderless work. And this is true whether it is paid or unpaid, whether its rhythm is determined by production or by consumption. But even though work is conceived as genderless, access to this activity is radically biased. Men have primary access to the paid tasks which are viewed as desirable and women are assigned those left over. Originally, women were the ones forced into unpaid shadow work, although men are now increasingly given these tasks, too. As a consequence of this neutralization of work, development inevitably promotes a new kind of war between the sexes, a competition between theoretical equals of whom half are handicapped by their sex. Now we see a competition for wage labour, which has become scarce, and a struggle to avoid shadow work, which is neither paid nor capable of contributing to subsistence.

Pax economica protects a zero sum game, and ensures its undisturbed progress. All are coerced to become players and to accept the rules of *homo economicus*. Those who refuse to fit the ruling model are either banished as enemies of the peace or educated until they conform. By the rules of the zero sum game, both the environment and human work are scarce stakes; as one gains the other loses. Peace is now reduced to two meanings: the myth that, at least in economics, two and two will one day make five, or a truce and deadlock. Development is the name given to the expansion of this game, to the incorporation of more players and of their resources. Therefore, the monopoly of *pax economica* must be deadly; and there must be some peace other than the one linked to development. One can concede that *pax economica* is not without some positive value – bicycles have been invented and their components must circulate in markets different from those in which pepper was formerly traded. And peace among economic powers is at least as important as peace between the warlords of ancient times. But the monopoly of this élite peace must be questioned. To formulate this challenge seems to me the most fundamental task of peace research today.

A Fourth World peace proposal

JOHN PAPWORTH

JOHN PAPWORTH was Convener of the First Assembly of the Fourth World in 1981.

The Political Conditions of Peace
If we accept the need for a human scale in public affairs we need to pose a question which has scarcely been considered since Plato: how big is the optimum size of a nation?

Plato himself postulated the pre-technological scale of a

community as the size of a gathering within the range of a speaker's voice, but in practice this figure for city states appears to have been, at its upper limit, around a quarter of a million, and this remained true, with exceptions, down to the Renaissance.

Technology has altered the basis of such calculations. Communication can now be globally instantaneous, and has yielded the unreal image of the global village. But even if one person's voice can be heard globally, world government could not mean other than an entity dominated not by the interests and the wishes of the generality of people (for how could it be?), but by those controlling the technology used to promote and sustain it.

Nevertheless, technology *has* made the democractically effective unit of government larger, and on a purely pragmatic basis of observing how existing governments behave we may agree with Professor Leopold Kohr and others in putting the upper limit at around twelve million. Beyond that, technology and manipulation increasingly intrude at the expense of democratic practice.

If we accept as a basic premise that no nation should exceed twelve million in size we are envisaging a global family of more than 350 nations (a figure based on a division of the world population by twelve million; the number will be larger than this since there are many nations with quite small populations, often below one million).

Let us assume a grand congress for global peace is summoned by general agreement of the nations both big and small to achieve this. What would its agenda be and how would it fashion its proposals so as to make them effective?

We ought first to note that of the 206 nations in the world most of them are already what we may call Fourth World nations, that is, they are below the critical size being postulated here of twelve million. In addition, the rest might well be grouped between the giants (or meganations), having each a population of between twelve million and, let us say, eighty million, and the supergiants (continental meganations) having populations above eighty million.

On such a division the following picture emerges:

Nations	164
Meganations	43
Continental meganations	7
(China, India, Russia,	
United States, Indonesia, Brazil,	
Japan)	

It is one thing to postulate a breakdown of nations; it is quite another, even if we disregard the imposing political obstacles to doing so, to accomplish it when we have regard to the diversities of regional, national, cultural and economic conditions which prevail.

Nor can there be any question of suddenly transforming or abolishing institutions and codes which have prevailed for centuries, and suddenly creating new ones of equally sweeping effect *en masse*. We cannot shatter the world to bits and then remould it nearer to the heart's desire, if only because such an approach is impractical, unwise, immoral and totalitarian. Besides we may be mistaken! All we can do is set out some objectives towards which we feel the global community should be working, as distinct from those, insofar as there are any at all, which are now lodged in people's minds.

Our primary concern is with the abolition of the threat of global war; the suffering such an event will entail is surely its own spur for people to make quite considerable adjustments in their way of life in order to achieve it; what is important at this stage is to bring the nature of the changes required into the centre of the arena of serious political discussion.

Action Programme

1. The Association Of Fourth World Nations
To draw up a plan or blueprint for the creation of a human-scale non-centralized global order would be as foolish as it would be futile. If the *principle* of the human scale is accepted then, clearly, each human-scale community will be concerned to work out its own way of life, in accordance with its own judgements, and any suggestion of acting in

accordance with a centralized plan would be the extension of a disease rather than the application of a remedy.

But men will only act in accordance with a principle if they understand and accept the principle itself and to that end a major and multi-faceted drive to educate and generally to promote the principle of the human scale is now a task of the utmost urgency.

Everything must have a start and a point of origin somewhere and what follows are simply certain proposals for action which could advance the principle to wider acceptance; they are neither comprehensive nor exclusive, they are the product of a number of trends already beginning to emerge, trends which appear to be moving in the direction of human control by means of the human scale and away from giantism, and to yield the promise of further useful developments.

The first proposal relates to the establishment of a global association of small nations, the nations of the Fourth World. Membership will be confined exclusively to those nations whose population numbers less than, let us say, twelve million.

It is proposed that the objects of the association (AFWN) shall be as follows:

1. To defend the political, economic, geographic and cultural integrity of its member nations, especially against the expansionist tendencies of the bigger nations and those afflicted with giantism.

2. To do everything possible to promote the principle of the human scale throughout the world.

3. To give support to ethnic or other human-scale groupings, such as regions and bioregions, in their struggle for autonomous independence either individually or in concert with fellow members, with economic or financial support and by giving diplomatic status and recognition to such peoples who may wish, if need be, to establish a government in exile.

4. To achieve the maximum degree of non-centralized political and economic operation in each country within its own frontiers.

5. To reduce global war dangers by refusing to participate

in any military, political or economic alliances with bigger nations.

6. To withdraw from membership and to refuse to give any further support to the United Nations Organization, its specialist agencies or any of its subordinate or associated bodies and to promote the principle of neutrality in foreign relations.

It should be clearly understood that what is being proposed here is not some kind of incipient mini-world government or any similar global inanity. What is proposed instead is that in those areas where a clear functional need for an international body and for a common global acceptance of specific regulations exists (such as a postal union, maritime law, the use and control of oceanic resources, pollution controls, the containment of epidemics, emergency and disaster contingency provision, some forms of crime prevention, etc.) that separate bodies for each of these needs shall be established and that each should have a clear locus of control stemming from the basic unit of government within each country. It does not follow that there need be a representative of every village in the world on the governing councils of such bodies, what does follow is that the means must be established whereby any substantial body of citizens of any region should be able, if it feels the need, to make its views known and be able to secure changes through its voting power if it so wishes. *How* this shall be done will doubtless vary considerably from one body to another, what humankind dare not risk is the danger of the kind of global tyranny on a world scale of which the Nazi and communist dictatorships of the twentieth century have shown is all too feasible if we are foolish enough to permit centralized forms of power to coalesce around one centre.

The emphasis of the organization will be on the human scale and on human control. To that end the new body will be simply an *association* with absolutely minimal executive powers. The nearest comparable structure which comes to mind is that of the Commonwealth (formerly the British Commonwealth of Nations), yet even here there appears to be an undue emphasis on its secretariat and a disposition to develop organizationally in an increasing number of directions as is common to governmental bureaucracies everywhere.

The new body will be wise to insist on an annual change of presiding officer and perhaps a triumvirate of senior executives, each of whom will serve for a maximum of three years and one of whom, each year after serving as top executive, will resign.

Responsibility for *all* arrangements for its regular global assemblies will be taken turn about by individual host governments and *not* by the secretariat. Any specialist bodies it needs to establish (disarmament? peace-protocol? economic protection?) will be on an *ad hoc* basis, situated each in different countries and manned as far as is practicable on a voluntary basis.

It needs to be recalled that at least one third of the peoples of the world already live in Fourth World countries; their most immediate task is to band together to advance the cause of the human scale among the giants as an indispensable prerequisite to world peace. There is no other way in which the danger of global war can be removed.

And let them remember that among the remaining two-thirds there is taking placed even now an astonishing resurgence of localized ethnic spirit which is a new (and still much neglected) phenomenon on the world stage. The Inuit (Eskimo) peoples of the far north are at one with the Nagas of the Indian subcontinent, with the Mollucans of the Indonesian archipelago, the Aborigines of Australia, the tribes people of Africa, the Indians of the Americas, the Scots, the Irish, the Welsh, Bretons, Basques, Andalusians, Georgians, Sami, Armenians, Ukrainians, Assyrians, Walloons, Flemings, Frieslanders and numerous other ethnic groupings of Europe whose identities until only yesterday, as it were, were submerged in bigger, artificial nation-state entities they are now repudiating as they assert their inalienable historic national identities.

2. Fourth World study and research bureau

The second proposal concerns the setting up of a bureau of

studies and research relating to the problems of the human scale and of non-centralized forms of political and economic activity. The whole concept of the Fourth World is essentially a battle to challenge and change a number of widespread and leading misconceptions about the nature of government and power in the modern world. A battle of ideas needs a constant stream of factual information by way of ammunition, as well as numerous additions to the range of Fourth World literature already extant which tackle some of the deeper problems of the concept.

The bureau will be a non-governmental body even if it receives government assistance from Fourth World countries; it will be essentially a global network of scholars and doubtless organized from a number of different centres, but its work will give equal weight to the task of researching the problems of the human scale and that of making the results known as widely as possible.

3. Fourth World assemblies and forums
The third proposal, that of continuing the initiative of holding each year an international assembly of the Fourth World, will have the following objectives:

(a) To promote a greater understanding of Fourth World objectives
(b) To strengthen the bonds of understanding and common purpose among those who seek to promote the human scale.
(c) To provide a venue for the advertisement of results of scholarship related to problems of the human scale, for an exhibition of the work of the Fourth World in different countries and of the literature on Fourth World concerns.

4. Fourth World commissions
This proposal relates to the establishment of specific and, to some degree at least, specialist commissions. These will, in broad terms, consist of two main groups: those for the problems of particular trouble spots in parts of the world where war is brewing or actually being waged, and those for specific problems such as unemployment, inflation,

trading relationships, urban renewal, ecology, resource conservation, pollution, etc., etc.

In both groups it is envisaged that those sponsoring a particular commission will seek out interested parties, and those with specialist knowledge who accept the basic premise of the need for the human scale, and who will prepare reports which contain proposals based on the principle of the human scale with its concomitants of division and decentralized power structures.

These reports will be in draft form as a basis for generating discussion and proposals for amendment from participants in as many countries as possible by means of informal global networking initiatives and consultations.

It is hoped that besides opening new avenues to practical peace-making and the fashioning of draft instruments of government policy by private citizens, these commissions will go a long way towards giving the members of many peace and public interest organizations that now exist a positive and responsible role in policy formulation as well as equipping them with carefully researched proposals as a basis for campaigning action.

5. Fourth World action centres

The final proposal relates to human scale action centres. These will stem from a multiplicity of interests or concerns; no two will be much more than approximately similar, each will be entirely autonomous, self-governing and self-directing and there will be no question of affiliating to a national or international body, or of being subject to any rules or regulations stemming from larger organizations (apart from the framework of law which already prevails and which in many respects they will be working to change).

Their concerns may be with the danger of global war, with the ecology crisis, the cause of ethnic identity, with the threat of nuclear energy or weaponry, of the abuse of animal life, or with the wastage of the world's finite resources; or they may be working to restore the vitality and integrity of local community life in countless ways, by reasserting local control of matters such as hospitals, schooling, policing, transport, taxation, administration and so on, or initiating local economic enterprises in the field of banking, insurance, shops, travel, bakeries, building, journalism, furniture-making, tailoring, and so on.

What will unite all these centres, whatever their concerns and whatever they call themselves, is a common awareness of the overall danger of giantism to all humankind and an awareness of the need to respond to it by establishing human-scale structures as a means to human control of global affairs.

To this end they will be concerned not with trades unionism, but *local* trades unionism, not with public ownership or private enterprise, but with *local* forms of one or the other or both, not with cooperative forms of production or trading, but with *local* cooperatives, and similarly with numerous other questions such as workers' control, economic planning, resource allocation, social welfare and so on.

There is, of course, nothing new about much of all this; what is new is the awareness which now exists of the relationship between all these matters and the global war danger and, in the light of that danger, the need, consciously and explicitly, to reject overgrowth of form and organization wherever it rears its head and to promote always the human scale with its emphasis on the local in its place.

Human scale action centres already abound in almost every part of the world; they are the blood cells of a new global polity, and as their number increases they will supersede the old giantist forms and pave the way towards global peace for a quite simple reason: communities based on a human scale of operations will lack the resources for a global war; we may note too that monster weapons of mass destruction have a retaliatory effect which, assuming no small nation desires to immolate itself in death, rules out their use. These considerations do not apply to meganations and even less to continental meganations; it is reported that the USA is planning for the contingency of fighting a nuclear war lasting several years... and with a casualty figure of sixty million deaths...

Conclusion

This then is one person's answer to the global crisis of power which now hovers over the entire future of the human species. It is in no wise complete, nor can it be, nor need it be; for a decent future is surely one which each individual spark of humanity can help to build. All that is being asserted here is the obvious point, that if we are confronted with the prospect of a vast breakdown in the functioning of our societies then we are making false assumptions with regard to the basic principles on which we *think* they should be run. We are thinking wrong; we are thinking that we can safely accept giantism as a normal factor of life – even when we are on the brink of being destroyed by it.

So that if we wish to see the world saved from the wrack of violence we need to think again, and to think small instead of big. The future does not belong to giantism, for giantism can now only destroy the prospect of any future for any of us. The future belongs to all of us; more particularly it belongs to each one of us, and it surely behoves each one of us to act now to save the future while there is time.

(A copy of the full forty-five page proposal is available from John Papworth, 24 Abercorn Place, London NW8, UK. Current price on application to John Papworth.)

11 The Fourth World Movement

Fourth World Declaration

Four hundred delegates assembled in London for the First Assembly of the Fourth World in July 1981. The rallying call that helped attract them was the 'General Declaration', drafted by Assembly Convener, John Papworth. The document has a lengthy preamble, but its rousing declaration concludes as follows.

I   We are the people of the Fourth World, we represent a broad global spectrum ranging from ethnic, cultural and linguistic, to religious, economic, ecological and community concerns, many of which have been submerged to one degree or another by the disastrous onrush of giantism of the last two centuries or more. We are united in our determination to defuse the prevailing anarchic crisis of power by seeking to create our own social, cultural and economic patterns as we see fit in our own localized communities.

II   We declare that it is only through small social units which are capable of being subject to the control of their members that the peoples of the world will ever defeat the dangers of global war. We call for the breakdown of all giant nations into entities of no more than twelve million or so, and for all nations to practise and respect the principle of non-centralized, human-scale, democratic decision-making at the village level. We insist that the political and economic power within each nation shall be so localized that no central government shall ever again encompass the capacity for any large-scale act of aggression against its neighbours.

III   In the same way it is only by such means that they

can resolve the problem of excess human numbers, make effective a proper respect for their material environment so as to defeat the ecological peril, and end the curse of alienation from life and fellowship which now afflicts millions upon millions of people in many parts of the world. We and our neighbours seldom desired this development of giantism, very often it was fiercely resisted, it was rarely accepted and now we proclaim of it our total repudiation.

IV   We assert in its place our inalienable right to live as free, independent, autonomous and self-governing peoples and we reject the validity of any arrangements, however long-imposed, especially by giant political units, which seek the continued denial of this right.

V   We further assert our right in our own villages or urban parishes to operate and control our own schools, hospitals, police force, banks, industries, commercial trading and transport arrangements, forms of taxation and other matters of community concern as seems best to us, without external interference or coercion.

VI   We accept the need for many forms of association and cooperation across local and national frontiers, if only to realise the potential enrichment of human life such cooperation can achieve; we are happy to acknowledge this need and while repudiating the bleak, unthinking nonsense of 'world government', which could only be a global dictatorship based on a monstrous bureaucratic nightmare, we look to a far greater degree of transnational cooperation in specific political, economic and social spheres than prevails today. We affirm our readiness to participate in such cooperation wherever the mutual or general interests of the people are thus best served, but in so doing we reserve to ourselves the inalienable right to decide in what ways we shall participate, and the full freedom to withdraw from any such arrangements at any time.

VII   In general terms we assert that any state which exceeds modest, human-scale dimensions is at serious risk of being unable fully to control its own affairs and is thus a danger to its own and other people in terms of war, ecological excess and economic dislocation: the bigger the state, the bigger the danger.

VIII   The grim lesson of political life of the twentieth century, which has already inflicted more murder, suffering and infamy on the common people than has been perpetrated in any previous period, is that the only safe form of power is shared power. We therefore further affirm that even within such human-scale nations, in order to overcome the dangers of war and the overgrowth of human numbers, to check the spread of the spiritual void of mass alienation, and to widen the boundaries of freedom, there is an urgent need for a new respect for the rights and powers of decision-making and control of both political and economic institutions by the members of localized communities in their villages, wards and parishes as the case may be, in every part of the world. Such a programme of non-centralized political and economic power as is here envisaged is an essential safeguard to prevent the power of the state being seized by any group for the purpose of war, aggrandizement or oppression.

IX   For the same reason we hereby affirm our unreserved opposition to any attempts to increase the size or the scale of political units or any moves towards further governmental centralization. We denounce such trends as likely to lead to yet a further loss of human control, to result in further assaults on freedom and a further increase in the prevailing global dangers.

X   *War* We call on people everywhere to end the curse of global war by repudiating the uncontrollable giantism which is the chief cause of it; we urge the dismemberment of all giant entities of power into sensible, human-scale, controllable nations of no more than twelve million people which shall be governed on the basis of the maximum degree of non-centralized power by vesting all powers of government in the hands of village communities.

XI   *Ecology* Unless we transform our lifestyles and make a more realistic appraisal of the resilience of the mutual support systems of the biosphere, large parts of our planet could, in a few more generations, become uninhabitable. We urge every village and village-sized community in the world, especially in the advanced world, to examine the impact of its mode of life on the ecology of the planet and order those changes which will ensure that what is now ecologically malignant is made stable and benign.

XII   *Resources* The lifestyle of rich nations is making demands on the finite resources of the planet which can only widen the gulf between rich and poor peoples and beggar the posterity of both by degrading the habitat. We call for an immediate reappraisal of this lifestyle, especially by communities in rich countries, in all particulars where finite resources are being consumed, in order to establish a way of life which is beneficially sustainable for all peoples.

XIII We call for an end to waste and an end to policies which presume a subservience of the resources of the habitat to a quest for unlimited economic expansion. We call instead for a profound sense of reverence for all the elements of the natural order and a deliberate policy of thrift and careful husbanding of all planetary resources in place of the present policies of exploitation and abuse, with their dangerous disregard of the consequential effects on the interlocking equilibria of the biosphere, on which the well-being of all life depends.

XIV   We condemn the rapacious manner in which the finite resources of the globe are being squandered as being ignorant, foolish, wasteful and immoral. We urge the adoption of standards of consumption which make a minimum demand on such resources, and which are served by a maximum reliance on self-renewable resources. We urge people everywhere to reject products which make needless demands on finite resources which constitute the heritage of all our posterity temporarily in our keeping.

XV *Population* The largely unconscious biological mechanisms which control numbers in the animal world were also operative in human societies until quite recent times. They operated on the basis of decisions made consensually (and frequently instinctively) in small groupings. Today there is a need for those responses to be reinforced by a conscious process of reasoning; instead, we have largely destroyed the small communities which were their basis. This is the real cause of the population crisis. No small community would allow itself to be swamped by its own numbers without doing something to prevent it *if it had the power to do so*. We declare that the need for base power in our village societies is imperative if the crisis in human numbers is to be resolved. No government of a mass society can solve this problem except by means which are totalitarian and an assault on human dignity. Community responsibility for community affairs is a precondition for the control of community numbers. It follows that community power is a precondition for community survival.

XVI *Alienation* Human fulfilment is realized in religion, work, culture and family life; the blind pursuit of economic growth as an end in itself and the giant forms of organization it promotes put a discount on moral purpose, degrade human labour to being a mere appendage of machines, devitalize culture by destroying the basis of the power to create and to decide upon which it flourishes, and undermine the historic basis of family life by substituting considerations of the cash nexus for the bonds of mutuality, and reverence for relationships, which are the core of any worthwhile civilization. We denounce this experience as being destructive of human happiness.

XVII   We call on all the peoples of the world to affirm their membership of the human family and their duty to advance its well-being in terms of peace, freedom and ecological sensibility by joining with us to establish the Fourth World, a world where power is fully shared by the people in societies which are modest enough in size to do justice to the majesty of the human spirit and to serve the noblest accomplishments and potentialities of its creative genius.

XVIII   We pledge ourselves to work unceasingly for the liberation of peoples everywhere in these terms.

Long live the Fourth World!

Fourth World chronology

1966   Founding of *Resurgence*, 'The Journal Of The Fourth World, For Small Nations, Small Communities And The Human Spirit'.

1981   Founding of *Fourth World News*.

First Assembly of the Fourth World (London).

1982   Second Assembly (Berlin).

1983   Third Assembly (Larzac, France).

Founding of the Academic Inn (London), a convivial open university for Fourth World issues.

1984   Fourth Assembly (USA).

Establishment of the Fourth World Peace Commission on South Africa.

KEEP IN TOUCH!

Fourth World Review is one of the journals of the Fourth World. It carries crisply-written articles on current events from a human-scale stance, items on the ethnic struggle (worldwide), ecology and numerous local initiatives in many spheres of citizen concern; alternative, concerned book reviews and news of Fourth World developments in different countries.

Edited by John Papworth, 24 Abercorn Place, London NW8, UK. (01 286 4366). Subscription costs £10 sterling or 20 $ US.

The idea of some form of planetary government has dominated a great deal of human thinking. I find such thinking glib, bogus, dangerous and totalitarian. We need a greatly expanded consciousness of world problems and of the common identity of humanity, but we do not need world parliaments or world governments or world citizenship. That way lies death, destruction and disintegration of such remnants of civilization as have survived the giantism of the twentieth century.

Long live the forward march of the common people towards their true and just inheritance in their fully autonomous, small-scale localized communities.

Long live the Fourth World!

John Papworth

'My God how near the end we seem to be! It is almost as though the leaders of the "great" powers have all gone mad together. I feel we are very near the edge of the Gadarene cliff. But we must still go on hoeing our manglewurzels. Hwyl fawr...'

(from a letter to the editors from John Seymour)

Index